THE RISE OF NATIONALITY IN THE BALKANS

The Rise of
Nationality
in the Balkans

By R.W. SETON-WATSON

HOWARD FERTIG

NEW YORK   1966

First published by Constable and Company Limited
in 1917

HOWARD FERTIG, INC. EDITION 1966

Library of Congress Catalog Card number: 66-24354

PRINTED IN THE UNITED STATES OF AMERICA
BY NOBLE OFFSET PRINTERS

TO

MY WIFE

25 Marc , 1917.

NOTE

OWING to his departure from London on military service the author has not been able to finish this book: it is, therefore, not the true fulfilment of his intention. But, as the substance of it is in its final form and nothing is wanting except a preface and the statement of general conclusions, his publishers believe that the value of the book as a guide to critical affairs in the Balkans is in no way impaired. They therefore present it to the British reading public with full confidence that, alike in its intrinsic worth and by the acknowledged authority of its author, it will help to serve the great purposes of the War.

25 March, 1917.

CONTENTS

CONTENTS

THE RISE OF NATIONALITY IN THE BALKANS

CHAPTER I

BYZANTIUM AND STAMBUL

THE master of Constantinople, said Napoleon, will rule the world, and his reputation for political prophecy has given an unnatural lease of life to what is merely a dangerous half-truth. In a conjunction of circumstances such as ten centuries may not bring, and under the guidance of some universal genius of peace and war, Byzantium may resume that supremacy which it enjoyed under its Imperial founder and to a lesser degree under the great Justinian. But even then it will be for the future historian to consider whether other causes, such as undermined the fighting powers of Rome and diverted the trade routes of the Middle Ages, were not the main factors in the revival with which he will be concerned, and whether Constantine would have been any the less supreme had he refrained from founding a New Rome upon the shores of the Bosphorus. That it may in the future dominate the European situation none would be rash enough to deny; to assert that it must of necessity do so would be little short of an open defiance of the past. For history shows us that, despite its commercial importance and its ancient traditions of culture, Constantinople has for many centuries played a purely negative part in the politics of Europe, and that even under such great and war-like sovereigns as Basil II., Mohammed II., and Suleiman the Magnificent, Europe, though it rang with their victories, was never the tool of their policy.   To-day, more than ever, the straits between Europe and Asia possess a potential rather than an actual importance, which is intimately connected with the fate of the territory separating them from the Balkans and the Taurus.   On the other hand, for purposes of defence, communication, and administration, its strategic position is unrivalled and bears witness to the genius of its founder. Geography, indeed, goes far to explain alike the stubborn survival of the Eastern Empire as a trunk-less head and the frequent recoveries of the Sick Man from a seemingly hopeless illness.   In a word, Constantinople is a key which, in the right hands, may work wonders, but which only acquires full value when key and lock are in the same possession.   For the past two years history has been writing the proof of this assertion in letters of fire across Europe, and the fate of Constantinople is one of the most decisive issues of the Great War.   The definite establishment of German control would at once convert the dream of "Berlin to Bagdad" into the most practical of realities, while its acquisition by Russia would change the whole centre of gravity in Eastern Europe by assuring to the greatest of Slavonic Powers its access to the sea and removing the chief incentive to political activity in Persia or the Middle East.

The victories of Belisarius and Narses in Italy and Africa (533–554) were the last serious acts of aggression in the West committed by the so-called "Byzantine" Empire.   Henceforward its military resources were devoted on the one hand to retaining or reasserting its hold upon the Balkan Peninsula, and on the other to holding back the advancing tide of Islam from its Asiatic provinces. For ten centuries after the fall of the West before the repeated onslaughts of the barbarians (476), the East held Asia at bay. While the rest of Europe was sunk in the depths of barbarism and anarchy, Constantinople preserved, with much that was corrupt and decadent, many of the great traditions of the ancient world. Recent research and a wider conception of history have restored it to its place as the true centre of culture during the Dark Ages. Indeed, for a long time the Moorish Court of Cordova was its only serious rival as a repository of learning and science; it was only later that the great scholastic centres of Bologna and Paris, of Oxford and Prague, began to assume a real importance in the history of thought and civilisation.

It is true that in the sultry atmosphere of Byzantine ceremonial all initiative had long been stifled; but the West was now ready to receive the treasures so long hoarded on the Bosphorus, and it is hard to exaggerate the impetus which their dispersal after the Turkish conquest gave to the Italian renaissance, and the consequent revival of art and learning throughout Europe.

Internal decay and stagnation had rendered the fall of the Byzantine State inevitable, nor need its dissolution have been a cause for regret, had its conquerors possessed either the inclination or the capacity to accept its great traditions and transfuse them with their own fierce virility. Unhappily, the very opposite occurred. Religious fanaticism and military prowess combined to inspire the Turk with contempt for the conquered Greeks. By a glorious death the last Constantine vindicated his own honour, but could not conceal the craven spirit of his subjects, while the corruption of the Eastern Church served to render the art and culture which centred round it peculiarly abhorrent to a race which followed the purer tenets of Mohammed.

By the middle of the fourteenth century the collapse of the Empire had become a mere question of time, and in the year 1355 we find a Venetian diplomat treating it as the certain prey of the Turks.[1] Yet the great strength of its strategic position enabled the imperial city to postpone its downfall for a whole century after the Turks had gained their first foothold in Europe. The additional respite afforded by the onslaught of the Mongols on the Turkish rear came too late to save either the Empire itself or the loosely-knit Slavonic states of the peninsula, to whom the triumph of the Crescent meant national ruin. In the ninth and tenth centuries (807–1018) the Bulgars, under the leadership of the savage Krum and his great successors, Boris and Simeon, had seemed more than once on the point of sweeping all before them, but the ferocious energy and military prowess of Basil II. reduced them to complete subjection for 170 years. The second, or Roumano-Bulgar, Empire of the Asenid dynasty,[2] and the still more formidable Serb Empire of Stephen Dushan, both proved unequal to the task of uniting the peninsula against the infidel. The fatal battle of Kosovo (1389) —the Flodden of the Southern Slavs—which has been immortalised by a wonderful cycle of popular ballads, assured to the Turks a dominant position in the Balkans. It was followed in a few years by the subjection of Bulgaria (1393), while Serbia and Bosnia were reduced to the defensive, and were only permitted to survive in uncertain vassalage, until the Sultan, after planting the Crescent upon the Golden Horn, was ready for an advance into the heart of Europe. Even to-day the

[1] Marino Falieri, cit. Hopf, Geschichte Griechenlands, p. 488.
[2] See Chapters III and VI.

claims of rival propagandists are based upon the
doubtful and fluctuating frontiers of mediæval times.
Each race naturally tends to exaggerate the achievements of its ancestors and to ignore the claims of its
neighbours. But even upon a perfectly sound historical
basis it is possible to make out a good case for at
least three mutually exclusive and irreconcilable programmes. Meanwhile, it may safely be asserted that
none of the three states referred to was so exclusively
national in character as those who read the present into
the past would have us believe. During the fifteenth
century the indifference and disunion of Christendom
favoured Turkish ambitions. The disastrous battles of
Nicopolis (1396) and Varna (1444) crushed what were
at best isolated, if gallant, efforts. In the West, Pius
II. alone showed some perception of the issues at stake;
but his noble enthusiasm and personal example, while
shedding a dying lustre upon the pre-Reformation
Papacy, produced no tangible result. For a whole
century the Magyars and Roumanians were left virtually unaided to stem the Turkish tide. Their heroic
leaders, John Hunyády and Stephen the Great, proved
in many a desperate battle that the Crescent was not
invincible; but their efforts would have been more
effectual had Stephen been a contemporary, not a successor, of the great Roumanian voivode, and had the
two nations acted conjointly instead of on parallel lines.
Even Hunyády's son, King Matthias Corvinus,
admittedly one of the greatest figures of the fifteenth
century, would seem to have under-estimated the
Turkish danger, for his campaigns in the south were
mere spasmodic efforts compared with the energy and
resources squandered in repeated aggression against
Austria and Bohemia.

The writers of historical text-books have often
selected purely arbitrary dates for the opening of some

new era, but it was a sure instinct which fixed upon the fall of Constantinople in 1453 as a decisive landmark in European history. Henceforth a barbarous Asiatic Power, to whom law and administration were a sealed book and the argument of the sword the sole reality, was to make its capital in the city of Constantine and Justinian. The Imperial tradition of the Cæsars, which had survived within narrower limits, but in a more recognisable form, in Byzantium than in the shadowy Empire of the West, was rudely shattered by the might of the Crescent. The fragments of its literary treasures were transferred to Italy and Germany, and gave added strength and a new direction to the humanistic current which is known as the Renaissance, and which, on its spiritual side, was to merge in the reforming movement of Luther, Calvin, and Knox.

The destruction of the Eastern Empire involved the establishment of an essentially barbarous Power cemented by military organisation and an insatiable lust of conquest. The records of Turkish rule in Europe are one long catalogue of bloodshed and rapine, at first directed by the genius of one of the most remarkable dynasties which the world has seen,[1] but never from first to last inspired by the faintest traditions of culture. In marked contrast to other Moslem Powers, the Turks have never shown a trace of creative genius; when not actively engaged in the cause of destruction, they have remained sunk in the lethargy of fatalism. The learning and culture of Bagdad and Cordova, the architectural and artistic triumphs of the Indian Moguls or the Fatimite Caliphs of Egypt, were never rivalled by the Turks. Even their literature, despite its

---

[1] From Osman (+ 1325) to Suleiman I. (+ 1566) are ten generations in lineal descent; and with the possible exception of the two Bayezids, all were men of commanding ability, and at least two of real genius.

numerous votaries, is in the main an imitation of Persian and Arabic models.[1]

The Turks entered Europe endowed with the savage virtues of the primitive warrior; confronted with so utterly alien a civilisation as that of Byzantium, they could only assimilate its worst qualities, which acted upon their martial spirit as a slowly corroding poison. Their apologists are fully entitled to extol the dignity and the virtues of the individual Turkish peasant, and even to contrast them with the unlovely qualities of the enslaved rayah; but no effort can conceal the supremely negative nature of the Turkish character, the utter incapacity for constructive work or probity of administration displayed by the governing class. The essential distinction between Islam and the Turks cannot be emphasised too strongly in a book dealing with Balkan problems, for there is at the present day a foolish and unfounded tendency to assume that severe criticism of the latter necessarily involves hostility towards the former.

The final and unanswerable condemnation of Turkish rule in Europe consists, not in recounting the periodic massacres and outbreaks which its discontented subjects have provoked, but in contrasting the material and moral condition of the various provinces before and after the conquest, and still more their condition a generation before and a generation after the expulsion of the Turks. Every province which they have held has become a desert under their blighting influence, and has only blossomed again when the blight has been

[1] Even the historian, Hammer-Purgstall, who in his monumental work on Ottoman poetry introduces over 2,000 "poets and versifiers" to the West, has to admit that the Turks "are not inspired by any native and peculiar poetical genius, like the Arabs and Persians," though they have assimilated the literary treasures of those two peoples. See *Gesch. des osmanischen Reiches*, Bd. II., S.683.

removed. The rose garden replaces the dung hill, and flourishing modern cities the foul and mouldering hamlets of a century ago. Whether it be Hungary, Croatia, Serbia, Greece, Roumania, Bosnia, or Bulgaria, the story is invariably the same. The proverb which declares that grass does not grow where the Ottoman hoofs have trod, merely gives poetical expression to a fact which is as indisputable as the law of gravity.

With the triumph of the Turks the Eastern Question —which has its root in the secular rivalry of Europe and Asia—assumed a new phase, in the course of which there was a faint revival of the old conception of European solidarity, which the Crusades had kindled into flame but which the decay of the Holy Roman Empire had done so much to obscure. But it was only with the decline of Ottoman power that it entered upon the stage which has been so familiar to recent generations, and which ended amid the cataclysms of 1912.

A period of 550 years separates the day on which the Turks, still flushed with their conquest of Adrianople, routed the allied Serb and Bulgar armies on the Maritza near that city (1371), and the day on which Adrianople surrendered to the victorious Bulgars and their Serbian Allies. This period falls naturally into two divisions: one of expansion and aggrandisement (1357–1595), in which the capture of the Dardanelles was the first and the conquest of Cyprus (1571) the last of an unbroken series of military triumphs,[1] and one of slow but constant decline (1595–1912), in which province after province was severed from the decaying trunk of the

---

[1] A further period of expansion occurred under the great Viziers of the later seventeenth century. The conquest of Crete from the Venetians (1669), and of Podolia and the Ukraine from Poland (1676) marked the high water line of Turkish conquest. This revival closed dramatically with the unsuccessful siege of Vienna in 1683.

Ottoman state. At the height of its power Turkish pashas ruled in Buda, Belgrade, Sarajevo, and Athens; Wallachia, Moldavia, Transylvania, and Ragusa paid annual tribute to the Porte; while the Empire and Poland felt the menace of the Sultan's power.

The strength of the Turks lay in their skilful combination of the military and feudatory systems, in the still more ingenious adaptation of slavery by the blood tax, and in the position of the Sultan as the spiritual head of Islam.[1] From the very first the whole organisation of the conquering race rested on a military basis; war was their true profession, and foreign aggrandisement was the surest road to fame and advancement. The child tribute, by which the famous corps of Janissaries was recruited, was a double source of strength, for on the one hand it made good the comparative sterility of the Turks, and on the other drained the best forces of the subject population. Thus, by a refinement of cruelty, the unhappy Christians saw the flower of their youth converted into the deadliest instrument for prolonging their subjection. It was only when, towards the end of the sixteenth century, the Janissaries were permitted to marry, and under the degenerate successors of the great Suleiman were appeased at each fresh accession by extravagant largesse, that the first symptoms of decay became apparent. When marriage was once allowed to them, the admission of their children to service in the same corps became a mere question of time; and from the moment that this practice became common, the blood tax inevitably fell into disuse, and the drain upon the Christian population ceased. The growing lack of discipline among the Janissaries coincided with the transformation of the old military tenure of the Timars: the luxury and extravagance of

[1] *Cf.* Ranke, *Fürsten und Völker Südeuropas im XVI. u. XVII. Jahrhundert,* cursim.

the Court kept pace with the rapacity of the troops.
The incapacity of the later Sultans naturally increased
the influence of the harem, and all these causes combined to deplete the Treasury and thus weaken the
offensive power of the Empire.

Like a vampire, the Ottoman state could only flourish
by draining the life blood of its victims; and this process
still further whetted its appetite, until at length the
overgrown body fell an easy prey to decay and corruption. The art of government has always been a sealed
book to the Turks, whose peculiar talent has been
strictly limited to war and diplomacy; and nothing illustrates this more strikingly than the circumstance that
so many of their greatest statesmen have been of other
than Turkish origin, owing their advancement, not to
race, but to the unifying bond of Islam.

CHAPTER II

TURKEY IN DECLINE

THAT the inevitable process of Turkish dissolution has been prolonged over several centuries is due, not so much to the patient's powers of resistance (though these must not be underestimated) as to the mutual distrust and animosities of the Christian States of Europe. The same short-sighted indifference, the same selfish calculation on their part which permitted the fall of Constantinople, left the Turks in undisturbed possession of their prey, and on more than one occasion actively supported their designs of aggression.[1] It is an unhappy fact that one of the central events of European progress, the German Reformation, should have contributed materially to this result. The clash of warring religious systems and the bigotry displayed on both sides gave rise to the conviction that the Papacy was a deadlier enemy than the Turk, and led for the first time to co-operation between a Protestant and a Mohammedan Power. Nowhere was this more marked than in Hungary, where the opponents of the Habsburg dynasty and its Jesuit allies often preferred the rule of Islam to that of a rival Christian sect. During the late sixteenth and early seventeenth centuries their very

[1] *Cf.* the encouragement given by Francis I. to Suleiman's invasion of Hungary, inspired by the French King's desire to injure the House of Habsburg.

zeal for the Catholic faith proved to be the chief handi-
cap of the Habsburgs in their great designs for the
recovery of Christian territory from the Turks. The
Thirty Years' War, in which the Protestant North
linked hands with Gabriel Bethlen and the Calvinists
of Hungary, served as a diversion in favour of the Turks
and delayed the Christian advance for at least two
generations. But if the Bethlens, the Tökölis, and the
Rákóczys, instead of following their ancestors' example
as the foremost champions of Christendom, were content to remain the vassals of the Porte, this is to be
explained and condoned by the gross intolerance and
persecuting zeal displayed by the House of Habsburg
towards the Hungarian Protestants—a frame of mind
which coincided with a despotic tendency to override
all constitutional traditions. Despite this stain upon its
scutcheon, however, it is to the House of Habsburg that
we must assign the chief glory in the task of turning
the tide against the Turks. For a century and a half
(1526–1687) the great central plains of Hungary
remained in Turkish possession, and for the greater
part of that period the Habsburgs were forced to act
upon the defensive. The exigencies of German politics,
involving the future of the dynasty and of the Roman
Church, and at the same time Magyar hostility to a
foreign king and the strategic value of Transylvania as
a focus of national resistance, all combined to render
an aggressive policy virtually impossible. But defence
at least was not neglected, and the sixteenth century
saw the organisation of the Croatian Military Frontiers,
which at once stemmed back the Turks from the
hereditary provinces and threatened their flank in the
open Hungarian plain. This frontier work was an
essential preliminary to the task of reconquest, and its
success was demonstrated by the gradual extension of
the system of soldier-settlers along the whole northern

bank of the Save and Danube as far east as the Transylvanian Alps.

The famous siege of Vienna in 1683 marks the last serious effort of the Turks at European conquest. The danger was averted by the joint efforts of the Imperialists and their Polish allies under the great Sobieski, and the moment of extreme peril was immediately followed by the heroic era of Habsburg advance. In a series of glorious campaigns under the Duke of Lorraine and Stahremberg, and their still greater successor, Prince Eugene, the Imperialist armies drove back the Turks from the greater part of Hungary and Transylvania (1685–1699), and at length—after an interval caused by European and Hungarian opposition [1]—not merely expelled them from their last foothold on Hungarian soil, the Banat of Temesvár, but also occupied the fortress of Belgrade and large portions of the modern Serbia and Roumania (1716–1718).[2]

The designs entertained by the Court of Vienna for the extension of Austrian power in the Balkans took practical form in the manifesto addressed in 1690 to the Christian subjects of the Porte, and as a result the Serb Patriarch Arsenius abandoned the ancient metropolitan see of Ipek and settled with many thousand Serb families in the Southern plains of Hungary under the protection of a special Imperial charter. Nine years later the Treaty of Karlowitz recognised the Emperor's right to intervene on behalf of the Christian subjects of the Porte, who in their turn looked more and more to Vienna for their political salvation. In the Eastern policy of Leopold I. an almost equal share may be assigned to the traditional theories of the Holy

---

[1] The War of Spanish Succession (1702-1713), and the rising and prolonged resistance of Francis Rákóczy (1703-1711).

[2] The north of Serbia as far as the Morava, Drina and Una rivers, and Little Wallachia as far as the Aluta (Olt) river.

Crown of St. Stephen and to the fanatical desire for the advancement of Catholicism. The ambitious dream of Leopold's counsellors, who set Constantinople as the goal of their endeavour, appeared to be no longer so fantastic under Prince Eugene as in the preceding century. The Treaty of Passarowitz[1] (1718) seemed to render Austria's complete absorption of Serbia and Bosnia a mere matter of time.[2] But the fatal dual tendency which has so often paralysed Austria's action —the sure outcome of her geographical position between east and west—prevented more than a very partial fulfilment of these designs. The double-headed Eagle, facing both ways, had already become the symbol of Habsburg rule. The mirage of universal dominion— the tradition of their ancestor, Charles V.—fascinated the gaze of Leopold I. and his successors, and tempted them to waste the favourable moment when a determined concentration might have crushed the Ottoman power in Europe, and when there was as yet no serious rival to dispute the spoils. The Spanish War of Succession had left its legacy of exhaustion, financial embarrassment, and the fear of Western complications; and the Treaty of Passarowitz, though it marked the farthest point of Austrian advance to the south, bore no relation to the expectations which had been aroused.

The incapable successor of Prince Eugene failed to

---

[1] Požarevac.

[2] It is instructive to note the claims put forward by Austria as the result of her victorious campaign with her actual achievement. She demanded Serbia with Niš and Vidin, Western Bosnia as far as the Una river, all Wallachia and the greater part of Moldavia. She actually acquired the Banat of Temesvár, Belgrade with the western districts of Serbia, a frontier revision in Bosnia, and Little Wallachia. In 1736 Austria hoped to acquire all Bosnia and Albania to the river Drin, Wallachia as far as Braila and Moldavia as far as the Pruth! *Cf.* Beer, *Die Orientalische Politik Oesterreichs*, p. 16.

hold what he had won, and the shameful Treaty of Belgrade (1739) restored to the Turks all the territory south of the Danube. But there can be little doubt that the position would have been retrieved but for the cruel diversion created by Frederick the Great's invasion of Silesia and the desperate struggle which alone preserved Maria Theresa's throne. As so often in their subsequent history, events in the West afforded respite to the rapidly decaying Ottoman state. The history of Austria is a record of wasted opportunities. The brief period in which expansion to the south could have been effected almost without a challenge was destined never to recur. Parallel with the decline of Turkey came the rise of a new Colossus in the North; the two great historical processes which were to transform the political system of Europe interacted more and more closely upon each other. While Austria, France, and Prussia filled the middle of the century with their rivalry, Russia, building upon the sure foundations laid by the genius of Peter the Great, consolidated her power under Anne and Elizabeth, and by the time Maria Theresa had finally assured her dynastic position, was already firmly established as a dangerous rival in what is now known as the Near East, but then seemed, save to our empire-builders in India, "the East" *par excellence.*

The Eastern Question, which for the first quarter of the eighteenth century seemed to be a monopoly of Austria, enters upon a new stage in the year 1726. For the remainder of the century Austria is content to seek, in alliance with Russia, what she had lacked the energy to secure single-handed, and, indeed, only too often to leave all initiative to her Ally. The Austro-Russian alliance of that year was renewed on four separate occasions,[1] but for the greater part of the reign

[1] 1756 against Prussia, 1772 against Poland, 1781 against Turkey, 1795 against the French Revolution.

of Maria Theresa—indeed, until the influence of her son upon public affairs became apparent—its motive power, so far as Austria is concerned, is directed northwards and westwards rather than southwards. Kaunitz, who towards the middle of the century described Turkey and Prussia as the two worst enemies of the House of Habsburg,[1] appears to have soon come to regard the former as more or less innocuous. Indeed, his neglect of Near Eastern problems in favour of Germany and Italy set an example which many of his successors in office have imitated.

Characteristic of the negative policy adopted by Austria, under Maria Theresa and her Chancellor, was the indifference which they showed alike towards the Swabian and the Serbian settlers in the Banat and Bačka. The latter especially had to face the double hostility of the Magyars, who regarded their reception as a violation of the Hungarian Constitution, and of the Ultramontanes, who actively disapproved of the favoured position secured to the Orthodox Church. But even though Austria failed to realise the potential value of her new Serb subjects as a weapon of central authority, the Habsburg dominions remained for over a century to come the centre of such Southern Slav culture as had survived the Turkish flood. Nowhere was the Habs-

---

[1] *Cf.* Beer, *op. cit. p.* 17. In a long and highly interesting memorandum submitted to the Empress in 1776 Kaunitz lays down as the first of 27 "speciale Staatsgrundsätze" the axiom that Prussia "is in the meantime the most dangerous neighbour and secret enemy" (dermalen der gefährlichste Nachbar und heimliche Feind), who is "never and under no circumstances to be entirely trusted" (niemalen und in keinem Fall vollkommen zu trauen). "According to this system our entire state system is to be weighed." See Denkschriften des Fürsten Kaunitz, in *Archiv für österreichische Geschichte,* vol. 48, p. 78. This conviction Kaunitz carried to his grave. How different is the attitude of Austrian Statesmen towards Berlin to-day!

burg tradition stronger than in the Croat, Serb, and
Roumanian Military Frontiers, where a system of military land-tenure, organised on remarkably democratic
lines, gave rise to numerous fighting families inspired
from generation to generation by keen personal devo-
tion to the Emperor and his house.

The process of historic evolution to which we have
alluded above—the decline of Turkey and the corresponding rise of Russia—brought with it as one of its
chief symptoms the destruction of the Polish "Republic." For many generations the policy of the Porte
had been deliberately to encourage the growing anarchy
in Poland, with a view to paralysing a probable ally of
the Imperialists in their advance southwards. The
success of Russian intrigue at the Court of Warsaw,
and the dominant position acquired by Catherine II.
through the election of her lover Stanislas to the Polish
throne, at length aroused the Turks to a belated sense
of the intimate connection of their own fate and that of
Poland. But Turkey's espousal of the cause of Polish
independence led to the war with Russia (1768), and
precipitated the very catastrophe which it had sought to
avert.

The alarm with which Vienna regarded the first
appearance of a Russian fleet in the Mediterranean
(1769–70), the ineradicable distrust with which
Frederick the Great inspired Maria Theresa and
Kaunitz, and Frederick's insistent view that the survival
of Turkey was Prussia's best guarantee against Russian
or Austrian aggression—these three main threads of
policy and the numerous complications introduced by
the attitude of the Western Powers seemed to many
observers to be the precursors of a fresh European
struggle. But common dynastic interests overshadowed
national, religious, and economic jealousies, and Poland
was sacrificed to avert a rupture. At the first partition

(1772) Catherine the Great consoled herself with the lion's share and with a knowledge that a further partition had been rendered inevitable.

The policy of Kaunitz at this eventful period of European history was rather that of the professional diplomat than of the far-sighted statesman. His enmity towards Prussia, and the designs which he entertained for the recovery of Silesia and for the reversion of Bavaria,[1] made him deaf to the overtures of Russia. In 1769 we find Count Panin suggesting a triple alliance against the Turks, "who had survived so long solely because of the jealousies of the Christian Powers." But the extinction of Turkey did not suit Frederick the Great, who looked to the Sublime Porte to create a useful diversion in favour of Prussia in the event of any possible coalition between Vienna and Petrograd. He therefore spared no effort to impress upon Joseph II., during their famous interview at Neisse (1769), the grave dangers which the growth of Russian power involved for Europe. His arguments carried weight even with his old enemy the Austrian Chancellor. Needless to say, Kaunitz never acted save upon well-considered motives, and in this case there were weighty arguments in favour of an attitude of reserve. Prussia's consent to Austrian and Russian aggrandisement against the Turks could only be secured by granting her a free hand to annex the northern provinces of Poland; and while their possession would immensely strengthen Prussia's economic and strategic position, there would, Kaunitz contended, be no corresponding increase of strength for Austria as the result of annexing territory which had been desolated and exhausted by two centuries of Turkish misrule. But in allowing such considera-

[1] On the extinction of the elder branch of the House of Wittelsbach. This event, when it at length occurred in 1777, led to the war of Bavarian Succession.

tions to control his policy he was assuredly playing the
game of Prussia. In resisting Russia's invitation (1768)
he wasted a highly favourable opportunity for territorial expansion south of the Danube. In accepting the
Porte's advances and contracting the first Austro-
Turkish alliance (1771) he displayed to the full his talent
for diplomatic intrigue, but at the same time aroused
general resentment in Europe, isolated Austria, and thus
directly paved the way for Russia's greatest triumph,
the Treaty of Kutchuk Kainardji (1774). The Turks on
their part soon had cause to regret their action. The
victories of the Russian Army had forced them to look
about for fresh allies, and in their eagerness to secure
Austria they bated their hook with a proposal for the
dismemberment of Poland, which till then had met with
genuine disapproval at Vienna. Thus the war which
had begun in defence of Polish Independence was the
signal for the first partition, in which Austria, as a
result of her half-measures, gained less than either of her
fellow-conspirators. For the moment, however, she
succeeded in diverting Russian aggression from the
south to the west, since in order to gain a decisive control
over the Polish situation it was necessary for Catherine
to relax the vigour of her assault upon the Turks.

Balkan history in the eighteenth century is overshadowed by the relations of Austria and Russia, sometimes in jealous rivalry, but quite as often in amicable
partnership for aggression. After the middle of the
century it became a question of parallel spheres of
influence, of Austria on the west and Russia on the
east of the peninsula. Russia had two notable points
in her favour—her racial kinship with the Balkan Slavs
and her ecclesiastical position as the stronghold of
Orthodoxy and the Byzantine Church tradition; but
Austria still preserved the advantage of closer contact.

The age whose crowning infamy was the Polish Partition was full of similar projects for the partition of the Ottoman dominions. But in all these complicated actions dynastic interests and ambitions were the determining factors : the benevolent despots of whom that age of polite scepticism was so prolific reckoned with nations and provinces as with pawns upon a chessboard. At length, as the century drew to a close, the stately castle on the sand, erected at the pleasure of a few monarchs and diplomats, began to crumble before the incoming tide of a great idea. The principle of Nationality was leavening the dead mass of the Balkan population, and was soon to complete the ruin with which internal corruption was already threatening the Turkish state.

CHAPTER III

THERE is one factor of capital importance to the student of national movements in the Balkans—the position of Christianity under the Turks. One of the most striking characteristics of the Byzantine state had been the subordination of the ecclesiastical to the civil arm; the long struggle between Empire and Papacy had no counterpart in the East. The victorious Sultan allowed the Patriarchate to linger on in a condition of precarious vassalage, which speedily led to utter spiritual stagnation. The monk Gennadios, whom Mohammed II. installed as Patriarch a few days after his entry into Constantinople, really enjoyed a position which was in many respects far more authoritative than that of his predecessors under the Eastern Emperors. In Islam the twin conceptions of State and Church are completely intertwined, and the very idea of their separation is utterly alien to the Mohammedan mind. Mohammed II., then, saw in the conquered Christians of his new dominions another "millet" or religious community, and was entirely disinclined to distinguish between the various shades of national feeling. To him Greek and Slav were alike Christians and rayahs. Hence the Patriarch became the intermediary between the Sultan and his Christian subjects, the visible expression of their

religious life, and not least of all the individual upon
whom pressure could be conveniently exercised when it
was necessary to bring them to reason.   The Patriarchate, the real focus of the Eastern Church at that
period, and with it the whole ecclesiastical framework,
fell entirely into Greek hands, with the result that a
veneer of Greek language and culture was spread over
the whole Christian population of Turkey.   In the West
there grew up the highly inaccurate habit of referring
to all branches of the Orthodox or Eastern Church as
"the Greek Church," and more than one distinguished
historian and traveller was guilty of the most ludicrous
errors.   Even a Kinglake could describe his journey
through what is now the kingdom of Bulgaria without
making a single allusion to the existence of the Bulgarian race.   From the fifteenth to the beginning of the
nineteenth century Western Europe had virtually lost
sight of all the Balkan races save the dominant Turk
and the pliant Greek.

With a foreign conqueror as absolute master in the
state, and with Greek influence supreme in the Church,
the wretched Slav rayah seemed doomed to national
extinction.   There were, indeed, two fragmentary survi-
vals from a happier era—the autocephalous Bulgarian
and Serbian churches of Ohrida and of Ipek; but the
former had become entirely Hellenised even before the
Turkish conquest, while the latter, on the initiative of
the Patriarch Arsenius himself, transferred itself with
thousands of its adherents to the Habsburg dominions.
The last fragments of Serb and Bulgar Church autonomy
were destroyed by decree of the Sultan in the year 1767.
For several generations after this event the influence of
the Phanariot clergy—so-called from the Phanar or
Lighthouse quarter of Constantinople, in which the
Greek Patriarch resides—was paramount.   There was
the same corrupt traffic in episcopal sees and even in

less important Church offices as in the case of the vassal thrones of Wallachia and Moldavia, to obtain whose precarious tenure the Greek patrician families of the Phanar outbribed each other at the Sublime Porte. Greek was the language of culture and of fashion among the Balkan Christians, just as it was the language of the liturgy and of commerce. The Slav and Latin dialects of the peninsula were despised as barbarous jargons. National feeling seemed to be virtually extinct, or at best flickered here and there—in the monasteries of Wallachia and Moldavia, in a few prosperous Vlach towns on the fringe of Albania, in the Serb centres of Karlowitz and Neusatz (Novi Sad) on the Danube, and in the tiny Slav republic of Ragusa (Dubrovnik).

The events of the nineteenth century were to show that nationality, though long latent and seemingly extinct, was capable of truly volcanic outbursts. It is this new factor which is destined to transform so radically what many generations have known as the Eastern Question. In its earlier form it may be defined as the never-ending problem of rivalry between Europe and Asia, aggravated by the same religious and economic causes which were to lead at a later date to the colonisation of America and the partition of African territory. But with the decline of Ottoman power it assumed the form of an acute and increasingly complex competition for the legacy of the Turk. After this competition had lasted for well-nigh two centuries, the appearance of new and hitherto despised competitors in the field seemed to promise a worthier solution of the problem on the basis of the famous catchword, "The Balkans for the Balkan peoples." Unhappily, the conflict of interests was too great to permit of a solution without interference from without, and thus sowed the seed of a mightier conflagration.

Balkan history, then, during the last two centuries is

dominated by three central facts—facts so obvious as almost to be commonplace. The first is the long and apparently hopeless struggle of the subject Christian races against an alien rule of the most savage and incompetent kind. The second is the perpetual interference of the Great Powers in Balkan affairs in their own purely selfish interests, and the consequent formation of a thick network of intrigue and counter-intrigue with one main thread running through it all—the rivalry of Austria and Russia. The third is the rise of national feeling steadily leavening the dead mass until, in the Balkan wars of 1912–13, the final stage of liberation was reached, only to be succeeded by partial disillusionment and a transference of the struggle to other fields.

CHAPTER IV

THE SERBS AND THEIR STRUGGLE FOR INDEPENDENCE

OF all the nations of the Balkan Peninsula, the first among whom national sentiment revived and took a practical form was the Serbian, nor can it be emphasised too strongly that the movement among the Serbs was spontaneous, that its success was due in the main to their heroism and endurance, and that they received far less external help than any of their neighbours. The centre of the movement was the Šumadija, the wooded upland district south of the Save, which to-day forms the backbone of the little kingdom. But it is well to note at the very outset two peculiar features of Serbian history. Not merely have the frontiers of the Serbian state changed more frequently in the course of the last 1,000 years than perhaps those of any other European state, but they have never included, and do not even to-day include, the whole of the race; indeed, the fact that they do not is one of the causes of the present war.

The two kindred tribes, Serbs and Croats, trace their mythical descent to two brothers, who led their invading hordes in the seventh century into the territory still in the possession of the race. But almost from the first geography acted upon them as a centrifugal force and shaped their fate into varying channels. The rival cultures of Rome and Byzantium tore them in two oppo-

site directions and moulded their outlook, alike in matters
civil and ecclesiastical. The great Slav apostles, Cyril
and Methodius, themselves natives of Salonica, were the
decisive influence in the conversion of both Serbs and
Croats. But their memorable missionary efforts had
taken place at a period when the Eastern and Western
Churches were once more in communion. When the
conflict again broke out, and this time became final, the
western, or Croat branch, of the race naturally fell under
the influence of Rome, while the eastern, or Serb branch,
remained attached to Byzantium, whose power had very
markedly revived under the great emperors of the
eleventh century.

The breach was all the more effectual because the
ecclesiastical schism, confirming existing geographical
tendencies, coincided roughly with a period when the
kingdom of Croatia was on the eve of the extinction of
its independence, and when the young and vigorous
kingdom of the Serbs was steadily rising into prominence under the guidance of the Nemanja dynasty. The
eighth and ninth centuries saw the rise of these two
shadowy states, and the scanty fragments which survive
in the little museum of Knin (in the hinterland of
northern Dalmatia) show that the Croatian Court at a
period contemporaneous with William the Conqueror
and Robert Guiscard was not devoid of the first elements
of culture. After a brief interlude of glory, in which
Zvonimir, the greatest of the Croatian kings, was
crowned in Spalato by a legate of Pope Gregory VII.
(1076), Croatia fell under the sway of the Magyars
(1102), and although it has always succeeded in pre-
serving an autonomous existence, its fortunes have for
the last eight centuries been in the main dependent upon
those of Budapest. Meanwhile, the rise of the Serbian
state represents a natural growth from a primitive community, in which the family, in its widest sense, was the

unit and the Zadruga, or communal association, the superstructure. The power of the elder (or Starješina) developed into that of the župan, or clan chief, and an ever-expanding group of Zupans came to centre round the Great Župan (veliki župan), whose office, after passing from one great family to another, at length crystallised into an effective overlordship for the Nemanja family. It is essential to remember that the foundation upon which the Serbian state rested, even in its mediæval form, was the free peasant community.

In early centuries the rivalry of the Byzantine and Bulgarian Empires had been successfully exploited by the Serbs to secure relative immunity from attack. After the fall of the latter the young Serbia had to reckon with the powerful mediæval kingdom of Hungary, which, stretching out across Croatia, established a somewhat shadowy and varying claim to Bosnia and portions of Dalmatia, both peopled since the seventh century by a purely Croat and Serb population. The Serbian rulers of the thirteenth century found it necessary to enter upon closer dynastic and political engagements with the Hungarian kings, and even to court the favour of the Papacy and hold out serious hopes of a conversion to Catholicism. Stephen Prvenčani, or "the First-Crowned," whose father, Nemanja, had ended his days in the garb of an Orthodox monk, allowed himself in 1217 to be crowned by a Papal legate with the high-sounding titles of "king of Serbia, Diocletia, Travunia, Dalmatia, and Chum." Zealous monkish chroniclers record the story of a second coronation in the year 1222, by which his brother, the Metropolitan Sava, reclaimed him for the Eastern Church : but modern research rejects this as an invention of religious bigotry. St. Sava, who established his archiepiscopal see at Užice—the Serbian Mecca, as Ranke has called it—is the true founder of the Serbian National Church and one of the greatest figures in the history of the nation. His influence effectively checked the overtures made by Innocent III. to the Serbian king, and finally identified the cause of the National Church with Constantinople rather than Rome.

The twelfth and thirteenth centuries represent the golden era of the Serbian national state. After steadily gaining strength under a series of able rulers, it reached its zenith in the twenty-four years' reign of Stephen Dušan (1331–55). Those who may distrust the natural enthusiasm of Serbian historians will find ample evidence of his military power and governing capacity in contemporary Greek chronicles. His Court became a centre of dawning art and literature; the southern districts of the present kingdom of Serbia are studded with remarkable examples of Serbian ecclesiastical architecture,[1] due, for the most part, to the munificence of Dušan and his father, and from the battered fragments of fresco and mosaic which have survived four centuries of Turkish barbarism it is easy to trace the influence of those Italian artists who were welcomed to the Balkans when the Sienese and Florentine schools were still in their infancy. The rich mines of mediæval Serbia were exploited by the merchants of the Ragusan Republic, and formed a growing commercial link with Italy. Above all, Dušan's famous code reveals the fact that law and administration were already passing from the primitive stage and giving promise of a new culture.

In the thirteen campaigns which he waged against Byzantium he reduced the greater part of the modern Macedonia, Albania, and Montenegro to his sway, and penetrated as far as the Gulf of Corinth on the south, the Bocche di Cattaro on the west, and almost to the

---

[1] Notably the beautiful marble churches of Dečani (near Ipek) and Studenica, and those of Gračanica and Ravanica, both equally famous in Serbian ballad poetry.

gates of Adrianople on the east. Belgrade and its territory were wrested from Hungary, and Bosnia reduced
to the condition of a vassal state (1350). In 1348 he
had assumed the title of "Tsar of the Serbs and Greeks,"
and wore the tiara and other Imperial insignia. The
crown of the East was his acknowledged aim, and preparations for the conquest of Constantinople were made
upon the most formidable scale. His armies were
already in sight of the Bosphorus when the great Dušan
succumbed to a sudden illness (1355), which suspicious
contemporaries ascribed to poison, but which the more
sober historians of our own day attribute to natural
causes.

Unhappily, Dušan's greatness died with him, and his
loosely-knit dominions became the prey of warring feudal
lords, and soon dissolved into their component parts.
Only a generation later, on June 28th, 1389, Lazar, the
last of the Serbian Tsars, and with him the Serbian
Empire, perished in the great battle of Kosovo, the fatal
Field of the Blackbirds, which lives in countless national
ballads of equal beauty and originality, and keeps the
memory of ancient glories aflame even to-day throughout
the entire peasantry, not merely of Serbia and Montenegro, but also of kindred Croatia, Bosnia, and Dalmatia.
The victorious Turkish Sultan, Murad I., shared the
fate of his rival Lazar, and was buried on the field of
battle. But Serbia fell rapidly under Turkish vassalage,
and in 1459 her conquest was completed by the redoubtable Mohammed II.

Finally, in 1463, the Serb princes of Bosnia were also
reduced to subjection; their last despairing effort to
secure Western aid by the adoption of Catholicism drove
the population, Orthodox adherents of Byzantium and
heretic Bogomil sectaries alike, to welcome the rule of
Islam rather than that of the Roman Cardinal whom
the dynasty were prepared to welcome. In Bosnia the

nobility saved their lands by apostasy from the Christian
faith, and for long intervals of time remained virtually
undisturbed by their new rulers. But in Serbia no such
local concessions were possible. The nobility ceased to
exist, and the valleys of the Morava and Vardar, like
that of the Marica further east, had to submit to the
Turkish system in all its severity. Just as to-day Serbia
is coveted by the Central Powers as a route to the East,
the key to the possession of Salonica and Constantinople,
so for centuries she was held in the brutal grasp of successive Turkish conquerors as the route to the West.
For the success of their almost annual campaign in
Hungary the utter subjection of the Serb and Bulgar
countries was an essential preliminary. In short, the
real cause of their national extinction lies, not in any
racial inferiority, but in their unfavourable geographical
position, which assigned to them the front rank in the
defence of Christendom against the inroads of the Crescent. In the words of a French historian, "they were
the victims of a tragic calamity analogous to that which
in 1914 condemned Belgium to atrocious devastation."
The Serb, Bulgar, and Roumanian, each in his own way
and in his own degree, suffered centuries of national
extinction in order that Western Europe might pursue
undisturbed its task of civilisation.

From 1463 to 1804 the national life of the Serbs lay
utterly crushed. The rayah, the enslaved Christian
peasant, was exploited by heavy taxation, cowed by
restrictions, and, above all, by the horrible child-tribute
to which the renowned corps of the Janissaries so long
owed its recruits. The relations between conqueror and
conquered are best characterised by the single fact that
a Christian who failed to dismount from his horse on
meeting a Turk was liable to be killed on the spot. Two
things alone kept alive the Serb tradition—the splendid
popular ballads, unsurpassed in Europe for directness

and imagination, and the stubborn spirit of the Orthodox
clergy, who, amid ignorance, neglect, and oppression,
remained the repositories of the nation's conscience.
Only at two points did the flame of liberty continue to
burn—in the tiny mountain eyrie of Montenegro and
in the maritime Republic of Ragusa (Dubrovnik).

The history of the Black Mountain (Crnagora) is in
many respects the most romantic in all the chequered
annals of the peninsula. Its barren rocks and precipices
became a rallying-place for the Serb survivors from the
fatal carnage of Kosovo; and under Ivo Crnojevič,
renowned in many an ancient ballad as Ivo the Black or
Ivo Beg, this remnant of a warlike nation defended
itself desperately against all comers. Ivo's descendants
proved unworthy of him, and the little country was
reduced during the seventeenth century to pay occasional tribute to the Sultan, and even to provide fighting
men for the Turkish service. But the spirit of the
mountaineers was never wholly broken, and on Christmas Eve, 1702, at the instance of their vladika, or
bishop, they rose and massacred every Turk within their
reach. This ferocious incident lives in history as the
Slavonic version of the Sicilian Vespers; from it dates
the final independence of the Black Mountain. The
Vladika Danilo, of the family of Petrović-Njegoš,
became the founder of the dynasty which still occupies
the throne; the succession passed from uncle to nephew
until a second Danilo, the uncle of King Nicholas,
separated the princely from the priestly calling and
placed the dynasty on a purely secular footing.

With the exception of the Turks and the Venetians,
Europe had hitherto been ignorant of the very existence
of Montenegro. But the exploits of Danilo found an
echo in distant Russia. When war broke out, in 1710,
between Russia and Turkey, a certain Vladisavić, a
Herzegovinan Serb in the Russian service, proposed to

Peter the Great that an attempt should be made to raise Herzegovina and Montenegro against the Turks. Another Serb soldier of fortune in Russia was accordingly sent to Danilo with a proclamation of Peter, couched in grandiloquent terms, denouncing the alliance between the barbarous Turks and the heretic king of Sweden against Russia, and proclaiming the lively concern of the Tsar for the "Slav nation" and his determination "to liberate the oppressed Orthodox Christians from the yoke of the infidel."[1]   The proclamation produced a deep impression upon the Montenegrins, and this was but the first of many occasions on which the influence of Petrograd goaded them into action against the Turks.   It became a tradition among the Vladikas to visit Russia, and so implicit and unreasoning was the faith of the mountaineers in their distant kinsmen, that in 1768 an impostor, known to history as Stephen the Little, was able for a time to usurp the government of the Black Mountain by posing as the murdered Tsar of Russia, Peter III.   The renewed outbreak of hostilities between Russia and Turkey in the same year induced Catherine II. in her turn to prepare a manifesto "to all Christian communities of the Greek and Slav Orthodox nation, our co-religionists of the Holy Eastern Church," inviting their aid if they wished to "shake off the oppressive yoke of the infidels."[2]   Subsequent events, however, showed that Russian policy as yet regarded these peoples as convenient pawns in a game of which Constantinople and Santa Sofia were to be the reward.

Very different was the development of Montenegro's near neighbour, the republic of Dubrovnik, better known by its Italian name of Ragusa.   Originally founded by Roman refugees from the neighbouring town of Epidaurum, it acquired a Slavonic character as early as the seventh century, and has throughout its history played

[1] Milaković, *Storia del Montenero*, p. 88.   [2] *Ibid.*, pp 124-7.

a unique part as interpreter between the Latin and Slavonic worlds. Save for a century and a half of Venetian rule (1205–1358), the little town continued to defend its independence against all comers, and acquired a commercial position of the first importance throughout the Levant. In the fourteenth century the republic had special trading centres in Sarajevo, Skoplje, Prizren, Belgrade, Sofia, Vidin, Bucarest, and Adrianople, and leased three Serbian gold mines for an annual rent of 300,000 ducats, which, according to the calculations of Sir Arthur Evans, amounted to half the total revenue of Queen Elizabeth two centuries later. As an example of the enlightened policy of the Ragusans may be cited a decree issued by the Grand Council in 1416, by which all traffic in slaves was forbidden to citizens of the republic. Ragusan territory became an important centre of the shipbuilding trade, and the "argosies" which figure in the poetry of the Elizabethan era derive their name from that of Ragusa. Ragusan galleys took part in the battle of Lepanto and shared the disasters of the Spanish Armada. The republic reached its zenith in the early seventeenth century, when Ivan Gundulić formed the centre of a brilliant group of poets and dramatists and laid the foundations of Serbo-Croat as a modern literary language. The great earthquake of 1667 ushered in a period of decline; but when at last Ragusan independence was destroyed by Napoleon in 1808 the national spirit was once more awake among the Serbs. Dubrovnik, so long the solitary torchbearer of Southern Slav culture, sank exhausted under the rule of the Habsburgs (1814) to await in fitful slumber the hour of national resurrection.

Montenegro and Ragusa were but faint and isolated beacons amid the deep gloom of the Turkish era. Meanwhile the great mass of the Serbian race, to whom Russia was still unknown, naturally turned with eyes

of hope towards the north. Until the beginning of the
nineteenth century the world, so far as the ignorant Serb
peasant was concerned, fell into two halves—Carska
Zemlja, the land of the Tsar or Emperor (in other words
Turkey, for in every Slav tongue Constantinople is
Tsarigrad, the city of the Tsar)[1], and Cesarija-Zemlja,
Austria, the land of the Cæsar in Vienna. Even as early
as the fifteenth century many Serbs flying from Turkish
rule had settled in the southern plains of Hungary and
along the banks of the Danube, as far north as Budapest. After the defeat of Mohács and the Turkish Conquest of Central Hungary, these Serb settlers shared
the fate of their Magyar neighbours in the Alföld, and
depopulation and ruin was the fate of some of the most
fertile provinces in all Europe.

In the first period of chaos which succeeded Mohács
the territory between Drave and Save was guarded by
an army supported by the Styrian Estates, while the districts lying between the river Kulpa and the Adriatic
were left to the care of the Estates of Carniola. In the
course of time a special province, subject to the direct
authority of the Emperor, was formed under the title of
"The Military Frontiers" (Vojna Krajina). It was
divided into two "generalates," the Slavonian and the
Croatian, organised and governed on a purely military
basis. Every Graničar, or Frontiersman, was liable to
military service from his eighteenth year, and must at
all times be ready to bear arms against the invader; but
in return for this duty, successive emperors granted
substantial privileges, and the Graničari were justly
famous, not only for their military prowess, but also for
their sturdy independence of character. Every com-
mune elected its head, and all the communes of a capi-
tanate their joint judge, the election in each case requir-

[1] Hence the title "Tsar," invariably applied to the Sultan
in the old Serb ballads.

ing the sanction of the commanding officer. The Orthodox Church enjoyed the same privileges as Catholicism,
in striking contrast to the more northerly countries. In
the course of time the military frontiers were both modified and extended, and there grew up a race of hereditary soldiers and officers, holding their land on a military tenure but otherwise organised on strictly democratic lines and inspired by a tradition of personal devo-
tion to the Imperial idea such as not even the long
chain of errors and crimes committed by Vienna and
Budapest in their recent dealings with the Southern
Slavs have wholly availed to efface.

Towards the close of the seventeenth century the tide
turned very definitely in favour of the Christians. In
1686 the Turks were expelled from Buda, where a Pasha
had ruled for 160 years, and during the next twenty-five
years the armies of the Duke of Lorraine, Stahremberg,
Louis of Baden, and above all Prince Eugene, reclaimed
Central Hungary and even large tracts of Serbia itself.
It was under the impression of the earlier of these
splendid victories that the chief Serbian exodus into the
Habsburg dominions took place. In 1690 the Patriarch
of Ipek, Arsen Crnojevič, with many thousand Serb
families, migrated to Hungary and Slavonia, on the
direct invitation of the Emperor Leopold himself, and
occupied some of the territory which Turkish rule had
reduced to desolation. The Imperial charters of 1690
and 1691 assured to Leopold's new subjects their full
recognition as a nation, the free exercise of their religion,
national customs, and Church calendar, and the right to
elect their patriarch and voivode and to control their
own administration. These privileges were repeatedly
confirmed, but Jesuit influences at Court and the hostility
of the Hungarian Estates combined to prevent their
due execution. The consequent discontent provoked a
rising in 1735, which led to a further curtailment of Serb

rights and to the re-emigration of large numbers of the settlers to the south of Russia, where they have long since become merged in the surrounding population. None the less, large numbers remained behind and flourished exceedingly.

As we' have seen, the Treaty of Karlowitz (1699) secured for the Emperor the formal right to intervene on behalf of the Balkan Christians, who in their turn looked more and more to Vienna for their political salvation. The Treaty of Požarevac (1718), which crowned the victorious campaigns of Prince Eugene, not merely expelled the Turks from their last foothold on Hungarian soil, but secured the fortress of Belgrade, northern Serbia, and western Wallachia for Austria. This seemed to render Austria's complete absorption of Serbia and Bosnia a mere matter of time. But the fatal dual tendency which has so often paralysed Austria's action —the sure outcome of her geographical position between east and west—prevented a fulfilment of the designs which some of her statesmen harboured. In the Balkans Austria had a start of several generations over any of her rivals, but she failed to use it, and her history is a record of wasted opportunities. The successors of Prince Eugene proved incompetent to defend his conquests, and the ignominious Peace of Belgrade (1739) restored Serbia and Wallachia to the Turks. The Austrian occupation left many memories among the Serbs, whose intercourse with their kinsmen on Habsburg territory it had strengthened. But it was followed by nearly fifty years of negative policy in the Balkans. Throughout that period the whole attention of Maria Theresa and her advisers was concentrated upon the long struggle against Frederick the Great, and all their surplus energy was devoted to that elaborate series of administrative reforms by which the survival and evolution of modern Austria was rendered possible.

Catherine the Great's first war against Turkey was undertaken without Austrian co-operation, and Maria Theresa was a reluctant accomplice in the partition of Poland. But her son, Joseph II., despite his preoccupation with agrarian, linguistic, and ecclesiastical innovations, fell more and more under the spell of Balkan adventure. In combination with Catherine II. he worked out an ambitious scheme for the partition of the Ottoman Empire, and in the pursuit of this aim Laudon succeeded in planting for a brief period the Imperial Standard on the citadel of Belgrade (1789). But the death of Joseph transformed the situation. Leopold II. was more concerned for the fate of the Netherlands, his relations with Prussia were extremely difficult, and the growing complications and unrest of the French Revolution paralysed his Balkan policy. When peace came Belgrade was restored once more to the Turks, and the Serbs were left to their own resources.

The joint action of Austria and Russia against the Turks had aroused great expectations in Serbia, and when the war ended in a virtual restoration of the *status quo,* the disillusionment and bitterness were unbounded. A very characteristic outburst was that of the Serbian leader Aleksa Nenadović, who roundly declared : "The Emperor has deserted me and the whole Serbian nation, just as *his* ancestors deserted *ours.* I will go from cloister to cloister and bid every monk and priest take note of it, so that in future no single Serb may ever believe the Germans." National feeling had been so thoroughly aroused that the Turks, when taking over one of the fortresses evacuated by the Austrians, called out to the latter : "Neighbours, what have you done with our rayahs?" Henceforth the Serbs relied upon themselves, and happily fortune, in teaching them the bitter lesson of self-reliance, also provided them with peasant leaders of real genius. The insubordination of the Janissaries, which already seriously menaced the Sultan's power, was especially flagrant in the distant province of Belgrade; and their arrogance and depredations, culminating in 1804 in the massacre of a number of Serbian notables, provoked a serious insurrection. George Petrović, better known as Black or "Kara" George, was the son of a prosperous peasant in the central, or Šumadija, district of Serbia, following the national profession of pig-breeding. He was a man of commanding figure, indomitable resolve, and fierce passions, ignorant and even barbaric as the world counts wisdom, but endowed with those qualities of leadership, personal magnetism, torrential bravery, and diplomatic skill which in times of crisis are needed to rally a nation behind an individual. Among the first leaders of revolt there was no idea of asserting independence; their only desire was to shake off the oppressive rule of the Dahis and to secure from the Sultan the sure guarantee of local privileges. It is, however, well to note the part played by the Orthodox clergy in the movement for liberty; not content with merely encouraging their flocks, many of them were foremost in the ranks of the combatants. In the whole career of Kara George, Katić, Jakob Nenadović, Luka Lazarević and others of their comrades it is easy to trace something of the spirit with which the peasant bards of Serbia have for centuries past clothed their national heroes. Under Kara George, as Supreme Chief, "every tree became a soldier"; the flower of the Turkish Army was more than once defeated by the Serbs, and Belgrade fell into their hands. A first primitive senate was formed, and the rudiments of an administrative and educational system were introduced. But after a heroic resistance of nine years there followed a sudden collapse, accentuated by internal dissensions among the Serbian chiefs and by the complications to which foreign, and especially Russian, intervention gave rise. Turkish rule was restored, and Kara George was forced to take refuge on Austrian territory.

The liberation of Serbia was to be completed by a rival leader, Miloš Obrenović, a man of equal energy and superior statecraft, and unquestionably one of the most remarkable rulers of his age. On Palm Sunday, 1815, Miloš unfurled anew the standard of revolt, and speedily won the entire country to his side. Within two years he was the undisputed ruler of Serbia, was proclaimed as "supreme prince" (Vrhovni Knez), and found himself free to organise the administration on purely national lines. Unhappily, his triumph was stained by the treacherous murder of his rival, Kara George, whose head was dispatched as a hideous trophy to placate the Sublime Porte (1817). Thus originated the fatal dynastic feud between the Obrenović and Karagjorgjević families, which has embittered modern Serbian history and done so much to retard the country's progress.

It was not till 1830 that the Sultan could be induced to recognise Miloš as Prince. But despite the uncertainty of the preceding decade, the growth of Serbian independence was sure and steady. None the less, the need of a strong military organisation was so obviously the sole means of maintaining the liberties which they had won that the Knezes, or district leaders, were very soon compelled to submit to the personal domination of a single man. Miloš made the most of his double position as the acknowledged chief of the nation and as the accredited representative of the Porte. He soon came to disregard the advice and complaints even of his most influential followers. While concentrating all administrative and judicial power in the "supreme national court," which continued the traditions of Kara George's short-lived Senate, he at first insisted upon its following him whenever he changed his residence,

and reserved to himself the right of pronouncing the
death sentence. Miloš was a truly patriarchal ruler, such
as is only possible in a primitive form of society; while
his wife, the Princess Ljubica, cooked for him as Pene-
lope may have cooked for Odysseus, kept order in his
semi-Oriental establishment, and occasionally resorted
to very drastic measures to rid herself of rivals in her
husband's graces. In private intercourse Miloš treated
the Knezes as his equals, but unhesitatingly declined to
accept their control in public affairs. "Am I the
master," he would exclaim (using the word "Gospodar,"
by which he was most widely known to his countrymen),
"and shall I not be at liberty to do as I please?" After
the advent of the Orleans dynasty in France he was
even heard to declare that Charles X. would never have
lost his throne, had he understood how to govern as he
himself did in Serbia.[1] Unhappily, his uncontrollable
temper and greed of money led to many scandalous
abuses, the most notorious of all being his control of the
salt monopoly and of certain articles of export. By
degrees his autocratic leanings caused general discontent and estrangement, and in 1835 he saw himself forced
to introduce a Constitution and to allow the Skupština,
or popular assembly, to meet and express itself. The
interference of foreign Powers in the internal affairs of
Serbia began to gain in strength, and by a curious irony
Britain and France, whose consuls were very active at
this period in Belgrade and Kragujevac, favoured the
extension of the Prince's absolutist powers, while autocratic Russia contended for a restriction of his authority.[2]
The numerous restrictions which the charter of 1838
imposed upon the Prince proved intolerable to Miloš,
and led inevitably and rapidly to his abdication and exile
(1839). A month later his eldest son Milan succumbed
to a protracted illness without ever having been able to

[1] Ranke, pp. 252, 256.   [2] Ranke, *op. cit.,* p. 264.

assume office, and was succeeded by his younger brother
Michael. But the politicians who had engineered the
movement against the father did not feel secure with the
son as their ruler, and, having secured the approval of
the Porte for their plans, started a military revolt which
forced Michael in his turn to take refuge on Austrian
territory (1842). Michael was replaced by Alexander
Karagjorgjević, son of the murdered Kara George.
Russia's opposition to the change naturally forced the
new Prince into the Austrian sphere of influence, and
this tendency was strengthened by the events of 1848.
The Serbs of the Banat and Slavonia, under the leadership of the Patriarch Rajačić, eagerly espoused the
Habsburg cause against the Magyars; and the restoration of the Serbian Voivodina and the further concessions promised to them by the Emperor won for him
and for Austria the sympathies of the Serbs of the principality also, many of whom crossed the Save and
Danube as volunteers in the Austrian Army.

During the Crimean War Russian influence upon the
Prince and his Court declined still further; but his feeble
and vacillating policy alienated the masses, which had
never ceased to be Russophil. In 1858 Alexander, who
had hitherto governed through the Senate, for the first
time ventured to summon the national assembly, which
promptly voted his deposition and the recall of the
veteran Prince Miloš. His long exile had failed to curb
Miloš's autocratic leanings, and he celebrated his return
by the expulsion or imprisonment of several of the leading Serbian statesmen. But his death in September,
1860, restored Michael to power and marked the close of
what may be described as the patriarchal era of Serbian
history.

Michael was in many ways the wisest ruler whom
Serbia has produced, combining the native untrained
wit of the founder of his dynasty with the education and

wider outlook of a new generation. The arbitrary and slipshod methods of his father were superseded by a genuine zeal for constitutional procedure. Numerous administrative reforms were introduced, a national militia was created under French officers, and the old semi-Turkish Constitution of 1830 was remodelled on Western lines. Serbia found in Michael a jealous guardian of her rights against any encroachments on the part of the suzerain Powers. In 1862, as the result of an affray, the Porte consented to the demolition of the Turkish quarter of Belgrade and to the dismantling of the Turkish fortresses of Sokol and Užice. Finally, in 1867, as the result of Michael's firm attitude, the few remaining garrisons were withdrawn, and on May 6th the last Turkish soldier quitted Serbian soil.

To Michael's far-sighted view Serbia was but the advance guard of Balkan unity. Her liberation of Bosnia from Turkish rule was to be the first stage towards the emancipation of her Bulgarian kinsmen, whose eyes in those days were still turned towards Belgrade with hope and sympathy. The growing perception of kinship among all branches of the Southern Slavs was eloquently expressed by Michael's contemporary, Danilo of Montenegro, who addressed him with the words : "Form the kingdom of Serbia, and I shall gladly be the first to mount guard before your palace." No less cordial were Michael's relations with the great Bishop Strossmayer. The first germs of a Balkan League may be traced in Michael's relations with Prince Alexander Couza of Roumania and his youthful successor, Charles of Hohenzollern, with the Bulgarian Committee in Bucarest, and with Kossuth, the exiled Governor of Hungary. But with all his enthusiasm for the Jugoslav ideal he did not go far enough for Garašanin, the most audacious and speculative of Serbian statesmen : and the conflict which ensued, coupled with his relapse in internal affairs into the autocratic habits which he had avoided earlier in his reign, aroused the enmity of the younger generation, and above all of the Omladina, an active society which had its headquarters in Southern Hungary and dabbled in secret revolutionary propaganda. On June 10th, 1868, he was assassinated by a group of partisans of the rival dynasty, and though their conspiracy proved abortive, infinite harm was done to the cause of Serbia by the removal of so wise a statesman and by the accentuation of the fatal dynastic feud.

Michael was succeeded by his cousin Milan, then a boy of fourteen. The Regency, presided over by Jovan Ristić, may be said to have inaugurated constitutional government in Serbia, though on distinctly oligarchical lines. The Constitution of 1869 created a single chamber based upon almost universal suffrage, but modified by the Prince's powers to nominate one-quarter of the assembly. Its members had no powers of initiative; the introduction of new laws, and the convocation and dissolution of the Chamber, lay entirely in the hands of the Prince. The only definite advance upon earlier practice was the establishment of Cabinet responsibility.

Prince Milan typifies a class of which the Balkan Peninsula has been only too prolific during the past century—a class which has discarded the primitive virtues of the peasant and imitated the more superficial vices of the West without its more solid virtues. Heredity and education were alike against him. Excess had plunged his father into an early grave, while his mother was notorious as the mistress of Prince Alexander Couza of Roumania. He himself grew up in an atmosphere of intrigue and flattery such as might have undermined far stronger characters than his, and proved quite unequal for the difficult problems with which the years 1875–78 were to confront him.

CHAPTER V

THE GREEK REVOLUTION

THE Serbs were the first Balkan people to shake off
the Turkish yoke, but the Greeks were not far behind.
The two races present a striking contrast. The former
were a peasant community, land-locked and isolated
among their upland mountain ranges, though their Croat
kinsmen of the Dalmatian coast are among the finest
seamen in Europe. The latter fall mainly into two
categories—seafaring and commercial. The Ægean
was for many centuries before the Christian era a Greek
sea; but leave the coast, and to-day, as in the time of
Philip and Alexander of Macedon, Greek influences are
soon left behind. The Byzantine Empire, for the last
eight centuries of its existence, was essentially Greek
in spirit as in form. But its character was seriously
modified by the Latin conquest of the thirteenth century
—that famous Fourth Crusade which set out from Venice
to replace the Cross upon the Holy Places of Jerusalem,
but which rapidly degenerated into a freebooters' campaign, marked by the crowning incidents of the sack of
Zara and the conquest of Constantinople (1204–5). The
disintegrating effects of that conquest soon became
apparent in the crop of petty feudal states which were
sown all over the Near East, and struck deepest root in
what to-day is once more Greece. With the romantic

and parochial annals of Achaia and Athens, of Thessalonica, Euboea, and Naxos we need not concern ourselves.[1] They are of little importance save as a symptom
of decay and approaching dissolution. But it is worth
noting that the Byzantine nobility—'Ρωμαῖοι, to use their
own name—when they returned from two generations of
exile at Nicæa, assumed a more avowedly Greek
character than before.

The coming of the Turk reduced the Greeks to the
same dead-level of enslavement as their Christian
neighbours; all alike groaned under the *haratch* (poll
tax) and the blood tribute. But in the Morea there was
an interlude which did not come to the Slavs farther
north. From 1684 to 1718 the Venetians succeeded in
expelling the Turks, and the accounts which they have
left us of their new possessions afford eloquent proof
of what Turkish rule meant, even within a measurable
distance of time from the great days of Ottoman power.
Under Venice there were, of course, opportunities of
education and culture, even though the fortresses of
Morea, like the ports of the Dalmatian coast, were held
on the old colonial basis as objects of economic exploitation and strategic advantage, with no share in the privileges of the republic.

The gradual decay of Venice which followed the loss
of her Morean conquests coincided with a noticeable
revival of Greek commerce in the Levant, and there were
numerous Greek settlements in Wallachia and Moldavia.
There was also a growing connection, mainly ecclesiastical, with Russia. Monks from Mt. Athos and
occasional Greek and Roumanian bishops visited the
Court of the Tsar; and, indeed, in 1657 the Patriarch
Parthenius of Constantinople was hanged for plotting

[1] There are three standard English works on this subject—
Finlay's "History of Greece," W. Miller's "The Latins in the
Levant," and Sir R. Rodd's "The Princes of Achaia."

with the Tsar and with the Cossacks of the Ukraine, then an independent state. This sharp lesson intimidated the Greek clergy, and for a whole century to come Russia's relations with the peninsula were mainly confined to Montenegro and the Danubian principalities. But corruption contributed as much as fear to this result. The Phanariot *régime* [1] consisted, on its ecclesiastical side, in the shameless sale of bishoprics,[2] whose holders recouped themselves by virtually holding up minor Church offices to auction. The Patriarchate had been degraded to a mere instrument of the Sublime Porte, and was deeply infected by simony and similar malpractices. The parishes were burdened by all kinds of dues and tithes; there was a regular traffic in marriage dispensations, burial permits, and similar unjust perquisites of the priestly office. Monks entirely alien to the people and sunk in the crassest ignorance were intruded upon the villagers, and often called in the Turkish soldiery to enforce their extortions. Such a system was especially iniquitous in its working in Bosnia and Macedonia, where Greek prelates wrought their will upon the Slav peasantry. The Church was sunk in ignorance and materialism; only here and there a few humble parish priests and a handful of recluses in Mt. Athos kept the national flame burning.

Meanwhile, the rich Greek families of the Phanar rose to high ofice at the Porte, and, as flourishing bankers or even usurers, bought from the Grand Vizier or his colleagues as blank forms the firmans of nomination to various provincial posts and resold them at exorbitant figures, after filling in the payees' names. Their position brought them almost unlimited opportunities of

[1] See pp. 22 and 61.

[2] The price is estimated to have varied from 10,000 to 250,000 piastres.

exaction. The office of Dragoman of the Fleet, which came to be held almost invariably by a Greek, was especially lucrative, influential, and corrupt. Yet, in the apt phrase of a native historian, Greeks and Turks have remained distinct for centuries, like water and oil in the same jar.[1]

One section of the Greek population had always preserved some fragments of liberty—the islanders and mountaineers of what is now western Greece and southern Albania. The Klephts were wild brigands corresponding with the Slavonic Haiduks, who had defied the Turkish authorities and taken refuge in the hills; and in the ballads and legends of the Greek people "Klepht" (thief) and "Palikar" (hero) came to be almost interchangeable terms. In certain districts the Turks had found it necessary to recognise the formation of a rough Greek militia with national commanders, the so-called Armatoli; and these formed a nucleus of revolt when Russian agents appeared in the Morea during the Russo-Turkish War of 1769–74, and were backed up by the arrival of a Russian fleet in the Mediterranean. It is true that the Greeks were left to their fate when it suited Catherine the Great to make peace with the Sublime Porte. But at last the dry bones had been stirred, and the silence of the charnel house had been finally dispelled.

A long succession of degenerate Sultans had reduced the machine of state to real chaos, and before the close of the eighteenth century the fate of Turkey seemed to be sealed. She was rescued by the outbreak of the French Revolution and the European upheaval to which it led. But though there was a breathing space, internal disintegration continued. The Janissaries were completely out of hand, military insubordination became steadily

[1] Paparrigopoulos, "History of Hellenic Civilisation," *cit.* Cahuet, *La Question d'Orient,* p. 21.

more acute, and local pashas acted more and more according to their own good pleasure. Of these provincial tyrants none is more famous than Ali Pasha, the Lion of Janina, who began as an outlaw and a robber, but at the heyday of his fame negotiated on equal terms with Napoleon and other European Governments of the day. A considerable romantic literature has gathered round his name; Byron and other travellers introduced him to the notice of the West. The wily pasha played with the various envoys, fastened a tricolour cockade to his turban, and posed as a believer in the principles of the French Revolution, which in reality were about as effective a proof of his conversion to Western culture as the top hat on the head of a Nigerian chief. In short, he was a mediæval Oriental tyrant of the approved style. Ali's fierce and prolonged feud with the Suliotes—a tribe of Christian Albanians forming a rude and ill-defined republic on the Epirote coast—was one of the most notable incidents which led up to the war of Greek independence. He also exterminated some of the most flourishing Vlach colonies of the Pindus and Albania, notably the town of Moscopolis, or Moskopolje, from which more than one wealthy Roumanian family of Austria-Hungary traces its origin.[1] At that period, it is to be remembered, the main line of distinction in the Balkans was still between Christian and Moslem. Vlachs and Albanians were at one with the Greeks in regarding the Orthodox Church, in its Greek garb, as the chief champion of the enslaved rayah, and supplied the national movement among the Greeks with many of its leaders. Rhigas, the forerunner of the revolution, the author of the Greek "Marseillaise" and many stirring songs of battle, was a Vlach; and it is interesting to note that as early as the year 1798 he was trying

[1] *E.g.*, that of Dr. Dumba, the late Austro-Hungarian Ambassador in Washington.

to concert joint action between Greeks and Serbs, and paid for his rashness on the scaffold at Belgrade.

The movement among the Greeks was far more complex than among the Serbs, for there were Greek emigrants on every Mediterranean coast imbibing the ideas of the various Western countries at a moment when political thought was more than usually volatile. The island of Chios became a centre of Greek learning, maintaining fourteen professors and other subsidiary teachers. The influence of the French Revolution upon these men and upon their pupils was very great, and there was a rapid revival of national Hellenic sentiment. Parallel with this there was an equally rapid commercial expansion in the Ægean, due to the decay of the French Navy and of French commercial establishments in the Levant. The islands of Hydra, Spetsai, and Psara became flourishing shipping centres. Fortunes were made on all sides, and wealthy Greek traders in close touch with France and England educated their sons in Western ideas.

As Hellenic sentiment spread, its devotees came to look more and more to the Holy Alliance for deliverance. Fifteen thousand Greeks are believed to have joined the standard of the Allies. But the Congress of Vienna soon undeceived them. Dynastic, not national, interests ruled the day, and so far as the Eastern Question was concerned only Turkey and the Great Powers were considered. To-day the chief task which will confront the democracies of France and Great Britain after the war will be to prevent the formation of a new Holy Alliance for the deception of those small nations who set their faith, as one hundred years ago, in the high-sounding phrases of European statesmen.

For some years after 1815 the Greek movement was forced underground; the flame crept slowly over a double trail until the powder magazine was reached. On the one hand, the corruption of literary form, which had in the course of centuries so effectually divorced the modern Greek rayah from the glories of ancient Hellas, was repaired by linguistic reforms and the publication of popular versions of the classics. Korais and other learned Greeks laboured unremittingly and successfully to restore the lost continuity, and thus accomplished a process such as is vital to all national movements, and found its parallel in contemporary Hungary, Bohemia, and Roumania. But the men of letters, though they prepared the ground for the future, lacked the courage or initiative for political action. On the other hand, the Philike Hetairia, a secret society founded by three Greeks at Odessa in 1814 with the object of promoting a Greek rising against the Turks, struck rapid root in the Danubian principalities, notably in Bucarest, Jassy, and Galatz. Its organisation honeycombed the Morea and the islands, and within three years it already counted 17,000 adherents in Constantinople alone. About the same time a Greek educational society was founded in Vienna.

The Philhellene movement in the west of Europe kept pace with the organisation of the Hetairia, and a fresh focus for Greek feeling was provided by the Ionian Islands, which formed an autonomous unit under a British protectorate, and were granted a Constitution in the year 1817. In 1820 the Hetairia found a leader in Alexander Ypsilanti, the member of a noble Greek family which had ruled both in Wallachia and Moldavia, and a personal aide-de-camp of the Tsar Alexander I. It is typical of his visionary and unpractical outlook that he talked wildly of reviving the Eastern Empire, and that he decided to raise the standard of revolt, not in the real Hellas, but in the Danubian principalities. He entirely failed to realise that the population loathed the Greeks as representing the corrupt Phanariot *régime*. From

the lips of the Roumanian peasant leader Vladimirescu,
who headed a national movement in Wallachia at this
very moment, he received a blunt reminder that "Greece
belongs to the Greeks and Roumania to the Roumanians." In 1821 Ypsilanti issued a high-faluting
proclamation beginning : "Hellenes, the hour has struck.
It is time to avenge our religion and our country." He
then crossed the river Pruth at the head of a few
followers, but found no support, and soon had to fly
to Hungarian territory, where he was thrown, by orders
of Metternich, into the fortress of Munkács.[1] Ypsilanti's
adventure was the spark which fired the powder, but any
other spark might have done the task equally well.
Indeed, his action really had more effect on Roumania
than on Greece; for, even without him, Greece was
already in the throes of a revolutionary movement. Ali
Pasha, after years of intrigue and massacre, had
definitely revolted against the Sultan and invited the
Greeks to make common cause with him. In the spring
of 1821 the rising became general throughout the Morea,
and the capture of some strongholds was followed by
the massacre of Moslems. The Klepht song, "Not a
Turk shall remain," was acted upon only too well. And
here, in passing, it is well to refer to the patriotic sacrifices made by prominent Greeks, some of whom devoted
their entire fortunes to the national cause. Since then
private beneficence has become a tradition, and there is
no portion of the Near East where so many public and
charitable institutions are due to individual initiative.

The rising, and the excesses which it evoked, met with
a drastic answer from the Turks. Mohammed II., in his
rage, ordered the execution of the Greek Dragoman and
other leading Phanariots; and the Greek Patriarch

---

[1] His captivity at Munkács was the subject of a well-known
poem by the German poet Wilhelm Müller, father of the Oxford
Orientalist Max Müller.

Gregory V. was hanged from the gate of his palace. The body, after hanging for three days, was flung into the sea by the rabble of Stambul. Such an event only roused the insurgents to fresh efforts, and their cause seemed to prosper. In January, 1822, a Constitution was proclaimed for all Greece. But the Turks sent crushing reinforcements, overpowered and killed "the Lion of Janina" in his lake fortress, and then prepared to overwhelm the Greeks in their turn. The crowning horror of the war was the massacre of Chios, during which the entire Greek population was either put to the sword by the Turkish soldiery or sold as slaves or driven into exile. Utter ruin fell upon the most cultured and prosperous Greek community; the population sank from 113,000 to 1,800. It lies outside the scope of the present volume to recount in detail the story of the Greek revolution—the heroic guerilla warfare, the fierce discussions between the rival Klepht leaders, Botzaris, Kolokotrones, Odysseus, and others, the thrill which ran through Europe at the news of Byron's death at Missolonghi. Its dramatic episodes may be read in the classic pages of Finlay and Gordon and in other more recent works of historical research. In 1825 the war entered upon a new stage with the arrival, as Turkish generalissimo, of Ibrahim Pasha, the famous soldier son of Mehemet Ali of Egypt. The two main incidents of his campaigns were the fall of Missolonghi and the capture of the Acropolis. Finally, the brawls of rival chiefs ended in the selection of two foreigners to command the naval and military forces of Greece—Admiral Cochrane (afterwards Lord Dundonald), one of the greatest sailors the British Navy has produced, and Sir Richard Church, who had already made his mark by the extirpation of brigandage in Southern Italy. The turning-point of the war came in 1827, when Count Capo d'Istria, a Corfiote Greek born under Venetian rule, and a strong Russophil, was elected President of Greece, and when Britain, France, and Russia concluded a Treaty for mediation between Turks and Greeks.

The armistice which they tried to impose upon both parties was accepted by the insurgents, but disregarded by the Sublime Porte, and when their naval squadrons were fired upon by the Turks, action inevitably followed. In the memorable battle of Navarino (October 20th) the Turkish Fleet was annihilated by the Allies under Admiral Codrington. Thus the three Powers who after an interval of eighty years are once more operating in Greek territory may be said to have put the crown upon Greek independence. Canning's opponents in Parliament might describe as an "untoward event" what most people regarded, and still regard, as a "great victory"; but the essential fact is that Greece was saved. When in 1829 war broke out between Russia and Turkey, the Ottoman troops had to be withdrawn from Greek soil, and the last retreating army was routed in September by Demetrius Ypsilanti, the brother of the man whose action eight years earlier on the banks of the Pruth had begun the war.

In 1830 the protecting Powers drew up a Protocol regulating the status of the new Greece, but the frontiers were drawn upon so niggardly a scale that Prince Leopold of Coburg, afterwards Leopold I. of Belgium and grandfather of King Albert, declined to accept the new throne when it was offered to him. The kingdom of Greece was finally created by the Treaty of 1832, under the guarantee, not of the Concert of Europe, but of the three Entente Powers—a fact which is highly significant in view of the events of the present day. It is difficult to praise the new creation; it was notoriously incomplete, Epirus and Thessaly being omitted, and Samos and Crete expressly excluded—the latter to remain a festering sore for two more generations. The

austere but autocratic Capo d'Istria had been assassinated in 1831, and his death had been followed by faction
fighting. At last, in 1832, the crown was offered to
Prince Otto, the second son of King Louis I. of Bavaria
—an ardent Philhellene, whose artistic and archæo-
logical leanings are known to every visitor to modern
Munich. Under the new *régime* the three Powers provided a joint loan, and troops were supplied from
Bavaria. At first Nauplia was the capital, but by an
inevitable process it was transferred ere long to Athens.

It was only to be expected that Greece, after long
centuries of subjection, followed by those party feuds
to which the race has always been too prone, would fail
at first to develop proper constitutional government.
The National Assembly proved to be a mere farce, and
the administration was in a state of virtual anarchy. By
degrees administrative, judicial, and educational reforms
were introduced under the Bavarian Regents, and a
national University was founded. But there were
periodical local risings, and the tactlessness of Otto's
German advisers led at last, in 1843, to a revolution and
to the promulgation of a new Constitution, with a Parliament of two Chambers. One episode of Otto's reign
deserves special notice. During the Crimean War
attempts were made to raise revolt in Thessaly and to
extend that national unity which Greeks of to-day seem
afraid to carry to its final stage. The high-spirited
Queen was the leader of the war party, but Otto himself
was no less keen a nationalist. Greek action, however,
was paralysed by a Franco-British occupation of the
Piræus, which lasted from 1854 to 1857, and remains
one of the most humiliating memories of the Crimean
War—that futile war in which we helped the Turks to
repress nationality and liberty throughout the Near East.

The two vices of Greece were financial disorder in its
acutest form and local brigandage, due very largely to

economic causes. The next five years saw a rapid
decline in Otto's popularity. Though not a vicious ruler,
he was quite unequal to so difficult a task as presiding
over the infancy of a new state. While appearing
unduly arbitrary to his own subjects, he lost the support of the Powers, in very large measure because he
was too good a patriot and too devoted to the ideal of
"Greater Greece." In 1862 a revolution drove him from
the throne, and the upheaval was duly sanctioned by the
British Government, in whose name Lord Russell
affirmed Greece's "right to change its governing dynasty
upon good and sufficient cause." During the inter-
regnum the Duke of Edinburgh became the popular
candidate in Greece, but in 1863 the throne was finally
offered to Prince William of Denmark, who took the
title of George I. The new arrangement took the form
of a Treaty between the three protecting Powers and the
King of Denmark, Britain, France, and Russia once
more appearing in the *rôle* of godparents. The new
King brought with him as a present the Ionian Isles,
which were made over by Gladstone as a contribution
to Greek National Unity. Thus, if our behaviour in
1854 had gone some way towards effacing the effect of
Navarino, this act may certainly be said to have restored
the balance in our favour. The long rein of King
George opens a new era in Greek history—an era of
growing pains in the body politic, not unlike those which
affect our early childhood.

CHAPTER VI

MODERN ROUMANIA

WHILE Greek, Serb, and Bulgar lay crushed under
the heel of the Turkish conqueror, the Roumanian was
saved by his geographical situation from complete
national extinction, though even his fate was far from
enviable. During the dark centuries of barbarian
invasion from the north-east no country suffered more
severely than what is now Roumania; but when the
chief menace came from the. south-east with the Ottoman advance, the great natural obstacle of the Danube
afforded protection, and to some extent diverted the
stream of invasion. The fate of Serbia and Bulgaria
was decided by the fact that they blocked the Turkish
line of advance westwards, just as to-day Serbia had to
be crushed by the Central Powers because she lay across
the path of the victorious German *Drang nach Osten.*
These elementary facts, so lightly ignored by the statesmen in whose hands our fate as an Empire rests, spring
to the eyes of every intelligent student of the Near East.

The origin of the Roumanian race has formed the
subject of much speculation and heated discussion. A
purely academic question has been distorted to serve the
purpose of rival parties and to prove or disprove the
claims of racial supremacy. Certain points cannot, and
never will be, cleared up for lack of evidence, but the
main lines are absolutely clear, and no amount of poli-

tical special pleading can succeed in distorting them.
The modern Roumanians are the descendants of those
Roman colonists whom Trajan planted for the defence
of the Empire against the northern barbarians. After
the first conquest, which has been immortalised in the
reliefs of Trajan's Column at Rome, Dacia rapidly
became a flourishing province, and included the greater
part of the modern Roumanian kingdom and of Transylvania—its chief town, Apulum, being in the, latter
(now Karlsburg or Gyulafehérvár).[1]

In the year 270 the colony was abandoned by the
Emperor Aurelian, and for a thousand years this whole
tract of country has nothing which can even be remotely
described as history. It can boast an almost unique
record of anarchy and chaos, with practically no
memorials of literature, architecture, or art. The whole
period is shrouded in impenetrable obscurity, and it is
not till the thirteenth century that the veil is lifted. By
that time we find the country racially what it is to-day
—Roumanian. This fact is not disputed;. but there are
two rival explanations, each worked out on the ground
of a political thesis. The one view is that the native
population preserved its identity virtually unimpaired
through a thousand years of invasion and disturbance;
the other that the population was withdrawn to the south
of the Danube, remained there for a thousand years, and
only began to return in the twelfth and thirteenth
centuries. By putting forward this latter theory, Magyar
controversialists have established to their own satisfaction, but certainly not to that of any external observer,
the right of one race which has been nine or ten centuries
in a country to destroy the national identity of another
race which has only been seven centuries in the same
place. As usual, the truth is to be found half-way

[1] Perhaps best known under its mediæval name of Alba Julia or
Alba Regia.

between the two rival theories. The Roumanians are unquestionably descended from the Roman colonists of Dacia. Their Latin origin is obvious to anyone who walks through the streets of Bucarest, still more to anyone who visits the remoter villages of Transylvania and sees the pure Roman types among the peasantry. Above all, the Roumanian language is an unanswerable proof of linguistic continuity, its grammar and syntax being predominantly Latin. On the other hand, there is a considerable admixture of Slavonic words in the vocabulary such as clearly proves the presence of other elements in the race.

Perhaps the best proof that the Roumanian tide did not set from south to north, as Magyar apologists argue, but from north to south, is supplied by the position of the various capitals.   In Wallachia, the original centres were Câmpulung and Curtea de Argeş, which were superseded first by Târgovistea and finally by Bucarest, while the capital of Moldavia was transferred from its original seat in Suceava (in what is now Bukovina) to Jassy. In each case it is a gradual descent from the northern mountains into the plains of the Danubian system.

Not all the efforts of modern scientific research have availed to throw light upon this extremely obscure period of history. For our present purpose it is sufficient to point out that by the thirteenth century the kernel of modern Roumania was forming in the two principalities of Wallachia and Moldavia; 1290 and 1349 are the dates usually assigned for their emergence as national States.   The whole territory lying east and north-east of the Iron Gates consisted of a number of loosely-knit voivodes or principalities—each owning a varying and ill-defined allegiance to the Hungarian Crown, and living a precarious existence between the second Bulgarian Empire now tottering to its fall and the rising kingdom of Hungary. By the reign of Louis the Great (1340-1382) the northern voivodes had been assimilated by the Magyar nobility, while the sister states of Wallachia and Moldavia had taken definite shape between the Carpathians, the Dnjester and the Danube. But, unhappily before the consolidation could be achieved, the Turks had made their first appearance upon the scene, and the greater part of five centuries were to be consumed in a struggle for existence such as rendered progress or culture well-nigh impossible.

The part played by the Roumanians in the defence of Europe against the Turks has not received sufficient recognition in the West. To their race belonged the famous hero, John Hunyády, who led the armies of Hungary to repeated victory, and whose son, Matthias Corvinus, occupied the Hungarian throne during the period of furthest Magyar expansion. Nor should we pass over the exploits of another Roumanian hero who ascended the throne of Moldavia within a year of the great Hunyády's death. For almost half a century (1457-1504) Stephen the Great held the Turks at bay, and amply earned a place with Hunyády, Sobieski and Eugene as one of the four chief bulwarks of Christendom. "The high deeds which thou hast accomplished," wrote Pope Sixtus IV. to Stephen, "against the infidel Turks, our common enemies . . . have rendered thy name so glorious that all of one accord sing thy praises." In the chaotic annals of Wallachia and Moldavia Stephen stands head and shoulders above all other rulers : Mircea the Old, Alexander the Good, Vlad the Impaler do not deserve more than a local fame or notoriety.

The death of Stephen the Great ushers in a period of steady decline from warlike independence to abject vassalage. Yet the Principalities, as Wallachia and

Moldavia came to be called, never succumbed to Turkish rule with the same completeness as Serbia and Bulgaria, or even as Hungary in the sixteenth and seventeenth centuries. Instead of imposing Turkish pashas, the Sultan had been content with exacting a heavy tribute as the recognition of his suzerainty. While in Serbia the native aristocracy was exterminated, and in Bosnia adopted the faith of Islam as a means of saving its lands, the Roumanian boyars remained well-nigh undisturbed, and the native princes continued to be elected by the joint influence of the boyars and the higher Orthodox clergy. The nation was enslaved and neglected, but never annihilated like its neighbours. Indeed we are confronted by the strange paradox that at the very moment when Buda was the capital of a Turkish pasha, a Roumanian prince, Michael the Brave, laid for a brief space of time the foundations of a "Greater Roumania," comprising Wallachia, Moldavia, Bessarabia, Transylvania and Bukovina (to use the nomenclature of our own century—ere long, we hope, to be dismissed to the historical lumber room), and till his death in 1601 held Turks, Magyars, Poles and his own rebellious subjects alike at bay. His exploits not unnaturally fired the imagination of the race, and to-day his statue in Bucarest is to Roumania what Nelson's Column, in Trafalgar Square, is to London—the scene of political, and, above all, of patriotic demonstrations.

But Michael's reign was, in the words of Roumania's latest historian, nothing more than "a brilliant intermezzo." During the seventeenth century the two principalities lay between the upper and the nether millstones, and their degenerate rulers became the victims of Turkish, Austrian and Polish rivalry. In 1716, even the election of native princes, powerless phantoms as they were, was ignominiously forbidden by the Porte, and for the next century the thrones of Wallachia and

Moldavia were shamelessly put up for auction to the highest bidder. The Phanariot princes, to whom more than one distinguished family of modern Roumania traces its origin, were for the most part rich Greeks resident in that quarter of Stambul which took its name from the great Phanar or lighthouse. There was no lack of competition for an office which, however lucrative, was precarious and indeed not without its dangers; and, as on the one hand almost all the successful candidates sought to recover, by means of rapacious exactions from their new subjects, the money spent in bribing the Porte, and, as on the other, the Porte found an obvious interest in satisfying a new bidder, there were continual changes of ruler, and between the years 1716 and 1821 no fewer than thirty-seven and thirty-three Hospodars occupied the thrones of Wallachia and Moldavia respectively.

The outward and visible signs of this shameful period in a slumbering nation's history was the transference, at the hands of the Turkish suzerain, of two Roumanian provinces to alien rule—Bukovina to Austria in 1775, and Bessarabia to Russia in 1812. It is but just to point out that the Hospodar of Moldavia, Gregory Ghika, vigorously protested against this surrender of Bukovina, and with it of the ancient capital of Moldavia, Suceava; but even his threats of alliance with Russia failed to alarm the Porte, who knew only too well its vassal's impotence. At that period, moreover, Russia and Austria were marching hand in hand, and the latter's acquisition of Bukovina, following upon the first partition of Poland, filled only a small place in Joseph II.'s ambitious designs for the partition of the Sultan's dominions, by which he himself should obtain Belgrade and the Danubian provinces (in addition to the Dalmatian coast-line, then in Venetian hands), while Crimea and Bessarabia should fall to Russia and the remnants of Turkey should be guaranteed by the Great Powers. The war of 1789, with its crowning incident, the capture of Belgrade by Laudon, seemed to be the forerunner of such a partition, but the death of Joseph II. and the outbreak of the revolutionary wars soon put an end to all idea of Austria's expansion to the Black Sea. Indeed, so far from being free to acquire fresh provinces, Austria ere long found her own existence at stake, and in 1809, as the result of Napoleon's victorious campaigns, had to submit—in common with her future rival, Prussia—to a serious curtailment of territory, and even to her exclusion from the Adriatic. The influence of Napoleon throughout the Balkan Peninsula was, as everywhere else in Europe, that of an awakener, but the immediate result of the Napoleonic era was disastrous to the Danubian principalities. While endeavouring to exploit Polish national feeling for his own ends, Napoleon treated Wallachia and Moldavia merely as useful pawns in the game of setting Austria and Russia by the ears: and in 1812 the Tsar, whose army of occupation had governed the provinces for the past six years, received from Turkey as the price of evacuation the eastern portion of Moldavia, known as Bessarabia.

In the fifty years which preceded the Congress of Vienna, the Principalities had been exposed to equal danger from Vienna and from Petrograd; in the nineteenth century the dominant factor which determined their fate still continued to be the rivalry of Austria and Russia for influence upon the Lower Danube. Each time that Russia went to war with the Turks she occupied Moldavia and Wallachia, both as an obvious milestone on the road of territorial advance, and as a convenient hostage to bargain with at the close of hostilities. In less than sixty years there were no fewer than five foreign occupations, four Russian and one Austrian. Thus the Tsar's troops held Jassy and Bucarest from 1806 to 1812, from 1828 to 1834, from 1848 to 1849, and from

1853 to 1854, their place being filled during the Crimean War by the Austrian army. The solitary advantage which accrued to the inhabitants was the *Règlement Organique,* a Constitution which the Russians left behind them on their withdrawal in 1834, and which, inadequate as it was, at least showed some slight improvement upon its predecessors and contained the germs of future liberty.

This perpetual recurrence of foreign intervention not unnaturally gave a further impetus to reviving national feeling. Under the influence of the French Revolution the idea of nationality had made its entry, not only into Italy and Hungary, but also into the Balkans. The Serbs were the first Balkan people to assert their liberty.[1] But in Roumania also a popular movement broke out in 1821 under the peasant leader, Tudor Vladimirescu, and though the insurrection proved abortive, it none the less ended the Phanariot *régime* and secured for the two Principalities the right to elect their own rulers.

From 1821 till the outbreak of the Crimean War Russian influence was really all-powerful in the Principalities, which continued, as before, under the ban of Austro-Russian rivalry. But it was neither in Petrograd nor in Vienna, but in Paris, that the young Roumanians of the early nineteenth century sought the training and inspiration necessary to regenerate their country. The French influence, which for good or for evil has done so much to mould modern Roumania, owes its origin to the Phanariot princes, whose families, amid the barbarous atmosphere of Stambul, sought to link themselves with Western culture by a study of the French language. This outward veneer of civilisation followed them to their courts in Bucarest and Jassy. At first adopted as a

---

[1] Incidentally, it is worth pointing out that the movements for Greek, and later for Bulgarian, freedom were organised on Roumanian soil, Bucarest being the centre of the *émigrés.*

mere social pose by the young and wealthy boyars, French ideas began to strike root among the small educated class, and, as the spirit of nationality raised its head, were fostered by a growing consciousness of the Latin origin of the race. All the young Roumanian patriots made Paris their headquarters, and fell under the influence of the French Liberals and of Mazzini and his school. The revolution of 1848—"a stray spark from Paris," as it has been called—failed by reason of the inexperience of its promoters, their lack of any practical programme and the apathy of the masses, in whose mind the land was the all-absorbing question. But it brought to the front the future makers of Roumania, men like Kogalniceanu, Brătianu and Rosetti, and taught them the need for united effort.

The Russian armies which in 1849 crushed Magyar resistance to the House of Habsburg had no difficulty in restoring the *status quo* in Wallachia and Moldavia, and in imposing the Tsar's will upon the new Hospodars. Thus the *annus mirabilis,* as was only natural, did not leave the same impress upon the east as upon the west of Europe. The first vital change in the situation was caused by the Russian evacuation in 1854, rendered necessary by the attitude of the Western Powers in espousing the Turkish cause. No sooner had the Russians withdrawn than their place was taken by an Austrian army of occupation, which remained in possession until long after the close of the Crimean War. The Congress of Paris (1856), like its famous predecessor the Congress of Vienna and its successor the Congress of Berlin, showed but little consideration for the wishes of the peoples whose fate depended upon its decisions. One of its endeavours was to repress the growing movement in favour of union between the two Principalities. Indeed it is not too much to say that each of the Great Powers in turn—notably Great Britain, which in those days upheld as a dogma the integrity of the Ottoman Empire—ran counter to Roumanian aspirations, and assumed the attitude of a domineering schoolmaster rather than that of a powerful friend and mentor. Napoleon III. alone showed genuine sympathy and understanding for the Roumanian cause. When, in 1857, a secret Anglo-Austrian agreement led to a flagrant "cooking" of the elections in a sense hostile to the union, Napoleon compelled the Porte to declare them invalid, and in the same year his skilful diplomacy won over the vanquished Tsar to his own modified interpretation of the Eastern Question. The Conference in Paris, which resulted from the meeting of the two Emperors at Stuttgart, was the prelude to the birth of a new state in south-east Europe. The farce of separate legislatures, each electing its own prince, was still solemnly maintained, but a Joint Commission and a Supreme Court were instituted, and the paradoxical title of "the United Principalities" was conceded. Such an arrangement could only be provisional; the efforts of the Powers were of no avail to dam up the rising tide of popular feeling, and early in 1858 the two assemblies in Bucarest and Jassy elected almost simultaneously one and the same person as their prince. "We have," said Kogalniceanu, speaking in the name of Moldavia, "the same origin as our brothers (of Wallachia), the same name and language, the same faith and history, the same institutions, laws and customs; we share the same hopes and fears; the same frontiers are placed under our care. In the past we have suffered the same griefs, and we now have to assure for ourselves the same future."

At first the new prince, Alexander Cuza, was exposed to grave danger of intervention, and was obliged to submit to a double investiture and to maintain two separate ministries, but the outbreak of war between Austria and Napoleon III., by paralysing all opposition from Vienna, considerably strengthened Cuza's position. In 1861 the Porte conceded the union of the two assemblies, and on December 23rd of that year the prince was able to address to his people a proclamation which culminated in the words, "The Roumanian nation is founded."

The eight years of Cuza's rule (1858-1866) were marked by many internal reforms—notably the seques-tration of Church lands; the foundation of the two Roumanian universities; the severance of the Church from the corrupt and numbing influence of the Greek Patriarchate, and the emancipation of the peasantry, if not from all, at any rate from the worst, of their feudal grievances. But his virtues and his faults alike—on the one hand his genuine zeal for national progress, and on the other the scandals of his private life and his contempt for constitutional forms—aroused the antagonism of the great families, who had hitherto enjoyed and were anxious to retain a monopoly of government. The *coup d'état* of 1864 was an attempt on Cuza's part to follow in the footsteps of his patron Napoleon III.; but the prince, who owed his election precisely to the fact that he did not belong to what might be called the *papabili* families, lacked the prestige and endurance necessary to impose his will upon the country. Moreover, the liberal nature of his innovations was counter-balanced by the suspension of Press freedom—a measure all the more reactionary in a country where the Press was still in its first childhood. In short, he attempted to play at benevo-lent despotism tempered by universal suffrage, though he was fully conscious that the latter must be a mere farce among a population so unripe in political training. His wholesale imitation of French institutions and methods of government showed too little regard for the social and economic needs of his fellow-countrymen. It is not without reason that Professor Xenopol has described the Roumanian state as "the creation of France" : but there can be no doubt that Cuza's over-haste led to a slavish reproduction of French ideas, without any real effort to winnow the good from the bad.

In February, 1866, the dissatisfaction came to a head; Cuza was forced to abdicate and to cross the frontier, and disappeared completely from the scene. The vacant throne was somewhat hurriedly offered to the Count of Flanders—the father of King Albert of Belgium— and on his refusal to accept a position which seemed so precarious, the unanimous choice of the Roumanian Chamber fell upon Prince Charles, a younger son of the Catholic and South German branch of the House of Hohenzollern. Strangely enough, while King William of Prussia showed scruples in sanctioning his young kinsman's acceptance, his candidature was eagerly approved by the same Napoleon III., who four years later vetoed, with such disastrous effects, the candidature of Prince Charles's brother Leopold for the crown of Spain.[1] "Accept," Bismarck had said to the hesitating prince, "it will at any rate be an agreeable souvenir for your old age." The support of France more than counter-balanced the disapproval of Austria, and for the second time within a decade all possibility of active interference from Vienna was frustrated by the outbreak of war, this time between Austria and Prussia. Prince Charles, in the disguise of a bespectacled commercial traveller, passed down the Danube on an Austrian river steamer, and was welcomed on Roumanian territory by the Liberal leader, Ion Brătianu, whose active intervention in Paris had been one of the decisive factors in his selection. For many years the incident of his first entry supplied his enemies with a cheap gibe against "Brătianu's lackey."

The accession of Prince Charles may be regarded as the

[1] Charles's mother, it should be remembered, was related to the Bonaparte and Beauharnais families.

chief turning point in all Roumanian history. His long reign of forty-eight years has completely transformed Roumania from a corrupt and backward dependency of the Turks to much the most powerful independent state in south-east Europe, and a very large share of the credit for this transformation falls to King Charles himself, alike as statesman, as soldier and as organiser. At first hampered by the unfriendly attitude of the Powers, and by the strained resources of an undeveloped country, the new sovereign found it necessary on more than one occasion to submit to humiliating treatment from the Porte. For ten years his entire efforts were devoted to organising the Roumanian army on Prussian models, and to introducing order into the country's finances. It was to take twenty years before the chronic deficit disappeared : but a reform of the coinage, the sale of state lands, and the creation of a tobacco monopoly paved the way for that brilliant financial revival which was to mark the opening years of the twentieth century. At the same time, in circumstances of extreme difficulty, and in spite of many a scurrilous attack, Prince Charles consistently adhered to the principle of constitutional government. His natural sympathy with Brătianu and the Liberal party rendered him not a whit the less loyal in his support of their Conservative rivals when the Chamber brought them into power. Thus for a whole generation, while Serbia was the scene of repeated *coups d'état* and political scandals, while in Bulgaria, despite wonderful progress, the representative idea has always been ruthlessly subordinated to the will of the sovereign, while Turkey groaned under the Hamidian despotism and Greece still waited for the statesman who was to free her from the ban of political anarchism, Roumania, alone of all the Balkan states, could boast of an uninterrupted constitutional development.

CHAPTER VII

BULGARIA UNDER THE TURKISH YOKE

THE last of all the Balkan races to regain its liberty was the Bulgarian; yet even this is scarcely an accurate statement, since the freedom of Bulgaria was in the main won for her by others, not by herself. In approaching Bulgarian history, and, above all, the relations of Bulgaria and Serbia, it is well to remember that the two nations are to-day in very much the same stage of development as England and Scotland in the fourteenth or fifteenth centuries. In that period and even much later—as the result of the fatal policy of the first of England's "lawyer statesmen," Edward I.—the fierce mutual hatred of the two neighbours could hardly be exaggerated. And yet their eventual union was absolutely inevitable, though we, who are wise after the event, must be careful not to reproach our ancestors unduly for their national blindness. The same principle applies to the rival branches of the Southern Slavs, who have no real future unless and until they agree among themselves. Just as Scotland was too weak and poor ever to attain unaided to national greatness, but was always strong enough to hamper and endanger England's movements at every turn by an alliance with the French, so Serb and Bulgar by their internecine warfare have enabled alien Powers to overwhelm or in modern times to control the destinies of the Balkan Peninsula.

Just as the real greatness of England begins with the period when her relations with Scotland were at last put upon a tolerable footing, so a definite accord between Serb and Bulgar would obviously be the prelude of a new era in the history of Balkan independence. Just as Prussia's predominant position in Central Europe is very largely due to fomenting the Russo-Polish quarrel, so Austria-Hungary has tried to gain a foot-hold in the Balkans by fomenting the Serbo-Bulgarian feud, and only reconciliation between the two kinsmen can permanently redeem the situation.

The Bulgars are the most easterly of the four branches of the Southern Slavs. A certain school of modern writers claims descent from the ancient Thracians, who, they argue, were a Slavonic tribe; but this thesis cannot be proved for lack of evidence. A number of Slavonic tribes did, it is true, invade the peninsula between the third and seventh centuries, and doubtless some of their blood still flows in the veins of some modern Bulgarians. But the real Bulgarians were a Turanian race, related to the long since vanished Avars and Petchenegs and to the still surviving races of Tartars, Huns, Finns, Magyars and Turks.[1] Their original home lay between the Ural Mountains and the River Volga, from which the name "Bolgar" is generallly derived. At first forming a savage nomad state, warlike and polygamous, they moved slowly westward under their native Khans. In the year 679 they crossed the Danube and defeated the Emperor Constantine, while other hordes remained behind in the Volga districts and yet others penetrated into the southern plains of Hungary.

In the course of the next two centuries the Bulgars did

---

[1] Much controversy has raged over Bulgarian origins. The reader may still be referred to the works of two great Slavonic scholars; Safárik, *Slawische Altertümer,* and Jireček, *Geschichte der Bulgaren.*

what the Normans did in England and in Sicily, though
they undoubtedly formed the larger portion of the population.   After conquering the country and giving it
their name, they adopted its language and at last
became completely assimilated.   Even in the eighth
century we read that the Bulgarian prince had among his
counsellors men who spoke "Greek, Bulgarian and
Slav."   A certain parallel may perhaps be drawn between the Bulgars and the band of Scandinavian adven-
turers in Russia, who imposed upon a group of scattered
and disorganised tribes a definite state organisation and
a national name, and then became merged in the subjected population.

During the eighth century we find the Bulgarians involved in repeated and bloody conflicts with Byzantium,
of which the most notable were the seven campaigns of
Constantine V.   With the dawn of the ninth century
there arose the mightiest of all Bulgarian rulers, the
shadowy figure of Krum, whose kingdom stretched from
the Carpathians far into Thrace and included portions
of Southern and Eastern Hungary.   In 811 Krum defeated and killed the Emperor Nicephorus after fearful
carnage, and conquered Adrianople; but for his death
three years later Byzantium itself might have become his
prey.   Scarcely less remarkable as a ruler was Boris
(852-888), whose reign coincided with the epoch-making
activity of the Slav apostles, Cyril and Methodius.   These
two men, the sons of a high officer in Thessalonica, who
was probably of Slav birth,[1] were the inventors of the
so-called Glagolitic alphabet,[2] and thus the real founders
of "Old Slavonic," the parent language of Slav litur-
gies and literatures.   At this distance of time it is almost
impossible to determine what language they took as the

[1] Jireček, *Gesch. der Bulgaren*, p. 151.
[2] Based on Greek minuscule characters, but adapted to Slav
phonetics.

basis of their alphabet, but it is probable that they used the Slav dialect then spoken in Eastern Macedonia, adding various linguistic ingredients which we should to-day call Slovak, Slovene, and Wend. It is a matter of common knowledge that their chief labours were among the Pannonian Slavs, and in the powerful but short-lived Moravian Empire, whose capital, Nitra, was Methodius's archiepiscopal seat; and the chief Slavistic authorities of the present day are inclined to reject the theories which identify "Old Slavonic" with "Old Bulgarian" or "Old Slovene," but rather to treat it as a composite and theoretical language.[1]

The exact connection of the Slav apostles with Bulgaria is not known; but emissaries from the Court of Rastislav of Moravia appear to have brought Christianity to the Court of Boris, who, like many pagan chiefs before him, found its adoption to be indispensable if he was to hold his own against his Christian neighbours, and who eventually died in the odour of sanctity as a Christian monk.

Yet another name is worthy of mention among the early rulers of Bulgaria. Simeon (893-927) nearly succeeded in destroying the Eastern Empire, and gave public proof of his intentions by himself assuming the title of Emperor and proclaiming a Bulgarian Patriarchate. He thus aspired to make of his capital, Preslav, a town situated some 30 miles west of Varna, both the civil and ecclesiastical rival of Byzantium.

Under Simeon's successors Bulgaria fell into two halves, the eastern, corresponding to the Bulgaria of 1908, weakened by Russian invasions and finally crushed in 971 by the Byzantines; the western, corresponding to the Macedonia and Southern Albania of modern times. After the fall of the former the Bulgarian centre of gravity was transferred to Prespa and Ohrida, which

[1] See Jagič, *Zur Entstehungsgeschichte*.

became the capitals of a new dynasty. Samuel, during his long reign (976-1014), extended his frontiers as far as Durazzo and the future Montenegro, and was engaged in almost perpetual war with the reviving power of Byzantium. Finally his enemy, Basil II., won a decisive victory at the battle of Belašica, north-east of Salonica, and earned for himself the title of "Bulgaroktonos," by a deed of unexampled horror even in that cruel age. By his orders the 15,000 Bulgarian prisoners were blinded, every hundredth man being left with one eye, that he might serve as a guide to his helpless comrades; and it is recorded that when this mutilated remnant of an army reached Ohrida, the old Tsar died of mingled grief and fury. From 1018 to 1186 Bulgaria lay under the yoke of the Greeks; the dynasty came to an end, the Patriarchate was suppressed, though other essential features of the Bulgarian ecclesiastical organisation were allowed to survive.[1] But though the death of Basil was followed by growing corruption and inanition in the body politic, it was not till the end of the twelfth century that the Bulgarians were again able to raise their heads as an independent people.

Throughout this early period there was a remarkable spread of the mysterious Manichæan heresy known as Bogomilism. Its founder, Bogomil (beloved of God), was a ninth-century mystic, who in the solitude of his cell had assimilated and developed the strange doctrines which he imbibed on his travels in the East. His theory of the duality in religious life, of the struggle between a Good and an Evil Deity, is obviously Oriental in its origin. In the course of time his teachings were modified by his pupils. Satan was no longer regarded as a rival being to God since the beginning of time, but

[1] The Church of Ohrida remained autocephalous, but generally with a Greek prelate at its head. See Jireček, op. cit., p. 201, and Gelzer, Der Patriarchat von Achrida.

as a fallen angel whose power was not yet exhausted. The zeal with which the enemies of this sect destroyed their manuscripts leaves us to-day in some doubt as to their exact tenets, but there can be no doubt as to their ascetic enthusiasm for Christianity in its most primitive form, and as to their advanced views on social matters. Their influence spread rapidly through the Balkan Peninsula, taking especial root in Bulgaria and Bosnia, and finally perpetuating itself in the west in the form of the Albigensians, Patarines, Cathars and Waldensians. It was above all the brutal persecutions to which they were subjected in Bosnia that were responsible for the collapse of that kingdom before the Turks and for the wholesale conversions to Islam which followed.

The second Bulgarian Empire, or, as modern writers more accurately describe it, the Bulgaro-Rouman Empire (1186-1398) was founded by two brothers who were almost certainly Vlachs by race, though they claimed descent from the ancient Bulgarian Tsars. The greatest of all, Kalojan (Calojoannes) made Trnovo his capital, and in the year 1204 allowed himself to be crowned by a Cardinal Legate sent by the greatest of the Popes, Innocent III. This was, of course, a purely political move, intended to strengthen his position against Byzantium. How little he cared about the respective merits of Rome and Byzantium was very clearly shown by the attitude to the Latin onslaught upon Constantinople, when he played very much the same game as his astute successor, Ferdinand of Coburg, and remained watchfully neutral until Latins and Greeks had weakened each other. In 1205 he fell upon Baldwin, the first Latin Emperor, and captured him at the battle of Adrianople; rumour, but not history, records the victim's subsequent fate. Under Kalojan's successor John Asen II. (1218-1241) Bulgaria reached its zenith and established herself upon the three seas—the Black, the Ægean, and the Adriatic—to the possession of which Sofia's modern patriots aspire. Macedonia, Belgrade and Durazzo recognised his authority, and Trnovo, as capital of the Tsar and seat of the Patriarch, defied the anathemas of both Rome and Byzantium. But the later rulers of the Asenide dynasty were no longer worthy of its founder. Bulgaria soon lost Thrace and Macedonia once more, waning in the west before the rising power of mediæval Serbia and driven back in the east by the Greeks after the expulsion of the degenerate Latin conquerors. Serbia, as we have seen, reached its height in the fourteenth century under Stephen Dušan, who was actually threatening Constantinople at his death. But that event had been preceded by a fatal quarrel between Serbs and Bulgars, culminating in the battle of Velbužd in 1330. In it the Bulgarian Tsar lost his life, Serbian supremacy was assured for the moment and Bulgaria sank to the level of a vassal State. But the feud led inevitably to the undoing of both races, and made the entry of the Turks possible, just as to-day the old quarrel, fomented by Turk, German and Magyar in alliance, threatens to destroy Balkan independence once more. The desperate appeal of the Byzantine Emperor was disregarded by both Serb and Bulgar, though he is said to have warned them that they would rue the day when they left him unsupported. The jealousies of the small Christian Powers directly furthered the Turkish conquest, just as those of the Great Powers retarded time after time the day of deliverance, and just as since 1912 the jealousies of the Balkan Allies, skilfully played upon from without, have restored discord, weakness and misery to the reviving peninsula.

As we have already seen, the Serbian Empire perished at the memorable battle of Kosovo (1389); and that event was followed four years later by the fall of Trnovo, the death of the last Bulgarian Tsar, Šišman, on the battlefield, the removal of the Bulgarian Patriarch to Asia

Minor and the subjection of his Church to the Greek Patriarchate in Constantinople (1393). A few last fragments of independence still lingered in the peninsula. King Marko ruled in Prilep as a periodic vassal of the Turks, and has gone down to history as the hero of countless ballads, Serb, Croat, Bulgarian, and even Albanian. King Tvrtko of Bosnia for a brief space of time seemed about to create a new Slav state upon the Adriatic; but his death in 1391 left no one to carry on his ideas. Mircea the Old, as Prince of Wallachia (1386-1418), drove out the invading Turks and collaborated with the Magyars in their gallant attempt to save Bulgaria. But Sigismund suffered a crushing defeat at Nicopolis in 1396 and only with difficulty made his way back to Hungary. One final attempt was made to rescue the fast disappearing Balkan kingdoms from the Turkish flood; but Vladislav, who as King of both Hungary and Poland represented a really powerful combination, perished on the fatal field of Varna (1444). The last effort of Europe had failed, and only nine years later the victorious Sultan rode his charger into the church of Agia Sofia. Lack of unity and co-operation had delivered the Christians into the hands of the Turks. The last to fall was the celebrated Albanian Prince, George Castriota, better known as Scanderbeg, who is still the chief hero of a race which has fewer historical records and less traces of culture than any other in Europe. After his death in 1468 the old obscurity descends upon their mountain fastnesses, and seems to cling there without a single break until the second decade of the nineteenth century.

The causes of Bulgaria's fall are to be found mainly in the corrupting influence of Byzantium, in the Bogomil heresy and its corrosive force (corresponding to that anarchical trait which may be noticed in varying degree among all Slavs, but which is especially marked among the Bulgars and Ukrainians), and in the short-sighted selfishness of the great feudal nobles, playing for their own hands and failing to realise that they were working their own destruction. Turkish rule in Bulgaria did not differ in any essential feature from Turkish rule in Serbia or elsewhere, but nowhere was it so grinding and oppressive. This is, of course, due to the fact that it lay nearest to Stambul and formed the inevitable route of every Turkish advance westward.

One positive merit the Turkish *régime* can boast; it preserved more fully than any other state to all its subjects that career open to the talents which opens the road to true genius. There was one absolute condition, the acceptance of Islam, but that step once taken, all doors were open to the newcomer, just as in modern Hungary the renegade Slovak or Roumanian can always be sure of a smooth political career. Nothing is more remarkable than the spread of Slav influences in the Turkey of Suleiman the Magnificent and his successors. In 1531, the historian, Paulus Jovius, tells us that almost the entire corps of Janissaries spoke Slav. The Turkish privileges granted to Ragusa during the fifteenth and sixteenth centuries and all correspondence of the Sublime Porte and with the Republic were written in the Serbian language. John Zápolya[1] corresponded with the Grand Vizier in Serb, and Sultan Selim II. spoke it fluently. More than one of Turkey's greatest Viziers was of Slav parentage, notably Mohammed Sokolovič of Bosnia, and Mohammed Beg of Kosovo. Baron Ungnad, who established flourishing Protestant printing presses at Urach and Tübingen for the publication of books in Slovene, and in the Cyrilline and Glagolitic alphabets, seriously hoped by such means to spread Protestantism among the Turks. Indeed it is hardly an

---

[1] His great predecessor, Matthias Corvinus, also frequently used Slav, even in the Hungarian Diets.

exaggeration to say that at one time the Ottoman Empire bade fair to become Slavised.[1]

In Bulgaria the only remnants of ancient liberty that were allowed to survive were the "Vojnik" villages, occupied according to a rude military tenure and exempt from taxation. The most notable of these was Koprivština. Trade was concentrated mainly in the hands of the Vlachs, whose most flourishing centres were Moscopolis in the Pindus, Arbanasi, near Trnovo, and Kruševo, and of the Ragusans, who for centuries maintained colonies in every Balkan town of any importance—notably in Skoplje, Sofia, Belgrade, Novibazar and Sarajevo. Meanwhile the Phanariot *régime* dominated ecclesiastical life; Greek influence and the Greek liturgy were everywhere. After a precarious existence the two autocephalous Serb and Bulgar Churches, of Peč (Ipek) and Ohrida, were destroyed in 1767, as the result of Greek intrigue at the Porte. Hellenism sought more and more (and for a long time succeeded in the effort) to identify creed and nationality, with the result that the ignorant Bulgar peasant, when questioned as to his nationality, would answer with the misleading confession that he was a "Greek." It is this attitude which explains the failure of superficial travellers to detect the presence of Bulgarians in Bulgaria as late as the forties of last century ! A phenomenon familiar to all students of Balkan and Austro-Hungarian problems is the extraordinary levity with which many writers have placed themselves in the hands of only a single race of some extremely polyglot country, and have sometimes emerged from their travels almost without perceiving the very existence, far less recognising the national traditions and aspirations, of the others.

Towards the close of the eighteenth century anarchy seemed to have reached its height in the Ottoman Em-

---

[1] Jireček, *op. cit.*, pp. 369, 451.

pire, and speedy dissolution was regarded on many sides as inevitable. Grave symptoms were noticeable in the repeated outbreak of disorder in the provinces—the misrule of the Dahis in Serbia, which provoked Kara George's rising, the depredations of Ali Pasha, and the rise of other local tyrants at Skutari and Damascus, at Acre and in Egypt. Next to Ali Pasha none attained to such renown in his day as Pasvan Oglu, a Mohammedan Serb from Bosnia, who ruled as Pasha of Vidin, on the Danube. Bulgaria was at this time infested by the so-called "Kurdjalias," [1] who played a somewhat similar rôle to the Haiduks and Klephts of Serb and Greek history and to the more modern Komitadjis, and whose misdeeds and terrorism are still a living memory among the Bulgarian peasantry. Pasvan Oglu actively encouraged them and with their aid defied the Porte; but at the same time he always took care to pose as the enemy, not of the Sultan, but of his evil counsellors. In 1796 the Turks besieged Vidin with 40,000 men, but without success; and in 1798 the siege was resumed with an army of twice that size. But after six months the expedition ended in disaster, and the Sultan soon afterwards found it necessary to send a Pasha's horse-tails to Pasvan Oglu. The latter's arrogance was now unbounded, and his prestige enormous throughout the Moslem world. The French traveller, Pouqueville, records that in 1799 he heard a Turkish sailor openly chanting a song in honour of Pasvan, in the presence of a Turkish officer with two executioners at his side. It ran as follows: "After 100,000 bombs have been thrown at Vidin, I, Pasvan Oglu, the Sultan's hound, the slave of the Sultana Valide, have raised the standard of revolt. I, Pasvan Oglu, the hound of the Grand Seignor, I bark at his Ministers. I will do homage to my lord, I lick the dust from his feet, I, Pasvan Oglu." [2] Pasvan remained

---

[1] A Turkish word for "robbers."

[2] Pouqueville, *Voyage en Grèce*, Vol. I., 522.

undisturbed until his death in 1807. His career had contributed very considerably to the anarchy in Serbia and
to the consequent insurrection. Graphic descriptions of
the terrible misery inflicted upon Bulgaria by these
repeated conflicts are to be found in the memoirs of
Bishop Sofronij of Vraca, one of the earliest Bulgarian
patriots and writers.

Allusion has already been made to an outstanding
feature of all the various national movements in the Balkans and in Austria-Hungary—namely, the achievement
of a few philologists and historical students, in reviving
a dead mass and kindling a whole nation into flame.
This was especially marked in Bohemia, Hungary and
Croatia, but it is scarcely less true of Serbia, Greece and
Roumania; and if Bulgaria has produced no name which
can be placed beside Vuk Karadžić, Rhigas, Korais and
Radulescu, it would none the less be a grave error to
under-estimate the part played by literary effort in Bulgaria's awakening.

In 1762, Paisi, a Bulgarian monk on Mt. Athos,
composed "A History of the Bulgarian Peoples, Tsars
and Saints," which, though of no great historical value,
was of immeasurable influence by reason of its fiery
patriotism, its enthusiasm for a great past and a long-
neglected dialect. Copies of his manuscript soon found
their way through all Bulgarian lands. His most ardent
pupil and the perpetuator of his tradition was Bishop
Sofronij, who suffered terribly at the hands of the Turks
and died at Bucarest in the year 1816. The chief aim
of these two men was to restore the mother tongue to
the place usurped by Greek, especially in the Church,
and to combat the unspeakable corruption of the Phanariot *régime* both in ecclesiastical and civil life. It was
a difficult, uphill fight, for Hellenism had its claws deep
in the Bulgarian Church. The liturgy, the schools and
the clergy alike were Greek; and not content with this,

the Church authorities adopted a grossly reactionary and intolerant view, systematically tried to root out everything Slavonic and wrought deliberate havoc among the monuments and above all the manuscripts of the historic past. In this vandalism it was the bishops who set the example. In 1825, Ilarion, the Greek Metropolitan of Trnovo, made a bonfire of the old library of the Bulgarian Patriarchate, which till then had survived all the vicissitudes of the Turkish era. It is perhaps only fair to add that these habits of destruction and the kindred practice of forging historical documents or monuments have been adopted by every race in the peninsula at one time or another. Only the Turks were either too lazy or too contemptuous to indulge in such competition.

Under such circumstances it is hardly to be wondered at that even the most celebrated scholars of the Slavonic world, the founders of Slav philology, on a modern basis, men like Miklosich, Kopitar and even Šafařik himself, knew very little of the Bulgarian language. It is interesting to note, however, that the real pioneer of literary effort among the Bulgars was the Slovak scholar Venelin, whose books on Bulgarian history prompted the description on his tomb at Odessa as "the Awakener of Bulgaria." [1] They were directly responsible for the foundation in 1835 of the first Bulgarian school at Gabrovo, now the chief industrial centre of the modern kingdom. Since then schools have multiplied fast; for the Bulgar has in modern times shown a greater passion for education than any other Balkan race, save perhaps the Greek. A little earlier a Bulgarian version of the New Testament was printed in Bucarest.

The national revival naturally took two forms. The first, or more peaceful, expressed itself in educational work and in the demand for a national episcopate. In 1848 the first Bulgarian church was erected in Constan-

[1] Miller, *Ottoman Empire,* p. 340.

tinople, and its clergy omitted the name of the Greek Patriarch from their prayers. Shortly after the Crimean War certain Bulgarians made overtures to Rome, inspired, of course, by purely political motives, and tempted by the eclipse of Russia to look towards the west. Cankov visited Rome and induced Pius IX. to consecrate Sokolski, an ex-brigand turned monk, as the first archbishop of the Uniate Church of Bulgaria. That this movement was stillborn of course finds its explanation in the course which events took during the two following decades. Meanwhile, there was a growing revolutionary movement underground, on very similar lines to the Greek Hetairia. Bucarest became the centre of the Bulgarian political emigration, from which occasional disturbances were fomented in Bulgaria itself.[1] The real founder of this secret propaganda was George Rakovsky, poet, journalist, and guerilla leader, who published Bulgarian newspapers in Belgrade and in Novi Sad (Neusatz), was the friend of Jovan Ristič and Ion Brătianu and eventually died at Bucarest in 1867.

These patriots in exile tended to fall into two groups, the merchants and business men, who concentrated their financial efforts upon educational work, and the students, who followed the more subversive ideas of the Carbonarist Societies, the Hetairia, and the Serbian Omladina. Even among them there were two rival tendencies, one favouring a Southern Slav federation, with Prince Michael of Serbia as its natural head, the other wishing to see the Sultan proclaim himself as Tsar of the Bulgarians.

In 1864 Midhat Pasha, himself a native of Rustchuk, was appointed Governor of Bulgaria, and under him the country enjoyed for the first time a period of calm

---

[1] Perhaps one day a historian will trace for us the part played by Bucarest as a home for political refugees from Greece, Bulgaria, Serbia, Albania, and Hungary.

and prosperity. But the founder of Turkish Liberalism stood almost alone among Turkish statesmen, and even he held views on racial questions which accorded better with Magyar than with Western ideas. With the steady growth of national feeling in the Balkans, the Turks tended to modify their attitude towards the Christians. The method of Mohammed II. had been to recognise the Greek Patriarch and treat him as a medium between the Porte and all the Christian races. This worked admirably from the Turkish point of view, so long as Serb, Bulgar and Roumanian were sunk in drowsy apathy. When they awoke, the obvious policy was to play off one race against the other and to adopt the well-worn Habsburg motto, "Divide et Impera." In 1870 a firman of the Sultan created a special Bulgarian Exarchate, comprising almost all the Bulgarian territories and Niš and Pirot as well. Other places were free to transfer themselves to its authority, if two-thirds of the inhabitants voted for the change. The Exarch was to mention the Patriarch in his prayers and to receive the holy oil from him. But the Greeks opposed this innovation by every means in their power, and after blocking the appointment for two years, excommunicated the new Exarch and his clergy as schismatics. Ecclesiastical unity was at an end among the Christians of the Turkish dominions; and there followed an acute racial struggle under the thinnest of religious veneers, and above all a war to the knife between Greek and Bulgar, waged at times with every weapon of political intrigue and social, economic or ecclesiastical terrorism.

Each race at once realised the deep significance of the struggle, but the Bulgarian revolutionaries were far from satisfied with what many acclaimed as a national gain. In 1870 a secret congress was organised in Bucarest under Ljuben Karavelov and Levski, the chief of the wandering apostles, and it was roundly proclaimed that

"Bulgaria's freedom needs not an Exarch, but a rebel leader." Levski was a true prophet of subversion, who travelled tirelessly in every kind of disguise, till at length he was captured and executed by the Turks (1873). A monument to the national "martyr" marks the scene of his death on the outskirts of Sofia. Dissensions arose amongst his successors, Botjov and other active conspirators, and the insurrection which broke out at Stara Zagora in 1875 proved to be a tragic fiasco. In the following year a new revolutionary committee repeated the rising with equal lack of success. The Turks stamped out the Bulgarian resistance in the hideous massacre of Batak, where over 12,000 perished. The British Commissioner, Mr. Baring, in his report, describes this event "as perhaps the most heinous crime that has stained the history of the present century." He wrote in 1876. The twentieth century has outstripped the wildest dreams of Turkish savagery : in Armenia the Turk has learnt method from the bearers of German *Kultur*.

The Bulgarian massacres of 1876, first exposed by Mr. (still with us as the veteran Sir Edwin) Pears, inspired the famous philippic of Mr. Gladstone and roused the indignation of civilised Europe. The events to which they and the contemporary Bosnian rising gave rise can only be fully understood in their connection with the policy pursued by the Great Powers in the Near East.

CHAPTER VIII

AUSTRO-RUSSIAN RIVALRY IN THE BALKANS

THERE are two ways of approaching Balkan history—from within and from without—from the national and from the international angle. The former method treats of the rise and development of the various nations of the peninsula, both in each individual case and in their relations to each other; the latter lays special emphasis on their relations with the outer world. According to this second method each unit becomes a mere pawn in the vast diplomatic game which has come to be described as the Eastern Question. This has hitherto been the favourite method of studying Balkan history, and also the prime cause of the almost complete failure, on the part of Western public opinion and Western diplomacy, to fathom the somewhat turbid depths of Balkan psychology. Such a method is of course a survival of the old method of history, which dealt mainly in treaties, battles and genealogies, and perhaps, too, the unconscious survival of the atmosphere which prevailed under Frederick the Great, Catherine, Metternich and Castlereagh, and in which dynastic and family claims and the traditions of historic "state right" or ecclesiastical privilege predominated to the almost entire exclusion of the rights, interests and aspirations of the European nations, historic and "unhistoric" alike. In any historical survey of the Balkan problem it is essential to emphasise the need for shaking off this habit of mind : for it still lingers in the most unexpected places. Even in ultra-democratic news-papers which are proclaiming the necessity for consulting the people and the crime of compelling it to do anything which may not suit its momentary convenience, such phrases as "compensation," "territorial division," "access to the sea," and many others are continually allowed to crop up; and it is charitable to assume that their authors fail to realise that the phrases which they so glibly employ are in fact borrowed from the language of the reactionaries of the Holy Alliance and of the sworn enemies of all democratic ideas.

In the preceding chapters I have adhered to the first of these two alternative methods, and have tried to show as briefly as possible how national life again dawned after the long Turkish night. But in order to present the whole subject in its due perspective, it is equally essential to apply the second method also, before we can under-stand the most recent period of Balkan history. It will sometimes be necessary to cover portions of the same ground as that of previous chapters; but this is both inevitable and deliberate, for it is always instructive to approach the same facts from different angles.

That the Eastern Question is no new question, is clearly shown by its very name, which could only date from days when Asia was still only very partially and imperfectly known to Europe. Indeed, in our own day it has been found necessary to make good the deficiencies of the name by distinguishing between the Near, the Middle, and the Far East. The Eastern Question, then, dates back for many centuries; in the Middle Ages it took the form of the crusades : and both then and later its very essence has consisted in the perennial rivalry between Europe and Asia, between the Western and Eastern outlook upon life. The crusades were very largely inspired by the old mediæval conception of European solidarity, of Christendom as a united whole, under the dual, half-mystical, guidance of Emperor and Pope. The only modern conception which can even remotely be compared with this, is the wretched Concert of Europe, which is in theory as admirable as it has proved futile and unsound in execution, but which, if Europe is to have any future except that of the Apocalypse, it must be the endeavour of her statesmen to erect upon some solid base after the present war.

With its mediæval form we are not at present concerned. But with the arrival of the Turks it assumed a new phase, and it was only with the decline of Ottoman power in Europe that it entered upon the stage which was popularly known to our fathers and grandfathers as that of "the Sick Man," and which seemed to have ended in the cataclysm of 1912, but which, little as our simple-minded rulers realised it, was already even then leading inevitably to the far greater cataclysm of 1914-15.

The attitude of the European Powers, and notably of Austria and Russia, to the Turkish problem up to the close of the eighteenth century has already been briefly summarised,[1] and we have seen that Austria weakly squandered the advantages which both geography and history had conferred upon her. Save for occasional incidents, the relations of Russia with the peninsula were mainly ecclesiastical until the reign of Catherine the Great; at least she only began to be a serious rival to Austria when the Crimea and the Black Sea fell into her hands. Her relations with Montenegro have already been referred to. Her relations with Greece date from the appearance of a Russian fleet in the Mediterranean in 1770. Her relations with Roumania were determined by the simple geographical fact that Russian armies in fighting Turkey had to pass through Bessarabia and Moldavia; while so far as Serbia is concerned it is im-

[1] Chapter II.

portant to note that the Serbs only turned to Russia
after Kara George had appealed to Francis I. for protection and had asked for an Austrian Archduke as Viceroy
without avail.   The first official Russian agent appeared
at Belgrade in 1807, three years after the first rising.
Curiously enough the first serious Serb overture to Russia came in 1804 from the Serbs in Austrian, not in
Turkish, territory, and took the form of a memorandum
of the Metropolitan Stratimirovič, sent to the Russian
Foreign Minister, in favour of "the erection of a Slavo-
Serb Kingdom" under a Russian Grand Duke.   Thus
for the first time were ideas expressed which were to
bear fruit later in political aspirations with which public
opinion in the West is only gradually becoming familiar
under the stress of a world-war.

The war of 1788 was based upon the confident belief,
shared equally by Joseph II. and by Catherine the Great,
that Turkey would rapidly collapse, and in the latter
sovereign's case upon the dream of restoring the Eastern
Empire in favour of the Grand Duke Constantine.   But
the course taken by the war for the first time clearly
revealed the fact that the issue was not a simple one, but
inextricably interwoven with the whole fabric of the European state system.   The joint Austro-Russian offensive
produced very disappointing results, and the outbreak of
the French Revolution and the endless complications to
which it led in the West, compelled the Allies to postpone
almost indefinitely the realisation of their ambitions in the
Near East.   Moreover the Balkan policy of the two
Powers was profoundly affected by two new factors.   On
the one hand Napoleon, by his creation of an Illyrian
state, did much to revive national feeling among the
Southern Slavs, not only in Turkey but also in the Habsburg dominions.   In his eyes Dalmatia, Albania and
the Ionian Islands, as French dependencies, were but so
many stepping-stones on his path towards the dominion

of the East. On the other hand, the rapid growth of the commercial interests of the Western Powers in various parts of Turkey introduced new heirs to the sordid competition around the deathbed of the Sick Man.

During the Napoleonic period French ideas were as noticeable in the Balkans as farther west—acting upon Turkish conditions as a corrosive force, but also as a vivifying and renewing force among the subjected Christian races. They were unquestionably one of the chief influences in that new development which in the nineteenth century was to rescue the Balkan peoples slowly but surely from the conflicting designs of Austria and Russia. Thus modern Balkan history may be divided into three periods—the first in which Austria set herself the task of expelling the Turks, the second in which Austria and Russia combined in a policy of partition and worked on parallel lines; the third, in which the jealousy and competition which replaced their partnership was still further complicated by the growing influence and interference of other Powers. It is interesting to note that the diplomatic influence of France in the Near East turned the scale against the Austrian solution in 1793; while it is of course notorious that the influence of the French Revolution and the Napoleonic ferment were decisive factors in the awakening of Balkan nationality. In 1807 Napoleon signed a secret agreement with Alexander I. at Tilsit for the partition of Turkey, but stipulated for her retention of Constantinople. The tremendous events of the following years prevented the realisation of such designs, and led up to that breach with Russia which was to prove fatal to the career of Napoleon. But in the meantime Alexander was at open war with the Turks, and it was only through British pressure at the Porte that on the very eve of the Moscow campaign the Sultan could be induced to come to terms with Russia. The treaty of Bucarest (May 28th,

1812) marks the last stage in Russian territorial advance in Europe. The greater part of Bessarabia was abandoned by the Turks, and the river Pruth became the boundary between the two Empires. The Roumanians, who formed the great bulk of the population, were as yet too inarticulate to protest at their being thus arbitrarily severed from their kinsmen in Moldavia; indeed the blessings of Phanariot rule were not as yet sufficiently obvious to create resentment at the change. None the less it is to be regretted, as having sown the seeds of distrust between Russia and the most powerful of all the Balkan nations.

The Congress of Vienna, which may be described as one of the prime causes of the subsequent evils which have come upon Europe, almost entirely ignored Balkan matters. To it legitimacy was the keystone of the social order, and Turkey was a dynastic state under a legitimate ruler. In the words of M. Debidour, "the diplomats of 1815 took a year to provide Europe with bad laws. It was to take Europe a century to repair the evil which they wrought upon her." To-day we may push this view to its logical conclusion and maintain that the present war is the direct result of a stubborn refusal on the part of European diplomacy, even to try to repair that evil; nor have we to-day any very sanguine grounds for believing that the diplomats who control the fate of Europe will conduct the Congress of 1917 upon any more honest lines than its predecessors of Vienna, Paris and Berlin. Only a healthy and energetic public opinion can force the Greys, the Sazonovs, the Jagows, the Buriáns, the Sonninos, to apply true statesmanship to the national problems which await solution, and to abandon the prevailing habit of feeding the public upon vague and fulsome programmes, which only too often conceal acts of a thoroughly reactionary character.

The era which followed the Congress of Vienna was

dominated by the Holy Alliance, whose only aim, as expressed in the mystical ideas of Alexander I., was the regeneration of Europe into a true Christian commonwealth. That Alexander at that time was steeped in constitutional ideas is proved by his generous treatment of Poland and Finland and his friendy attitude towards the Liberal movement in Germany and Italy. But events soon produced a change in this unstable if wellmeaning visionary; and European politics fell under the domination of Metternich. This statesman, with all the cynicism of Talleyrand but with far greater superficiality, passed for a whole generation as the diplomat *par excellence*. It was he who said of the Holy Alliance "that it had for its author a moral significance, and for the other signatories not even that significance!"[1] It is true that Metternich was handicapped by the throned bureaucrat in whose service he worked. But the secret of his political survival lies in his practice of leaving internal politics in the hands of his reactionary and small-minded sovereign, who was thus enabled to gratify his consuming passion for red tape, and thus of securing for himself the almost absolute control of foreign politics. Metternich's system rested upon the double basis of legitimacy and the *status quo,* which in one sense may be regarded as different expressions of the same idea. In practice Metternich's theories took the form of the repression of all national movements in Italy, whether in the Austrian provinces or in the petty states of the peninsula, of strict measures against liberal tendencies in Southern Germany, and of opposition to the Greek rising and to the Polish movement. He failed to prevent the establishment of Greek independence, largely owing to the policy of Canning and to the consequent combination between Russia and the Western Powers. He also failed to prevent Russia's occupation

[1] Debidour, *op. cit.,* I., p. 99.

of the Principalities (1829–33) and her grant of a constitution—the *Règlement Organique*—in the latter year.

In this connection it is worth noting that autocratic Russia has always backed constitutional government in Greece, Roumania, Serbia, and to a lesser degree Bulgaria, the real fact, of course, being that she has always tried to secure the adhesion of the strongest party in each country to her politics. Above all, Metternich failed to prevent the secret treaty of Unkiar-Skelessi (1833), which virtually made Turkey the vassal of Russia, by imposing upon the Porte a defensive alliance with Russia and pledging the Sultan to close the Straits to the enemies of the Tsar. This arrangement, which was mainly directed against France and Britain, was soon followed by the conference of Münchengrätz, at which Russia and Austria agreed upon joint support for the Ottoman dynasty, and by Russia's evacuation of the Danubian Principalities. Metternich thus succeeded in bolstering up the crumbling policy of non-intervention; and the acute friction which arose between the Western Powers and the Tsar over the question of the Straits (1839-40) only brought Russia and Austria closer together. Throughout this period the traditional dream of the reactionaries, a league of the three Conservative Powers, Russia, Austria, and Prussia, reasserts itself from time to time. It is rare that all three are united except in the face of overwhelming danger from Napoleon, or as the result of the consummate statesmanship of Bismarck. The rivalry of Austria and Prussia within the bounds of Germany, the complications introduced by Austrian racial diversity, the influence of Italian and Balkan affairs, all contributed to confuse the issue. But the idea of such a league, advocated by Metternich as a sure bulwark of authority against the inroads of revolutionary and progressive ideas, has grown steadily ever since, and though rendered more and more difficult of realisation owing to the imperative claims of nationality, represents to-day more than ever the real inclinations of large sections of the governing class in Central and Eastern Europe. It is this tendency which is the real danger of the peace settlement; for a possible basis of union is provided by the Polish Question. It was the original crime of the Polish partition which created a bond of union between the three spoilers, and strengthened their alarm at the prospect of any change which might affect their ill-gotten gains. Thus the most revolutionary act of modern times —the wanton suppression of an ancient state and its national identity—was effected by the chief exponents in Europe of the doctrine of Divine Right, and of the unquestionable obedience of the subject. It must be the task of all who have the cause of European progress at heart to prevent the perpetuation of the evil by some fresh compact over the mangled body of Poland between the exponents of reaction in Prussia, Austria and Russia.

Metternich once boasted in a phrase which suggests the outlook of William II., that he had preserved peace in Europe for 33 years; and of course by sitting on the safety-valve it is always possible to preserve comparative quiet until the moment of the explosion. In the case of Metternich that explosion came in 1848, in the revolution of Vienna, Prague and Budapest, in the fierce racial war which overwhelmed Hungary, and in its climax, the deposition of the Habsburg dynasty by Louis Kossuth. Order could only be restored by the aid of 180,000 Russian troops, whom Nicholas I. sent across the Carpathians in the name of the outraged principles of legitimacy and autocracy.

CHAPTER IX

THE CONCERT OF EUROPE AND THE NEAR EAST

THE three chief characteristics of the Metternich era had been economic exhaustion following the Napoleonic Wars, the ascendancy of romanticism and the political reaction against revolutionary propaganda. The two bases of his policy, legitimacy and non-intervention, gradually crumbled away by reason of their own inherent rottenness. The liberal theories of the Tsar Alexander I. gave place to the black reaction and brutal autocracy of his successor, Nicholas I.; and Austrian rule even at its worst in Lombardy and Venetia was never so monstrous as Russian rule under Nicholas. The theories on which they rested were identical, and Nicholas was following a sure instinct when in 1849 he restored Hungary to the rule of the Habsburgs. But the doctrine of non-intervention proved to be a two-edged weapon, and led to results which were little short of comic. Austria, as the purest exponent of the absolutist doctrine, in her anxiety to preserve the *status quo,* found it necessary to *intervene* on behalf of threatened dynasties—notably Naples and Parma; while Britain, influenced by sympathy with liberal and progressive ideas on the Continent, favoured non-intervention in order to give these ideas a chance of asserting themselves. Metternich induced Russia and Prussia to join Austria in a declaration of principles, and in the refusal to recognise as a member of the European Alliance any state which was guilty of an internal revolution.[1] Thus in his eagerness to preserve a united front against "the revolution," he virtually incorporated the Right of Intervention into the Law of Europe. It was only a question of time for this right, which was intended only to benefit dynasties, to be applied in favour of nations also. Under Canning there was intervention on behalf of Portugal, and above all of Greece; and the war of Greek independence, culminating in Navarino, made a fatal breach in Metternich's political system. Russia was won to the British side, because her rulers were continually harking back to the idea of a Turkish collapse, and were equally fascinated by the dream of Santa Sofia, and determined not to leave to Britain or France a monopoly of the protection of the Greeks or of an Orthodox Church. Russia's share in this campaign involved her, as we have seen, in a long land war with Turkey, terminating in the treaty of Adrianople (1829), which secured access through the Straits for foreign vessels, and the dismantling of all fortresses on the left bank of the Danube. Russia remained in the occupation of the Danubian Principalities for four years, and only withdrew after the secret Treaty of Unkiar-Skelessi, which pledged the Sultan to close the Straits to enemies of the Tsar. Russia had thus established for the moment her predominance in the Near East, and seemed about to reduce Turkey to the position of a vassal. From 1833 to 1854 the central fact in European politics is the rivalry of Russia and Britain, or rather of Nicholas I. and Palmerston, of Absolutist and Liberal tradition. Throughout this period the issue was obscured by an interplay of forces, political, racial, religious, and economic, by the chemical process of Western ideas acting upon the decaying fabric of Ottoman rule. Just because there was no clear issue, and so

[1] Seignobos, *Histoire de l'Europe Contemporaine*, p. 719.

many *imponderabilia* in the situation, and because
every year and in every direction the states grew
greater than in any former epoch—for these very
reasons a growth of catchwords became apparent,
devised by essentially bureaucratic minds as the props
of an essentially artificial situation. "The Concert of
Europe" and "The Balance of Power"—conceptions
which, in their true proportion, are of great and fundamental value—became more and more the fetish of the
diplomatic world. The Eastern Question had become
so extraordinarily complex and delicate, and, above all,
so incalculable, that all the Great Powers—Russia,
Austria, Prussia, France, and Britain alike—favoured
the integrity of the Ottoman Empire.

In 1839-41 a fresh crisis was provoked by the revolt
of Egypt under Mehemet Ali. France found herself
isolated, the other four Great Powers backing the Sultan
against his rebellious subject, and it was this which split
the first Anglo-French Entente. In the winter of 1915,
certain British statesmen imposed a dangerous strain
upon the new and better Anglo-French Entente by again
opposing French policy in the Near East, and by urging
the cowardly and perfidious plan of abandoning a
common ally to her fate; but happily on this latter
occasion the bonds between us proved indissoluble. The
Egyptian crisis ended in 1841 in the so-called Convention of the Straits between the Great Powers and
the Sultan, which closed the Dardanelles to all foreign
warships. But just as Metternich's enthusiasm for
the *status quo* did not prevent him from annexing
the little independent Polish state of Cracow, so
Nicholas I., while the champion of extreme reaction
at home, dabbled in revolutionary schemes of foreign
policy. During his visit to England in 1844 he made
overtures for regulating the fate of the Turkish Empire,
but, receiving no encouragement, he had to drop the idea

for the time. During the troubles of 1848 he devoted his efforts to saving the cause of the dynasties; but when the danger had passed, his mind reverted once more to his former ideas. "The Sick Man of Europe" had already become the butt of international caricature when, in 1852, Nicholas approached the British Ambassador in Petersburg as to the need for "an agreement about the funeral." But the maintenance of Turkish integrity had become a fetish of British statesmen; and our steady hostility to Russia, supplemented by Napoleon III.'s desire for an ambitious foreign policy, led to the Crimean War.

It has become a commonplace to-day to say that the immediate cause or pretext of a great war is very rarely the true underlying cause; and the Archduke's murder supplies a classic illustration of this truth. If this were not so, we should have to admit that the origin of the Crimean War provided greater opportunity for the scoffer and the cynic than any other. For the trouble began with a dispute regarding the possession of the Holy Places at Jerusalem, based upon the rivalry of the Latin Catholics under French protection, and of the Greek Orthodox under Russian protection. It would, however, be a mistake to minimise too much the part played by what a witty French writer described as "a sacristans' quarrel"; for the dispute, deplorable as it was, has a profound significance, and has not lost it even to-day, as the crowds of Russian pilgrims to Jerusalem, and the rival German and Russian settlements outside the Holy City amply testify. It will be found at the end of this war that the fate of Palestine will not be a matter of indifference to Russia.

There were, of course, many other causes, though at this distance of time it is difficult to appreciate them, or to avoid regarding the war as a hideous and perfectly avoidable mistake. A great part was played in accentuating the quarrel by our Ambassador in Constantinople, Lord Stratford de Redcliffe, one of the greatest diplomatic figures of the century, and the soul of the Turkophil movement in England.   And scarcely less important was the influence of the British peace party in convincing Nicholas I. that Britain would never go to war—a miscalculation not altogether dissimilar to that of William II. in 1914.   It is typical of the illogical and ill-informed nature of British public opinion that, while a profound insular suspicion of Russia was excused and justified by the reactionary views of Nicholas and his advisers, the hideous corruption, disorganisation and tyranny under which the Christians of Turkey groaned did not in any way lessen the unreasoning enthusiasm of the British Turkophiles.   To-day it is curious to note that our Russophiles of the 'fifties were to be found among the extreme Radicals and Pacifists, so many of whom seem to have forgotten the great tradition of John Bright now that Russia is our loyal ally, and moving steadily towards constitutional reforms.

The course of the Crimean War lies quite outside my present scope.   Politically it was marked by two outstanding events, the vacillation of Austria, who, in the phrase of Schwarzenberg, astonished the world by her ingratitude, who alienated first Russia, then Prussia, then France and Britain, by her indecision, and finally ended by losing the prize of the Danubian Principalities : and that association of Piedmont as an ally of France and Britain, which marks the first entry of the future Italy into the ranks of the Great Powers, and which was pre-eminently the work of the great Cavour. The war was followed by the Congress of Paris (1856) whose work may be very briefly summarised as follows.   The integrity of the Ottoman Empire was guaranteed by the Powers.   The Sultan pledged himself to the introduction of far-reaching reforms, such as might be expected to regenerate the State and render tolerable the life of his Christian subjects. The navigation of the Danube was made free and international under the control of a mixed commission. The neutrality of the Black Sea was proclaimed; and as its waters were thus closed to navies, the maintenance of fortresses on its shores was declared to be unnecessary. The complete autonomy of Wallachia and Moldavia was recognised under Turkish suzerainty, and the southern portion of Bessarabia, which Russia had secured in 1812, was reunited to Moldavia. Never has an European settlement proved more futile or led so quickly to a diplomatic fiasco. Ere long every one of its main provisions had been riddled through. The aim of the Congress had been to dam back Russian advance upon Constantinople, and to restrain her within artificial bounds; and this aim had been prompted above all by ignorance and fear, and by a complete failure to realise that the growth of free national states in the peninsula was a far more effective barrier than treaties or political intrigues. Lord Salisbury was right when he said, with that bluntness which threw his habitual reserve into greater relief, that in the Crimean War we had put our money on the wrong horse.

In the years that followed the Congress of Paris, Europe was controlled by three prominent figures, Napoleon III., Cavour, and Bismarck. The Crimean War had deranged the old Concert of Europe, and before it had got into gear again, United Italy had been achieved. A year later, to the eternal loss of both Italy herself and of Europe, Cavour died; and the next ten years were devoted to a trial of strength between Napoleon and Bismarck. So far as the Balkans were concerned—and it was, of course, pre-eminently a Near Eastern settlement —the Congress of Paris prepared the way for the union of the two Principalities under a single ruler and the birth of modern Roumania. Brief allusion has already been made to the manner in which the Great Powers blocked the movement for unity, and to the skill with which their efforts were evaded and countered. Their attitude towards Roumania between 1856 and 1859 is one of the most striking of the many instances of futility and wrong-headedness of which the Concert of Europe has been guilty.

By an inevitable process leaf after leaf was being stripped from the artichoke; Roumania was now emancipated, though certain restraints of Turkish suzerainty survived; Serbia was gradually removing the last vestiges of Turkish rule; and Bosnia and Bulgaria were preparing for trouble. The Great Powers, then, in propping up the Sick Man upon his pillows and in blocking, whenever possible, the movement for the liberation of the Balkan Christians, had set themselves to fight the stars in their courses; and it was an irony of fate that the blackest of autocrats and reactionaries should have fought the battle of liberty against the liberal Powers of the West.

The Congress of Paris ushered in the period of Turkish reform—*lucus a non lucendo*—one of the most ignominious periods of European history. As early as 1839, Sultan Abdul Medjid, on his accession, had proclaimed a charter of reform, but like all similar documents in Turkey, it remained on paper, and the only direction in which any serious pretence at reform was carried through was the administration of the army, which was reorganised in 1843. It is the unfortunate habit of such reformers—and the Young Turks since 1908 have provided a striking confirmation of the fact—that they tend to build roads where they serve strategical purposes, and schools where they can be employed for military cadets, and that building operations are mainly devoted to the erection and extension of barracks. The Hatti-Humayun of 1856 pledged the Porte to the introduction of equality before the law, liberty of worship, equal taxation, judicial reform and mixed tribunals.   But it evoked general discontent among the Turks; for every true Moslem regarded it as a violation of the principles of the Koran, and having retained the natural outlook of a conqueror even in the evil days of Ottoman decay, keenly resented the bare idea of the rayah being treated as his equal. Thus reforms, which were so absolutely irreconcilable with Mohammedan law, simply remained on paper.   One point which was to acquire special importance in the twentieth century was specially debated.   Were Christians to be admitted into the army?   On the one hand there was no great competition among the Christians themselves for this doubtful honour, while on the other there was much hostility on the part of the Moslems, who would on no account have obeyed Christian officers, and who feared that by inculcating the Christians with military discipline they would merely be training soldiers for the future armies of the Tsar.   Finally, in 1869, a law was passed absolutely restricting recruiting to Moslems.

The whole judicial, and even administrative problem was infinitely complicated by the Capitulations, under which the various Great Powers possessed courts, post offices and special privileges of their own.   In view of the anarchical and corrupt condition of Turkish justice, and the incompatibility of European legal ideas with the Sheriat, it was obviously impossible to rescind these Capitulations, even if all the Powers could have been induced to agree.   In 1864, the Law of Vilayets reorganised the administration of the Empire.   Each vilayet or province, under its Vali, or governor, received an administrative council of its own and was sub-divided into Sandjaks or Arrondissements, each under a Mutissarif, Kazas, each under a Kaimakam, and Nahies or Communes, each under a Mudir or Mayor.

It is hardly necessary to mention the sordid fact that commercial and financial interests and jealousies lay at the root of the policy pursued by the various members of the Concert in Constantinople, and it was financial reform, the creation of the Imperial Ottoman Bank, the consolidation of an Ottoman debt, and the establishment of a Turkish *Cour des Comptes* which received the most persistent external backing. The pressure of the Powers exhausted itself in a dead mass of resistance and was neutralised by the peculiar workings of the Oriental mind and by the corrupt accumulations of centuries.

Throughout this period of reform the progress of gangrene leading to amputation continued. Wallachia and Moldavia were transformed into the flourishing state of Roumania. Montenegro's victory at Grahovo gloriously reaffirmed her defiance of the Turkish yoke. The accession of King George of Greece (1863), followed by the cession of the Ionian Isles, the grant of a new constitution and one of the more serious Cretan risings, marked the opening of a new era for Hellenism. In 1867 the last of the Turkish garrisons was withdrawn from Serbia.

The issue of the Franco-German War had a marked effect upon the Near East. France's influence was eclipsed, Russian prestige revived, while Britain showed the same hesitation in her Balkan policy as she subsequently displayed during the Balkan wars and during the eventful winter of 1915. Russia's revival was marked by two very striking successes, the repudiation of the clauses of the Treaty of Paris guaranteeing the neutrality of the Black Sea, and the creation of the Bulgarian Exarchate and the consequent strengthening of Slav nationality in the Balkans. Meanwhile the attitude of Austria had also been profoundly modified by the wars of 1866 and 1870. In the former year she had been expelled from both Italy and Germany, with the natural result that her eyes turned Eastward, while in 1871 the crown was set upon Prussian hegemony in Germany by the proclamation of the new Empire at Versailles. Count Beust, the Saxon statesman whom Francis Joseph summoned to Vienna to control his foreign policy, was dominated by the idea of revenge against Prussia; and that idea underlay the establishment of the Dual system between Austria and Hungary in 1867. But very soon an entirely different direction was given to it. Henceforth Magyar influence dominated the foreign policy of Austria-Hungary. Count Andrássy, the Magyar aristocrat, who was the first Hungarian Premier under the Dual system and succeeded Beust as Joint Foreign Minister, has even to-day not been assigned to his true place as one of the greatest statesmen of the nineteenth century. Like all true Magyars, Andrássy was anti-Slav; unlike some, he realised that this involved being pro-German. In short, he realised what Count Tisza realises to-day—that the creation or maintenance of the Magyar national state is only possible in alliance with Germany. This is one of the alphabetical truths of Continental policy which are still consistently ignored by British statesmen. Andrássy, then, prevented the introduction of federalism in Austria and vetoed the coronation of Francis Joseph as King of Bohemia, while, as we shall see, he laid the foundations of that alliance between Austria and Germany which dominates the European situation to-day. Andrássy's attitude was a natural supplement to that *rapprochement* between the three Empires—the three conservative elements in Europe—which had always been the goal of Bismarck's policy, and which was made possible by the kinship and personal friendship between William I. and Alexander II. Alexander thus based his policy on the dynastic and legitimist motives which had influenced his father and for the time being ignored Slavophil ideas. After 1870 Bismarck posed as the bulwark of general peace in Europe, and it would be unjust to suggest that except on one notorious occasion there was no sincerity in the pose. Between the years 1871 and 1876 he arranged a whole series of interviews between the two sovereigns.

As M. Seignobos justly remarked in 1896 : "The whole political history of Europe since 1871 has concentrated in the Balkan Peninsula." A new phase of the Eastern Question opened in 1875 with the outbreak of a revolt in Bosnia and Herzegovina. These provinces were then, as now, inhabited by Serbs and Croats, of whom rather more than one-third was Mohammedan by religion; and they naturally looked for deliverance to their Serb kinsmen in Serbia and Montenegro, and for sympathy to their other Serb and Croat kinsmen in Croatia and Dalmatia. From quite an early stage in the crisis Austria-Hungary seriously considered the occupation of the two provinces. Such a step was a logical sequel to her possession of Dalmatia, for it is obvious that if Bosnia fell into any other hands, Dalmatia would sooner or later be lost. Dalmatia is untenable without Bosnia, except so long as the latter is held by an uncivilised and decaying Power like the Turks.

A number of attempts were made to force a scheme of reform upon the Porte, but failed owing to the uncompromising demands and resistance of the insurgents. As usual, long and barren diplomatic negotiations between the Powers kept pace with growing anarchy in the disturbed provinces, and indeed in other parts of Turkey. In May, 1876, Bulgaria was the scene of the rising and massacre which roused Gladstone to his celebrated action; and in the same month a revolution broke out in Constantinople itself. The Sultan, Abdul Aziz, was replaced by his brother, Murad V., a brainless cipher in the hands of the Young Turks. The new *régime* found an able leader in Midhat Pasha, but his followers, though full of enthusiasm for Western ideas of constitutional government, proved quite incapable of assimilating the crude doctrinaire teachings which they had culled from some of the wilder writers of the French Revolution. Moreover, just as in Hungary the leaders of constitutional reform were grossly intolerant in their attitude towards the other nationalities, so the Young Turks were possessed by the Ottoman idea, which involved the assimilation and subjection of the Christian subjects of the Porte. Their efforts to gain control of the machinery of state were naturally encouraged by the internal anarchy in Turkey, by the storm of indignation in the civilised West and the rising tide of Pan-Slav feeling in Russia, which the Bulgarian atrocities had evoked.

On July 1, 1876, the two Serbian states declared war upon Turkey, after issuing proclamations which foretold the revival of Stephen Dušan's mediæval Empire. In this action Prince Milan of Serbia was certainly influenced by the fact that Prince Peter Karagjorgjević, the head of the rival dynasty, was one of the leaders of the Bosnian rising and was already proving his qualities as a soldier. The Serbian army, though led by a Russian General, Černajev, and augmented by many Russian volunteers, proved no match for the Turks, and was on the point of being crushed, when the Tsar imposed an armistice under threat of immediate war. It was during this eventful summer, when the Turkish Empire seemed once more threatened to its very foundations, that the phantom Sultan Murad was replaced by Abdul Hamid, who was soon to end the brief farce of the Turkish Constitution. The peace of Europe was in growing danger. Disraeli made a threatening speech at the Guildhall Banquet in favour of the unspeakable Turk, and his words were a glaring contrast to the speech of Alexander II. to the nobles of Moscow on the following day, when he declared that, "if he failed to obtain with the aid of Europe the guarantee which he was entitled to demand from Turkey, he would be obliged to act alone." If Disraeli had had his way, there would have been another unnecessary war between Britain and Russia to assert the right of the Sultan to misgovern and massacre at will. Providentially Gladstone's agitation on the Liberal side and the influence of sound commonsense among the Conservatives led to the dispatch of Lord Salisbury, the wisest of Conservative statesmen, to Constantinople. The negotiations of the representatives of the Great Powers with the new Turkish Parliament under Midhat shattered against the theories and racial fanaticism of the Turks, who insisted on "the integrity of the Turkish Empire." Just as Kossuth, the Magyar leader, on the eve of 1848 declared that he could not find Croatia on the map, so Midhat's followers affected ignorance as to the whereabouts of Bulgaria. After the failure of these negotiations war was only a question of time. Early in 1877 Pan-Slav feeling reached its height in Russia, and the Tsar concluded a military convention with Roumania.

The Russo-Turkish War, in which Serbia and Montenegro soon joined once more, lies outside the scope of the present narrative, which seeks to deal with causes and effects rather than with military details. The reverses at Shipka and Plevna, which followed the initial Russian success, were retrieved to a very great extent by the heroism of the Roumanian army under the able leadership of Prince Charles. The fall of Plevna on December 10, 1877, prepared the way for the Russian entry into Adrianople on January 20, 1878: and Constantinople was soon threatened by the victorious Russians. In February, Abdul Hamid took advantage of these disasters to get rid of his discredited Parliament and to suspend the Turkish Constitution. The Hamidian despotism under which Turkey groaned for the next thirty years was a worthy culmination of the process of decay which the importation of crude political nostrums from the West had been unable to arrest.

On March 3, 1878, the Treaty of San Stefano was concluded between Russia and Turkey, and its provisions revolutionised the whole situation in the Near East. The independence of Roumania and Serbia was definitely secured; but while certain territorial concessions were made to Serbia and Montenegro, Bessarabia was to be taken from Roumania, who only received the Dobrudja as a sorry exchange; and Bosnia-Herzegovina, instead of being united to their kinsmen on the East, were to receive an autonomy of their own. But the outstanding feature of the treaty was the creation of a Big Bulgaria, under the suzerainty of the Sultan, comprising the whole of Bulgaria proper, Eastern Roumelia with the town of Philippopolis and the whole of Macedonia, to the very gates of Salonica, and extending westwards as far as the Šar Mountains, Dibra and Koritza, and even eating right into the heart of Albania to the west of the Lake of Ohrida.

The Treaty of San Stefano was an absolutely impossible arrangement for two reasons. In the first place it was an essentially Slavonic settlement, which neglected or did grave injustice to the non-Slav races of the Peninsula, the Greeks, the Albanians and the Roumanians. In the second place it left Turkey with frontiers such as defied every law of geography, politics or common sense. Autonomous Bosnia was to retain its nominal connection with Turkey; but a narrow, wholly indefensible, and absurdly unnatural corridor through the Sandjak of Novibazar was still to connect Bosnia with the plain of Kosovo and to separate Serbia from Montenegro—a corridor infinitely less satisfactory and narrower by two-thirds than that which was actually created by the Treaty of Berlin. Salonica remained Turkish, but was entirely separated from its hinterland. Novibazar, Kosovo,

Albania, Epirus and Thessaly were left in Turkish hands,
as mere fragments, unworkable and disconnected.
Adrianople and the valley of the Arta were retained by
the Turks; but the whole connection between Adrianople
and Constantinople was directly threatened by the as-
signment to Bulgaria of an enclave of territory including Kirk Kilisse and extending south to within a few
miles of the river Ergene, near Lüleburgas. But if the
settlement was unjust and fatal on general grounds, it
is just upon *Slavonic* grounds that it had its most fatal
effect. For it would have aggrandised Bulgaria at the
expense of all her neighbours; and though it never became effective, its memory provided that tenacious race
with a programme which struck deep root in the minds of
its leaders, and has ever since been regarded by them as
their excuse and justification for aiming at the hegemony
of the Balkan Peninsula.

Meanwhile this settlement displeased and alarmed the
Great Powers on purely selfish grounds. Britain still
looked upon Russian control of Constantinople as a real
danger, and with more reason regarded with disfavour
the clauses which seemed to secure to Russia complete
control of the new Bulgarian administration and of the
Prince's election. Public opinion in England was influenced by the sentimental appeals of Indian Moslems
in favour of their Turkish co-religionists. Moreover,
Austria-Hungary was determined to have Bosnia for
herself and was highly displeased at an arrangement
which would have placed Bulgaria across her own path to
Salonica. The British Government took a strong line
in demanding a revision of the Treaty, and was backed
up by the mobilisation of Austria, and by protests from
the Greeks and other rivals of Bulgaria. Russia was not
prepared to risk an extension of the war and consented to
the convocation of an European Congress, which in due
course met in Berlin under the presidency of Bismarck

as the "honest broker" (June 13—July 13, 1878). The attitude and outlook of the Congress were at once revealed in its decision not to admit the Greek and Roumanian delegates to direct representation or to the vote, but merely to allow them to state their views. Thus the fate of the Balkan Peninsula for the next thirty years was decided by the Great Powers over the heads, and generally in defiance of the wishes, of the states and races concerned. If the settlement of San Stefano was unjust to all but the Slavs and did not draw a just line even between those Slavs themselves, the settlement of Berlin succeeded in being equally unjust to all. It was frankly based upon force, upon the interests of the Great Powers, and upon the negation of the rights of small nations. That is the root fact which it is necessary to bear in mind throughout the concluding stages of the present War— the more so in view of the ominous contrast between the professions and the practice of the statesmen who at present control the fate of Europe, in all matters that concern the principle of nationality.

It is interesting to note that Article LXIII. of the new Treaty declared the Treaty of Paris to be still in operation on all points not specifically abrogated. In point of fact it replaced the Treaty of Paris on virtually every point save three, viz., the international regulation of the Straits (X.) and of the Danube (XV., sqq.) and the recourse to arbitration before force. Only two stipulations definitely survived—the principle of the independence and integrity of the Ottoman Empire, which has now become a mere farce, and the admission of Turkey to the advantages of European public law, which was never applied.[1]

Under the provisions of the Treaty of Berlin the "Big Bulgaria" of San Stefano vanished, and Bulgarian unity, which the nation was to have won thus easily,

[1] Cahuet, La Question d'Orient, p. 401.

vanished with it. The Bulgarian race fell into three groups—the new Principality, with a population of about two millions, under a prince to be selected by the nation, subject to the approval of the Sublime Porte and the Great Powers, from one of the petty non-reigning dynasties of Europe; Eastern Roumelia with barely a million inhabitants, under a governor nominated for five years by the Porte; and the unredeemed Bulgarians of Thrace and Macedonia. Serbia finally acquired her independence and was allowed to extend her frontiers by the acquisition of Niš, Pirot and Vranja. The independence of Montenegro, which had long been a solid historical fact, was formally recognised by the Porte. The district of Nikšić and a fragment of Herzegovina, together with a few miles of coast line beside the roadstead of Antivari, were assigned to Montenegro; but the new frontier was so unnatural and produced such acute disorder between the Montenegrins and the Albanians, that in 1880 the Powers found it necessary to consent to a revision and to assign Dulcigno to Montenegro. The real injustice of this settlement as far as Montenegro was concerned lay in the circumstance that Spizza, which completely dominates Antivari, was left in Austrian hands, that Montenegro, though independent and not neutralised, was not allowed to possess ships of her own, and that the maritime control of her coasts was vested in Austria-Hungary; and that Austria's consent was necessary before Montenegro could build a railway through her own territory.

The Congress reached two far more vital decisions which affected the whole future, political and economic, of the two Serbian states. Bosnia-Herzegovina was assigned to Austria-Hungary. The long and bloody struggle of the Bosnians for union with their Serb kinsmen had thus been in vain, and the rights of nationality were again set at open defiance. The decision of the

Powers was resisted by force of arms, and the Austrian occupation could only be effected after a difficult and expensive campaign. A secret parallel arrangement between Austria-Hungary and the Sultan assured the latter that no steps derogatory to his rights as suzerain would be undertaken, and that the occupation was to be regarded as provisional. Meanwhile Austria-Hungary also obtained the right of garrisoning the Sandjak of Novibazar, and was thus enabled to drive a wedge between the two Serbian states, to complete the isolation of Serbia from the Adriatic and to keep open the line of advance towards Salonica and the Ægean which had long haunted the dreams of Austrian Imperialists. The fatal effect of these changes upon Serbo-Croat national feeling, and their share in producing the present war will form the subject of a later chapter.

The independence of Roumania was finally recognised by Europe, though, as in the case of Serbia, it was not till 1881 that Prince Charles assumed the title of King. A disgraceful and shortsighted provision was added by which Roumania was made to recoup Russia for the expenses of the war. Bessarabia, which had been acquired by Russia in 1812, but partially restored to its rightful Roumanian owners in 1856, was now reunited with Russia; while the barren and indefensible Dobrudja, lying to the south of the Danube delta, and peopled by a mixed population of Tartars, Bulgarians, Turks, Ruthenes, and Roumanians, was assigned to Roumania as compensation. It is difficult to explain this arrangement on any other theory than that of a deliberate desire to sow discord between Bulgaria and Roumania, and to provide the latter with a frontier open to strategical attacks from the south. At that time, it must be remembered, Russia expected Bulgaria to be little better than a vassal state, and, therefore, hoped to strengthen her hold upon Roumania by simultaneous strategical control from north and south. It is important to remember that from the very first Roumania vigorously protested against this new frontier, and repeatedly pressed for its revision, especially in the neighbourhood of Silistria, until the events of 1913 gave her an opportunity of making her claims effective.

The history of the next generation is the history of the non-execution of these clauses, and of ponderous and insincere negotiations between the Great Powers. At last, the period of the Concert of Europe ended shamefully in the bankruptcy of the Hamidian *régime*, the Young Turkish revolt, the achievement by a league of the small Christian states of what Europe had lamentably failed to achieve, and the wrecking of this new-found unity by the intrigues and selfish policy of the Great Powers.

CHAPTER X

THE Treaty of Berlin was the supreme effort of the European Concert. It asserted the right of the Great Powers to decide the destiny of those fragments which Turkey had contrived to rescue from the wreck of her European dominions. Just as in 1815 the allied Sovereigns portioned out Europe according to their dynastic interests, so the statesmen responsible for the settlement of 1878 followed the dictates of their own convenience and selfish interest. The young Christian states of the peninsula would have been helpless, even if they had been linked together in close alliance, instead of being separated by the stagnation and jealousy of centuries. Utterly lacking the strength to oppose the unanimous will of Europe, they had to submit perforce to an arrangement whose injustice many of them bitterly resented. Its effect has been forcibly summarised in the words of a Roumanian historian, as "the exploitation, in favour of the Great Powers, at one and the same time of the national right of the nations, and the historical right of the Turks." [1] The history of the thirty-four years which followed (1878-1912) is the history of the gradual process of crumbling decay to which that unnatural settlement was subjected—of Turkey's complete inability

---

[1] Iorga, *Histoire des États balcaniques,* p. 367.

113

and disinclination to introduce the promised reforms, and of an increasing tendency on the part of the Balkan states to correct the *status quo* whenever possible by presenting the sluggish Concert of Europe with a *fait accompli*.

The settlement had one most unpleasant sequel, upon which the full light of history has still to be shed; this was the highly questionable attitude of Disraeli. On May 30 he reached a secret understanding with Russia as to the conditions upon which Britain would consent to the Congress of Berlin. On June 7, he promised Austria-Hungary Britain's support for the occupation of Bosnia-Herzegovina. Meanwhile on June 4 he concluded a secret compact with Turkey, promising in the event of need the armed defence of Turkey's Asiatic possessions against Russia, and exacting as the price for this the occupation of Cyprus, which was only to be restored in the event of Russia's withdrawal from Armenian territory. This scandalous arrangement, which came to light prematurely, seemed in the eyes of Europe to justify the title of "Perfidious Albion." It makes it impossible for us to evade a heavy moral responsibility for subsequent developments—for the hideous sufferings of Armenia, for the incomplete solution of the Balkan problem, for the non-execution of reforms in Turkey, and for the consequent growth of anarchy and disorder and all the European complications which they inevitably involved. The sins of the European Concert have come back to roost, and this country is paying for its mismanagement of the Balkan problem a generation ago, by a situation in which French and British blood is being shed, and shed inevitably, upon the soil of Macedonia.

The Congress of Berlin ushered in a new epoch in the relations of the European Powers, an epoch of "armed peace" and ever growing armaments. It marked the height of the influence of Bismarck, whose permanent ideal was friendship between the three conservative empires—between the three spoilers of Poland, whose initial crime is so largely responsible for Europe's subsequent misfortunes. The true significance of 1878 lies in the fact that Bismarck made Andrássy his colleague and Disraeli his tool, and that he finally won and dominated Austria-Hungary without at the same time offending Russia.

The year 1879, then, saw the foundation of the alliance round which European diplomacy was to revolve for the next generation, the Dual Alliance of Germany and Austria-Hungary. The death of Alexander II. in 1881 ended the entente of the three Emperors; for Alexander III. did not share his father's warm personal feelings for William I., and though essentially pacific, was scarcely less Germanophobe than his wife the Empress Marie. Thus the 'eighties were a period in which autocratic Russia and Republican France, by a natural political process, slowly gravitated towards each other, but in which the process was delayed by Bismarck's ingenious "reinsurance" arrangement between Germany and Russia. France's isolation led her to console herself for failure in Europe by the foundation of a new colonial empire; and French and Italian rivalry in Tunis gave rise to a conflict which was promptly exploited by Bismarck. In 1883, the adhesion of Italy transformed the Dual into the Triple Alliance.

Meanwhile, with every year the rivalry of Austria and Russia fills a more noticeable place in European politics, though its significance is sometimes obscured by an artificially fostered jealousy between Russia and Britain. Cross currents and conflicting influences become so numerous that it is increasingly difficult for the onlooker to detect the plot of the play as a whole. But Austro-Russian rivalry remains as one of the dominant factors, and if after this war it is ever possible to acquire sufficient perspective for a general survey of the struggle, it will stand revealed as scarcely less responsible than the Anglo-German feud for the outbreak of the world war.

Quite a number of articles in the Treaty of Berlin proved to be impossible of execution, and had to be imposed by force. As we have seen, the Montenegrin frontier had to be revised in favour of the Albanians in the south, and in favour of Montenegro herself along the coasts. Greece succeeded in obtaining Thessaly after prolonged disturbance. Bosnia refused to submit to Austria-Hungary, and had to be conquered. A more peaceful dispute arose in connection with the new frontier between Roumania and Bulgaria, and was not finally settled till 1880. Silistria, the key to the Dobrudja, was left in Bulgarian hands. Russia's persistent neglect of Roumanian national sentiment and the lack of adequate support from France and Britain inevitably drove Roumania into the orbit of Austria-Hungary and Germany. Thus the two Latin sisters, Italy and Roumania, in return for the security and financial advantage offered by the Central Powers, renounced, at least officially, all irredentist plans for the emancipation of their kinsmen in the Dual Monarchy. Even Serbia, under King Milan, despite her keen resentment at the fate of Bosnia, found it impossible to escape from the Austrian sphere of influence; and for many years the Russophil party at Belgrade suffered a complete eclipse.

In the years that followed the Congress the chief centre of interest in the Balkan Peninsula was the new principality of Bulgaria. The Russian occupation, under Dondukov-Korsakov, was responsible for the beginnings of an educational and financial system, for the formation of a national bank and library and a State Press, and for the first draft of a new Constitution, which though ultra-democratic in form, left the chief power in the hands of the Prince. In April, 1879, the new throne was filled by the election of Prince Alexander of Battenberg, the son by a morganatic marriage of a Hessian prince. As the nephew of Tsar Alexander II. he was regarded by Russia as acceptable, and his youth and inexperience— he was only twenty-two—encouraged the belief that he might be a mere tool in the hands of his uncle. The establishment of manhood suffrage, single chamber government and virtually unrestricted freedom of the Press in a country which had for centuries groaned under Turkish rule, was a distinctly audacious experiment; and it is difficult to avoid the conclusion that the powers of Prince and people under such a Constitution were deliberately framed to counter-balance each other in order that the true power might rest with the Russian Tsar. Alexander found himself in a position of extraordinary difficulty. Bulgaria was entirely lacking in political traditions. Her people was a nation of peasants, endowed with more than the usual dose of suspicion which is inherent in most peasantries, and with a natural disposition to dislike all foreigners. Her politicians were untried men, trained in half a dozen different schools, and each desperately jealous alike of the person and the theories of his neighbour. Alexander himself was as inexperienced as the people whom he was called upon to govern, and soon tired of the Constitution, which he probably quite honestly believed to be unworkable. This change of attitude did not meet with the approval of the Tsar, but the assassination of the latter in 1881 provided the Prince with an opportunity of effecting a *coup d'état* —the assembly being induced by the threats of Alexander's resignation to vote the suspension of the Constitution for seven years. In effect, this step placed Alexander still further in the power of Russia. Russian generals assumed the offices of Premier and Minister of War, controlled the whole machinery of state and showed themselves anything but tactful or conciliatory. It is true that they organised the Bulgarian army, but otherwise they rapidly alienated public opinion, so far as it can be said to have existed in such a period of transition. In 1883 it was already found necessary to convoke Parliament once more, with a view to working out a new Constitution. Parliamentary life is a plant of slow growth, and it has never flourished on Bulgarian soil. On the other hand, the system of party groups and fractions has been steadily fostered by the attitude of Prince Alxander and still more of his unscrupulous successor Ferdinand, and in a more natural manner by the rise of several very remarkable men, Cankov, Karavelov, and, above all, Stambulov, whom his admirers were fond of describing as the Bismarck of the Balkans.

Meanwhile Eastern Roumelia, with Philippopolis as its capital, had been organised as an autonomous Turkish province, with a Government appointed for five years, and with an assembly of thirty-six members, of whom thirty-one were from the first Bulgarians.[1] The province became the centre of a secret revolutionary movement which gained ground steadily until on September 18, 1885, a successful and almost entirely bloodless *coup d'état* was carried out. The Governor was sent back to Turkey. The union of "the Two Bulgarias" was publicly proclaimed, and Alexander was invited to accept the new situation. This sudden display of energy and independent feeling gave great offence to so conservative a ruler as Tsar Alexander III.; and Russian apologists alleged that Prince Alexander, as recently as September 1, had given his word to the Russian Foreign Minister, de Giers, at Franzensbad to do all he could against the revolutionary movement in Roumelia.[2]

---

[1] It is worth noting that Mr. Gešov, afterwards Bulgarian Prime Minister and one of the makers of the Balkan League, drew up the first Budget of Eastern Roumelia with the aid of French financial advisers.

[2] Drandar, *Cinq Ans de Règne en Bulgarie*, p. 72.

Prince Alexander certainly hesitated to take such action as might alienate Turkey and Russia simultaneously. But he found himself between two fires; for Stambulov unquestionably voiced the feeling of the Bulgarian people when he bluntly told the Prince that if he did not advance to Philippopolis he had better retire to Darmstadt. Alexander accepted the union and ordered a general mobilisation, thus drawing down upon himself a furious telegram from the Tsar enjoining the resignation of all Russian officers in the Bulgarian army. But as usual the situation developed in an unexpected manner. The Turks refrained from any attack upon Bulgaria. Count Andrássy publicly declared in the Hungarian Parliament that the Berlin settlement of the Bulgarian problem had merely been provisional. Lord Salisbury, realising that the Bulgarians were developing a will of their own and were not disposed to remain mere instruments of Russia, gave Britain's support to the idea of union and thus tacitly reversed the policy of Disraeli.

The danger to peace came from quite another quarter. King Milan of Serbia constituted himself the champion of that Treaty of Berlin from which his own race had suffered most against the movement for national unity amongst his nearest neighbours and kinsmen. Even to-day it is difficult to apportion the blame for this fatal step. Milan Obrenović was corrupt in private life and addicted to gross favouritism. The corruption, alike administrative, elective and financial, and the repeated violations of the Constitution which characterised his rule, rendered him detested by all save the Court clique. Thus Milan tended to favour a policy of foreign aggrandisement and prestige for reasons not dissimilar to those which had inspired Napoleon III. in the closing years of the Third Empire. Milan was also alarmed by the growing popularity of the rival Karagjorgjević family, whose head, Prince Peter, had married a daughter

of Prince Nicholas of Montenegro.   But unquestionably
the main underlying cause of the catastrophe of 1885 was
the fatal rivalry of Austria and Russia for influence in
Belgrade.   This rivalry, which took the form of endless
political intrigue, has been the curse of the two Slav
states of the peninsula.   It has converted the splendid
ideal of Jugo-slav unity, as conceived by Bishop Strossmayer and Prince Michael, into a feud of two natural
allies, as deadly as the long feud which the ambition and
brutality of Edward I., the first of England's lawyer
statesmen, so needlessly created between England and
Scotland.

On November 13, 1885, Milan declared war upon
Bulgaria, trading upon the confusion which the withdrawal of the Russian officers might be expected to pro-
duce in a young and untried army, and expecting to enter
Sofia almost unopposed.   But overhaste, bad generalship,
the lack of equipment and cannon, and indeed the absence
of any serious strategical plan, proved fatal to the Serbian
arms.   At the battle of Slivnica the Bulgarians were
completely victorious, and their advance into Serbia was
only arrested by the arrival of an Austrian emissary,
Count Khevenhüller, in the camp of Prince Alexander,
to impose an armistice and to announce that any further
advance would be opposed by Austrian troops.   Alexander, opposed by Austria-Hungary and frowned upon
by Russia, fell back upon Turkish aid; a Convention
was rapidly concluded with the Porte by which the union
of the "Two Bulgarias" was recognised in return for an
offensive and defensive alliance between Turkey and
Bulgaria.   Upon this basis peace was restored, and
Milan returned discredited to Belgrade with no alternative save to become the political agent and vassal of
Austria-Hungary.   The scandals of his private life grew
steadily more violent, and culminated in his divorce
from Queen Nathalie.   In 1889 he saved himself from

an impossible position by pushing through a new and much more liberal Constitution and then immediately abdicating in favour of his only son Alexander. But though the regency was left mainly in the hands of Jovan Ristić, the ablest of Serbian modern statesmen, the old atmosphere of oriental intrigue and calumny remained. Milan and Nathalie flitted behind the scenes and kept Serbia in a state of intermittent political fever, until Alexander was ready to supplement the scandals of his parents by his own, and until the unhappy country could only escape from imminent disaster by a hideous crime.

Meanwhile the Bulgarian union had a dramatic sequel. On August 21, 1886, a *coup d'état* was organised by the friends of Russia. Alexander of Battenberg was kidnapped in his palace during the dead of night, hurried on to a Danubian steamer, landed on Russian territory, and then allowed to withdraw to Austria. But Stambulov put his shoulder to the wheel, and declined to allow the situation to be rushed by those who wished to be the slaves of Russian policy and who were not even ashamed to kneel in the mud outside the Russian Agency in Sofia in supplication to the Tsar. Alexander was invited to return to Bulgaria, and was received with the utmost enthusiasm. Then when the battle seemed already won, he wrecked everything by sending to the Tsar a telegram which culminated in the phrase, "Russia having given me my crown, I am ready to return it into the hands of her sovereign." Alexander III., who had never liked his cousin, made the most of such an opportunity and sent the following characteristic reply : "I shall abstain from all interference with the sad state of affairs to which Bulgaria is reduced so long as you remain there. Your Highness will understand what to do." On September 7, 1886, Alexander abdicated and withdrew to Austria, ending, as his successor began, as an officer in the Austrian army.

The course of events had thoroughly roused national feeling in Bulgaria. Stambulov, blunt and masterful by nature, had the nation behind him; and the extraordinary tactlessness of General Kaulbars, whom the Tsar sent to Bulgaria to lay the foundations of the new *régime,* only accentuated the growing desire of the Bulgarian leaders to manage their own affairs and widened the breach between Bulgaria and Russia. For many months the throne of Bulgaria went begging. At first an unsuccessful attempt was made to secure Prince Waldemar of Denmark, the brother of King George of Greece, and the brother-in-law of the Tsar. A little later King Charles of Roumania declined the suggestion of a personal union between the two countries. In view of the utter incompatibility of temperament between the two races, he may have acted wisely; and yet it is difficult to resist the conclusion that such a development might have saved the peninsula from many of its subsequent misfortunes. Finally, on April 14, 1887, Prince Ferdinand of Saxe-Coburg accepted the vacant throne, and on July 7 was formally elected by the Bulgarian Chamber. Prince Ferdinand was a member of the Catholic and Austrian branch of the house of which King George V. is the head; while his mother was a daughter of Louis Philippe, and his paternal grandmother, Princess Koháry, an heiress from whom he inherited rich estates in Hungary. No greater contrast could be imagined than that between the gallant and impulsive Alexander of Battenberg, and the subtle and calculating Ferdinand of Coburg, who has much in common with such Renaissance tyrants as Lorenzo de Medici or Pandolfo Malatesta.

For no fewer than nine years Russia remained irreconcilable and withheld official recognition from Prince Ferdinand, with the result that he could not be received at the various Courts of Europe. This was extremely galling to Ferdinand, but a matter of complete indifference to Stambulov, who as Bulgarian Premier acquired the position of virtual dictator, and governed with a strong hand in open defiance of Russia. In the words of Professor Iorga, "Stambulov was a man of Asiatic energy, passionate and cruel, a worthy pupil of his Russian masters, to whom he proved day by day that their weapons can also be employed by far feebler adversaries. He concentrated all his extraordinary energy upon delivering Bulgaria from the Russian tutelage in which he found her and from the Russian annexation which seemed to be in the future. To espionage he replied by counter espionage, to conspiracies by summary executions, to corruption by another variety of corruption, to cynicism by an equal cynicism. The Russian system in the East was destroyed in Bulgaria by its own tricks and its own violence." It would, of course, be unjust to quote so severe a verdict without at the same time pointing out that there have always been two currents in Russian diplomacy, reflecting more or less faithfully the dual nature of Russian political life at home—on the one hand the corrupt and brutal bureaucracy which is in its death throes to-day, on the other the ideal movement of Russian and Slavonic thought. These two tendencies sometimes mingle and interact upon each other; but it is easy to distinguish the conservative type of Russian diplomacy, imbued by Pan-Slavist feeling in its earlier form, from the more aggressive if abler tendency represented by Ignatiev, Čarikov and Hartwig.

Ferdinand, after submitting with growing impatience to the dictatorship of the great Minister, at last felt himself in May, 1894, strong enough to dispense with his services, and drove him from office by a rude telegram dispatched from an Austrian watering-place. Stambulov proved to be even less capable of supporting such treatment than Bismarck himself four years before, and carried on a Press campaign against the Prince which involved him in a serious libel action. Finally, on July 15, 1895, Stambulov was assassinated in the streets of Sofia by hired bravos, who added mutilation to their crime, and were allowed to escape in a manner which threw grave suspicion upon the authorities and led to open accusations of complicity against the Prince himself. The disgraceful scenes at the funeral of the murdered statesman, the manner in which the trial against the murderers was delayed, and, finally, the methods employed at their trial, only served to increase the suspicion and recriminations of the rival parties. But since 1895 Ferdinand himself has been the real force in Bulgarian politics, and has used Ministers and Cabinets as mere tools in his game.

In 1896 Ferdinand was reconciled to Russia, and baptized his son, Boris, into the Orthodox Church, in defiance of a solemn undertaking to his wife, a princess of Parma, and of the Pope's anathema. Meanwhile life in Bulgaria assumed a normal course, and material progress, especially in the matter of railways and schools, has been rapid and remarkable. Unhappily, Ferdinand imported with him from Hungary the specific Magyar quality of self-advertisement in the foreign Press, and a talent for throwing dust in the eyes of superficial strangers. Under the fair exterior of new public buildings and well-planned streets, attempts have been made to conceal the dearth of moral achievements and intellectual culture. In the West it became the fashion among writers on Balkan sujects to judge everything by a standard of mere material progress, and to assume that Bulgaria alone was worthy of serious consideration. If we were to accept this basis, it would be easy to show by a comparison of trade statistics and similar evidence that Roumania had made even greater strides than

Bulgaria during the past twenty-five years in every department of public life. But in reality the present war has demonstrated that material prosperity is not the main factor in the life of a nation, and that Serbia, however backward in hygiene and in modern scientific research, possesses those qualities of heroism and imagination upon which true progress depends.

In Greece there was more excuse till the advent of M. Venizelos for regarding the situation as desperate, and it is well to draw a veil over the financial exhaustion, the party wrangling and the administrative corruption which fill up the sordid annals of the 'eighties and 'nineties. Nemesis came in 1897 with the revolt of Crete, its occupation by the fleets of the European Concert, and the short but ignominious Greco-Turkish War, at the close of which the Powers had to rescue Greece from the consequences of her own rashness. Crete was placed under a special *régime* which satisfied nobody and continued to provide permanent material for friction.

Meanwhile Turkey lay for thirty years at the mercy of Abdul Hamid, a true Eastern despot, who governed by all the rules of murder, massacre, intrigue and espionage, but also a born diplomat and a man of profound knowledge and skill in handling the international situation. Profound horror for the crimes for which he is responsible need not blind us to his remarkable ability. But the fatal criticism to which his *régime* is exposed lies in the purely negative character of his policy. It is true that by an irony of fate he succeeded in reviving the spiritual side of his office and accentuating his position as the Caliph of Islam. But he never showed any signs of constructive genius, and was content to play for a whole generation the game of a consummate fencer who invariably contrives to take his opponents singly or even to play them off against each other. Under Abdul

Hamid all threads concentrated in the Palace of Yildiz Kiosk. Political espionage and delation were organised as a positive cult. Every man was set to watch his neighbour; prison, exile or death awaited the slightest false step. Life abroad offered the sole escape and it has been calculated that no fewer than 80,000 exiles returned to Constantinople after the restoration of the Constitution in 1908. The immediate result of such a system was administrative paralysis, degenerating into chaos and anarchy, of which the crowning example was the Armenian massacre of 1896. As we shall see, not the least odious feature of the Hamidian *régime* was the practice of playing off the various Christian races against each other and embroiling the various foreign states which were interested in their fate.

In the middle of the nineteenth century the question asked upon all sides by historical students was: Will Turkey be partitioned, and how? Since the Congress of Berlin a new idea has slowly ripened, an idea which no one did more to encourage than Gladstone, and which may be summed up in the phrase, "The Balkans for the Balkan peoples." Under Abdul Hamid, then, the real problem which lay behind the complicated intrigue and manœuvres of thirty years may be stated as follows:— How will the Balkan States succeed in dividing up the Turkish legacy? Will they do so with, or without, the participation of the Great Powers?

Abdul Hamid continued to play off the various Powers against each other; and as no British Government, either Conservative or Liberal, was willing to shut its eyes to the infamies of his rule, our influence in Constantinople naturally declined. The one great diplomatic figure of the period, Sir William White, a worthy successor to Stratford de Redcliffe, was unhappily infected by Russophobe tendencies. There was, however, one Power which did not scruple to associate on friendly terms with the assassin of the Armenians. The German Emperor was an honoured guest at Yildiz Kiosk within two years of the massacre, and followed up his visit by a theatrical entry into Jerusalem and by doing homage at the tomb of Saladin, a chivalrous but implacable enemy of his own crusading ancestors. German influence at Constantinople made itself felt in two main directions—in the reorganisation of the Turkish army by German officers and in the commercial penetration of Asia Minor, but reached its height in the secret Bagdad Agreement which Sir Edward Grey had concluded with Germany in 1913-1914, and which was awaiting final signature when the Great War broke out. Germany was fortunate in her two foremost representatives in the Near East, Marshal von der Goltz Pasha as Turkish military adviser and Baron Marschall von Bieberstein, who for twenty years presided over the German Embassy at the Golden Horn. Under their guidance German policy followed a conservative course and while favouring the *status quo* and blocking, as far as possible, every movement for reform, sought to build up in the Ottoman Empire a commercial hegemony in which such great political institutions as the Deutsche Bank played a notable part. The inner meaning of this policy cannot be better summarised than in the words of M. René Pinon: "For Russia and even Austria-Hungary the Ottoman Empire was an obstacle to a march towards the Ægean or the Persian Gulf; in the hands of England it was a barrier erected between the route to India and the Muscovite pressure. For Germany, it is the necessary ally, the collaborator without whom she could neither acquire nor hold the common outlets of the East and the routes of Asia. For England and Russia it was a *means*, for Germany it is an *end*; it is in itself the expanson hitherto lacking to German activity."[1] Germany's aim then was

[1] *L'Europe et l'Empire Ottoman*, p. 57.

to galvanise Turkey into fresh life, or if that should prove impossible, to secure for herself a special position in the patient's household at the moment of his demise. To-day we are witnessing the final stage of this process, but it is still too soon to prophesy as to the result.

Apart from the political atrophy produced by the all-pervading tyranny of the Sultan's police and the ceaseless diplomatic game between the Sultan and the Great Powers, the main feature of the Hamidian *régime* was the non-execution of the reforms which the Powers had extracted at Berlin in 1878. The two points at which the failure to enforce reforms led to specially acute trouble were of course Armenia and Macedonia. In Armenia distance and isolation made a policy of massacre the most practical form of solving the problem, and it was actually employed from time to time with complete impunity. It was Macedonia which eventually proved fatal alike to the Hamidian *régime,* to the Turkish reformers and to the Concert of Europe itself. The problem of Macedonia is the most complex of all the many Balkan problems which have come up for solution during the last century. With the single exception of Hungary, there is no part of Europe where the medley of race is so great; and it is not without justification that the word "*macédoine*" has passed into the French language. Among a whole series of causes which contributed to leave Macedonia longer than the neighbouring provinces in the hands of the Turks, was the absolute impossibility of providing it with genuine racial frontiers. If, however, the long record of Turkish misrule in Europe reached its height in Macedonia, it is also necessary to remember that the inhabitants of that province have since the dawn of history shown an unruly and restless disposition. Perhaps it is the influence of so corrupt and oppressive a *régime* that has made

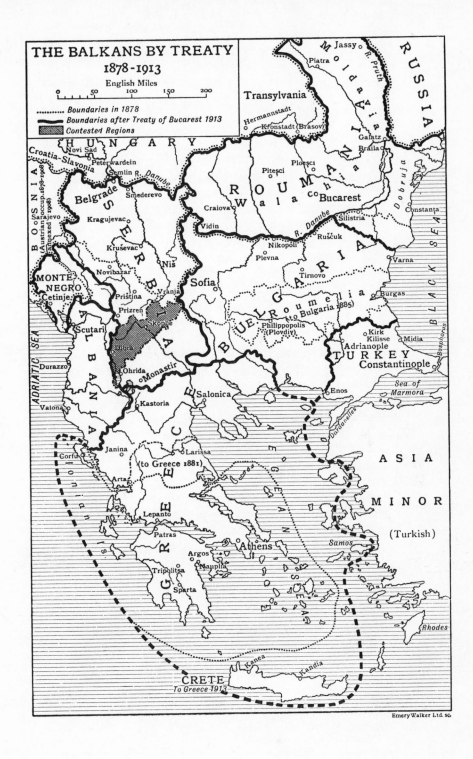

THE BALKANS BY TREATY
1878-1913

English Miles

0   50   100   150   200

.... Boundaries in 1878
—— Boundaries after Treaty of Bucarest 1913
▨▨ Contested Regions

RUSSIA

Jassy
Piatra
Moldavia
R. Pruth

Transylvania

HUNGARY
Novi Sad
Peterwardein
Hermannstadt
Kronstadt (Brasov)
Galatz
Braila
Semlin   R. Danube
Croatia-Slavonia

BOSNIA
Sarajevo
Austrian occup.1878-1908
annexed 1908

Belgrade
Smederevo

ROUMANIA
Pitesci
Ploesci
Bucarest
Walachia
Dobruja

Kragujevac
Craiova
Constanta

SERBIA
Kruševac
Vidin
R. Danube
Silistria

Niš
Nikopoli
Ruscuk

MONTE NEGRO
Cetinje
Novibazar
Plevna
Varna

Pristina
Sofia
Tirnovo

Vranja
BULGARIA
Burgas

Prizren
Skoplje
E. Roumelia
(to Bulgaria 1885)

Scutari
ALBANIA
Dibra

Philippopolis
(Plovdiv)
Kirk
Kilisse
Midia

Durazzo
Ohrida
Monastir
Adrianople
TURKEY
Constantinople

Valona
Kastoria
Salonica
Enos
Sea of
Marmora

ADRIATIC SEA
Janina
Corfu
Larissa
(to Greece 1881)

ASIA

MINOR

(Turkish)

Arta
Ionian Is.

Lepanto
Patras
GREECE
Athens
Samos

Argos
Nauplia

Tripolitsa
Sparta

Rhodes

AEGEAN SEA

Kanea
Kandia

CRETE
To Greece 1913

BLACK SEA
Bosphorus
Dardanelles

Emery Walker Ltd. sc.

the Macedonian so unattractive; but no one can deny his virility, nor the fierce tenacity and enterprise which has made him the source of perpetual discord to all the neighbouring States. Peopled by a fluid population of Turks, Albanians, Jews, Greeks, Bulgars, Serbs and Vlachs, Macedonia has been the home of ceaseless and varying racial animosities, of rival racial and ecclesiastical propagandas, each backed, as the Christian states of the peninsula grew stronger, by its particular racial affinity beyond the Turkish frontiers. Till the middle of the nineteenth century the Greeks easily held the field against their rivals. The religious traditions of centuries and the fact that the whole Church organisation was in their hands, gave them a very obvious advantage. In 1870, however, the Sultan, partly yielding to Russian pressure, but also in the hope of playing off his Christian subjects against each other, created the Bulgarian Exarchate, by which any district could be transferred from the jurisdiction of the Patriarchate to that of the Exarchate as the result of a petition by two-thirds of the inhabitants. This provided the Bulgarians with a powerful political weapon which they were not slow to use. At this period their success was almost automatic, for every Slav in Turkish territory who resented the pressure of the Greeks and was anxious to remain Slav, saw his salvation, and his only salvation, in the Bulgarian Exarchate. Serbia and Roumania agitated for the revival of the Serbian Patriarchate and for the creation of an independent Roumanian Church in Macedonia; but the Porte was by no means displeased at their alarm and made no effort to satisfy them, while Russia seemed for the time indifferent to any distinction between Serb and Bulgar. The schools and churches, then, became the main weapons of political propaganda, and outbid each other for popularity among the inhabitants. Children became a valuable commodity for which

the rival agitators paid in hard cash, and enterprising
fathers have been known to distribute their favours equally
among the rival propagandas, with the result that it is
by no means uncommon to find three brothers in a single
family professing three different nationalities. Numerous instances could be given of men who have changed
their names from Vlach to Greek, from Greek to
Bulgar and from Bulgar to Serb; and many of these
turncoats have doubtless during the past winter again
replaced the Serbian terminal "itch" by the Bulgarian "ov."

This discord was steadily favoured by the Porte,
which transferred its favours at irregular intervals from
one race to the other, but continued to act upon the
principle of "*Divide et Impera*." In 1890 Bulgarian
bishoprics were created at Ohrida and Skoplje, and four
years later at Dibra and Veles. In 1902 the first Serbian
bishopric was created at Skoplje, to the great disgust of
the Bulgarians; and in 1905 special concessions in church
and school were made to the Vlach propaganda. But
the Bulgarian school propaganda continued to flourish
more than any of its rivals. The Greeks were at a dis-
advantage when nationality was once aroused, because
for a Slav there could be no real choice between Greek
and Bulgar, but only between Bulgar and Serb, and the
Bulgar was almost invariably first in the field. The
Serbians in their turn were handicapped by the inaction
and incapacity of the Obrenović *régime*, now tottering
to its fall; while no activity on the part of the
Roumanians could overcome the obvious disadvantages
imposed upon them by geography. The intensity of
the Bulgarian movement rapidly created an educational
proletariat, which, finding conditions intolerable under
the Turks, transferred itself to free Bulgaria and
acquired an ever-increasing influence in the internal
politics of the Principality, and above all in the army.

In 1899 these emigrants were strong enough to form a Macedonian Committee at Sofia, which put forward the claim "Macedonia for the Macedonians," but which, while demanding autonomy under a Bulgarian Governor-General, aimed frankly at repeating the process which had led to the union of Eastern Roumelia with Bulgaria. Ere long they advanced from mere proclamations to the employment of force. Organised bands of Komitadjis made frequent raids across the Turkish frontier, and indulged in political brigandage, murder and forcible conversion. The kidnapping of the American missionary, Miss Stone, was deliberately planned by these bands, with the object of creating European complications. In the opening years of the new century it became more and more obvious that serious trouble was brewing, and that the European Concert was far too sluggish to enforce any remedy for the growing anarchy. At this stage Austria-Hungary and Russia, regarding themselves not unjustly as the two "most interested" Powers, took up the question without consulting their neighbours, and presented the Porte with a scheme of reforms known as the February Programme (1903). Hilmi Pasha was appointed Inspector-General of Macedonia, and reorganisation by independent foreign officers was promised. But this change, so far from producing calm, was a signal for a fierce insurrection during the sumer of 1903. The rising, which was mainly the work of Bulgarian Komitadjis, soon degenerated into a struggle of all against all. Unspeakable horrors were committed, thousands of peasants were rendered homeless, and finally the Turkish troops were encouraged to apply the most cruel methods of repression to the innocent and the guilty alike. British public opinion, wisely voiced by Lord Lansdowne as Foreign Secretary, clamoured for the prompt enforcement of reforms on a wider and more effective basis. Austria-

Hungary and Russia, still acting in harmony, forestalled[1] him in September, 1903, by the famous Mürzsteg Programme, which takes its name from the Styrian hunting-lodge at which Nicholas II. and Lamsdorff were the guests of Francis Joseph and Goluchowski. The main feature of the new scheme was the creation of an international gendarmerie for Macedonia, a special district being assigned to each of the Great Powers. Thus the Russians took over Salonica, the Austrians Skoplje, the French Seres, the British Drama and the Italians Monastir; the Germans alone held aloof. The chief command of the new force was assigned to the Italian General de Giorgis. The Macedonian gendarmerie proved quite inadequate to the task before it. It was very slow to move, and it failed to prevent the occasional recrudescence of guerilla warfare. This time it was the Greeks who organised bands of Komitadjis on a larger scale than ever before, and who, while challenging Bulgarian ascendancy, also turned with considerable violence against the Vlachs. Here and there this gendarmerie did admirable work, but it was none the less a striking proof of the bankruptcy of the European Concert in matters of Balkan policy.

The question of Balkan reforms was still further complicated by the Moroccan crisis, which was, of course, due on the one hand to Germany taking advantage of the paralysis of Russia—produced by the war with Japan and internal revolution—and on the other to her determination to prevent at all costs that reconciliation between Britain and France which was the great achievement of King Edward. During the eleven years which Count Goluchowski spent at the Ballplatz (1895–1906) Austria-

---

[1] Lord Lansdowne's proposals are believed to have reached Vienna only a few hours before the departure of Count Goluchowski for Mürzsteg, and to have been deliberately shelved until the Austro-Russian Agreement was concluded.

Hungary and Russia worked cordially together in matters of Balkan policy. Under his successor Baron Aehrenthal, who as Ambassador in Petrograd had acquired the reputation of a Russophil, but who in reality had merely supplemented his innate sympathy for the traditions of Metternichian diplomacy by a study of the worst methods of the Russian Police-state, the breach between the two countries rapidly widened. Russia's defeat in the Far East had encouraged Austrian Imperialist tendencies, whose natural and inevitable field was the Balkan Peninsula.

CHAPTER XI

THE YOUNG TURKISH REVOLUTION

FEW events have been more misunderstood than the Young Turkish Revolution of 1908. It was a *coup d'état* carried through by a small group of men of remarkable energy and lack of scruple. Some, like Niazi Bey, who took the first open step of rebellion, perished by assassination, that two-edged weapon which he himself had so readily employed. Others, like Enver Bey, still hold the field in Turkey, having extended the principles of scientific assassination from the provinces to the capital and applied them with equal success to a Commander-in-Chief, a Grand Vizier, and an Heir-Apparent, to say nothing of many minor personages. The Young Turks with whom Western Europe was in contact were men who had lived long in exile, divorced from Turkish life and thought, infected not so much by the true culture of the West as by the unbalanced theories of the wilder spirits of the French Revolution. Many of them enjoyed a doubtful reputation, and almost all were conspirators rather than politicians, inspired as much by motives of personal revenge and hatred as by patriotic considerations. The revolution which they promoted was above all the work of a single town. It was in Salonica, under the shelter of its masonic lodges, that the Committee of Union and Progress, the secret organism which overthrew the Hamidian *régime*, grew up and flourished. The real brains of the movement were Jewish or Judæo-

Moslem. Their financial aid came from the wealthy
Dunmehs and Jews of Salonica, and from the capitalists
—international or semi-international—of Vienna, Budapest, Berlin, and perhaps also of Paris and London.
Gradually the movement was joined by officers in the
army, upon whom its organisation naturally relied for
the necessary backing to their designs; and after the plot
had succeeded these men found it more necessary than
ever to dabble in politics, in order to counteract the
perpetual palace intrigues in favour of a restoration of
the old *régime*. The first shock of surprise was followed
by an ill-considered enthusiasm in Western Europe.
Skilled observers on the spot detected from the very first
the natural affinity which existed between the Young
Turkish leaders and the Prussian system, and predicted
that German ascendancy would in turn become even
more pronounced under the new than under the old
régime. What so utterly misled the West was the revival of the Turkish Constitution of 1876 and the fresh
emphasis laid upon its main provisions—crude, ill-
digested, doctrinaire pronouncements, transplanted, to
use a geographical expression, from the temperate to
the torrid zone. In this mock charter of Turkish liberties
two clauses stand out pre-eminent. Paragraph 8 declares
that "all subjects of the Empire are called Ottomans,
whatever religion (Millet) they may profess." Paragraph 17 runs as follows :— "All Ottomans are equal
before the law. They have the same rights and the same
duties towards the country, without prejudice in religious
matters." It is characteristic that in neither clause is any
reference made to nationality. Such doctrines overthrew
by a stroke of the pen the fundamental principles of
Ottoman government; indeed they represent a negation
of the whole past history of Turkey and are incompatible
with Islam itself. It ought to have been obvious from
the first that such theories either could not be made

effective in Turkey or would involve the destruction of
the religious and social foundations of Islam and the
Mohammedan world. The natural outlook of the true
Turk towards reform is summed up in a phrase with
which one of the deputies from Constantinople itself
interrupted a speech of the Grand Vizier in the Parliament of 1909. "Shame," he cried, "we have the Koran :
that ought to suffice. What need have we of European
laws?" Fire and water cannot mingle. The Ottoman
Constitution was from the very first a barren farce.

The main fact about the Committee of Union and
Progress is its essentially un-Turkish and un-Moslem
character. From the very first hardly one among its true
leaders has been a pure-blooded Turk. Enver is the son
of a renegade Pole. Djavid belongs to the strange Jewish
sect of the Dunmehs. Carasso is a Sephardim Jew from
Salonica. Talaat is an Islamised Bulgarian gypsy.
Achmet Riza, one of the group's temporary figureheads,
is half Circassian and half Magyar, and a Positivist of
the school of Comte. Energy and ferocity they have
certainly displayed, but never any sign of capacity as
statesmen or diplomats; indeed their chauvinism has
only been surpassed by their tactlessness. After the first
raptures of enthusiasm had passed, it soon became
apparent that new presbyter was but old priest writ
large. The old officials were replaced by the Committee's nominees. Baksheesh did not cease, and was
merely diverted into other channels. In effect the
Hamidian system was decentralised into a network of
local organisations, which were for the time virtually
sub-Governments. The revived electoral system became
the channel of unexampled corruption and violence, all
the most approved electoral methods of Hungary being
supplemented by open murder and bloodshed. The
crude mania for change at any price expressed itself in
such extraordinary proposals as the abolition of the veil

for Turkish women.   The whole of Turkish life was in
a ferment : uncertainty was the order of the day, and
economic stagnation was the natural result.

The revolution of July, 1908, was followed nine months
later by the counter-revolution of April, 1909.   The army
of Macedonia marched upon the capital.   Abdul Hamid
was deposed in favour of that amiable nonentity
Mohammed V., and deported to a villa on the outskirts
of Salonica.   The Young Turks assumed complete control of affairs, and their nominee, Hilmi Pasha, became
Grand Vizier.   The reign of liberty and fraternisation
had soon ended.   It was followed by a real orgy of
jingoism.   Turkification was proclaimed as a definite
policy.   The abstract principle of equality before the law
and the refusal to recognise any distinctions of race or
religion were soon interpreted in a reactionary sense.
Henceforth no race save the Ottoman was to be recognised, and, of course, it was unpatriotic to distinguish
between Ottoman and Turk, or to claim official recognition for any language save Turkish.   Clause 68 of the
Constitution makes ineligible for Parliament "those who
claim to belong to a foreign nation."   Applied as the
Young Turks began to apply it, this clause would soon
have enabled the authorities to prevent any Macedonian
who dared to call himself a Bulgarian or a Greek from
standing for Parliament.   The same spirit was abroad in
Turkey which has inspired the Magyars in Hungary
for the last three generations, which made the great
Magyar patriot, Kossuth, himself a Slovak by origin,
erect gallows for Slav patriots in 1848, profess himself
as unable to find Croatia on the map and refer a Serbian
deputation to the decision of the sword; which made
Coloman Tisza, as Hungarian Premier, deny the existence of a Slovak nation, and which prompted another
Hungarian Premier, Baron Bánffy, when he declared
that it was impossible to consider the consolidation of

the *legal* state until the existence of the *national* state
had been secured on extreme chauvinist lines. In Turkey
the elections were marked by exceptional brutality and
corruption, and the opposition was often not merely kept
away from the polls by military force, but also shot
down in cold blood. Two measures which created widespread discontent were the extension of military service
to Christians and Jews, and the attempt to impose taxation upon the whole Empire, and to ignore the immunity
which large sections of the Arab, Druse, and Albanian
population had hitherto enjoyed.

It is interesting to note that the first, most serious and
most persistent movement against the new *régime* came
from the most backward of all the European races of the
peninsula, and from that one which has most widely
accepted Islam. The Albanians are indeed the living
disproof of that superficial proverb which describes as
happy the nation without a history. Their hostility to
the Turks was due to two main reasons. On the one
hand their traditional attachment to the Sultan and the
old *régime* was at once the cause and the effect of their
exemption from taxation, and their enjoyment for
centuries past of a peculiar system of voluntary enlist-
ment, which has given to the Turkish Army many of its
best officers. The Young Turks in their officious zeal
insisted upon both taxation and recruiting being made
uniform throughout the Empire, and no longer adapted
to local conditions. On the other hand the Constitution
—a word which was, of course, entirely meaningless to
the mountaineers of Albania—aroused deep-seated
suspicion, which was only temporarily overcome by pro-
fuse assurances that Albanian local customs would be
respected, and schools and other national institutions
erected and encouraged. With their keen practical sense,
the Albanians were the first to realise, though few of
them perhaps could have expressed the idea in words,

that the Young Turkish revolution was essentially Turkish, nationalist and centralist in character. In July, 1908—within a fortnight of Niazi Bey's proclamation at Resna—ten thousand Albanian tribesmen assembled at Ferizović to swear the "Bessa," and to protest against the Hamidian *régime,* while disclaiming all hostility to the person of the Sultan. A month later the Albanians of Tirana and Elbassan were already framing their demands; and in November of the same year an Albanian congress met at Monastir and adopted the Latin alphabet for Albanian books, instead of Turkish characters. The Albanian propaganda spread very rapidly, and by 1910 they had reached the stage of claiming the unification of the four vilayets inhabited by Albanians, as a kind of autonomous "Great Albania." The wildest rumours were current in the mountains, and as an example of the tribesmen's frame of mind may be instanced the persistent rumour that taxes were about to be imposed upon eggs and upon beards.[1] The folly of the revenue officials and of the military, combined with indignation at the deposition of the Sultan, goaded the Albanians into a revolt, which was suppressed with extreme brutality by Shevket Torgut Pasha. Discontent became chronic, and in the summers of 1910, 1911 and 1912 regular military campaigns had to be undertaken against the rebellious Albanians. There were serious revolts in the Yemen and in Syria; but the Albanian trouble unquestionably did more than anything else towards undermining the Young Turkish *régime.*

The internal policy of the Young Turks, then, was based upon Turkification and terrorism; and one of its many pillars was the "removal" of political opponents. The art of assassination was first practised upon Shemshi Bey, then upon various "Liberal" journalists and minor

[1] *Die Türkei vor den beiden letzten Kriegen,* by an anonymous diplomatist, in the *Deutsche Revue* of June, 1913.

politicians in Constantinople, and finally upon such prominent personages as Nazim Pasha and Mahmud
Shevket Pasha. The machinery of state was clogged
more and more by personal jealousies and hates and by
the old corrupt and incompetent *régime*, revived in a
different and often cruder form. As time passed, it became more and more obvious that the sole hope of salvation lay in the army. Hence it was absolutely inevitable
that the Young Turks should fall under German influence since the Germans alone could be relied upon to
reorganise the army, without at the same time interfering
with the autocratic designs of the Committee of Union
and Progress. The lack of leaders with political experience and prestige compelled the Committee to recall to
power some of the Old Turkish leaders; and thus in
January, 1912, Said Pasha became Grand Vizier, and in
July of the same year was followed by Ghazi Mukhtar
Pasha. But this only served to accentuate the dissensions at headquarters. Never in all its long history had
Constantinople been the scene of more persistent intrigue
and counter intrigue.

The Albanian movement was steadily encouraged by
Austria-Hungary for her own ends. It is scarely necessary to point out that the road from Durazzo to Monastir
has throughout history been an alternative route to that
which follows the Morava valley. Austria's encouragement seriously alarmed Italy, and played its part in
deciding the Roman Cabinet to embark upon the Tripolitan expedition. It is still too soon to affirm posi-
tively whether Austria-Hungary encouraged Italy into
the African adventure in order to divert her attention
from the Adriatic and thus leave to herself a freer hand
in Northern Albania. We know, however, from the
Italian Green Book that Austria-Hungary vetoed Italy's
naval action against Turkey on the ground that it would
be a violation of the terms of the Triple Alliance.

Special stress has been laid upon the policy of Turkification,[1] not only because it provides the key to the internal policy of the Young Turkish *régime,* but also because from the moment it crystallised a combination of the Christian races in Macedonia and of all the kindred Balkan nations against the common danger became inevitable. The Young Turks in their arrogance and chauvinism pinned entire faith upon the army; and friendly observers outside accepted their estimate of its sound condition. The Balkan League did not share this opinion; it staked everything upon its more intimate information; and it won. During the first years of the new *régime* many foreign optimists fondly imagined that the reforms promised under the Treaty of Berlin, but never executed, would now at last be enforced under the menace of Balkan co-operation. But the Concert of Europe, always feeble, was paralysed by Italy's separate action and seemed afraid to push too hard. Britain had been without a policy since the death of King Edward, while Russia was working for her own hand, and France was absorbed by the internal problem of the Three Years' Service Bill. Meanwhile the Central Powers were too confident of Turkey's ability to deal with her upstart neighbours to make any serious effort to avert war. In August, 1912, a feeble proposal of reform was put forward by Count Berchtold on behalf of Austria-Hungary; but though it may be regarded as proving that nerveless statesman's personal leanings towards peace, it was at once obvious to everyone that the twelfth hour had already struck. The Balkan League, which in 1912 took the field against Turkey, was the outward and visible sign of the bankruptcy of European statesmanship in the Balkan Peninsula.

[1] Ottomanisation is a slightly less hideous but also less accurate word.

PART II

CHAPTER XII

THE BALKAN LEAGUE

THE thirty-four years which followed upon the Treaty of Berlin were, so far as the Balkans were concerned, a period of arrested development, during which the Great Powers, under pretext of enforcing the will of Europe, really secured a free hand for the Turks. The settlement actually imposed in Berlin was no less arbitrary and artificial than that which Russia had sought to enforce at San Stefano a few months before. Its crowning error lay in the fact that it subjected once more to the Ottoman yoke large tracts of territory which the war had liberated, and yet entirely neglected to enforce the guarantees for which it had stipulated. Despite this injustice and the great misery which it involved, it is possible to regard the Treaty of Berlin as the instrument which eventually rendered possible the liberation of the Balkan peoples by their own unaided efforts, instead of by the aid of a foreign Power. The enforcement of the San Stefano programme really would have left Russia supreme in the Near East. The disappointment and resentment aroused by the reversal of this programme created a very different atmosphere throughout the Balkans—a feeling compounded of the recog-

nition of their own inability to resist the rulings of the
Concert and the cynical but natural determination to
exploit for their own ends the jealousies of the rival
Powers. Such an attitude was fully justified by the
cavalier manner in which the Roumanian, Serbian and
Greek delegates were treated at the Congress of Berlin,
when the diplomatic world, repeating the errors of the
earlier Congress of Vienna, displayed a superb indifference to the wishes of the population whose fate it was
deciding.

The indignation with which the Balkan Christians
greeted this betrayal of their interests not unnaturally
revived the idea of a Balkan League. To theorists such
a League was by no means new. Mazzini, Michelet,
Lamartine, Edgar Quinet, Louis Blanc, and many other
political thinkers of their time had advocated in one
form or another that combination of forces which the
pioneers of Balkan freedom—Karageorge, Miloš,
Ypsilanti—had vaguely set up as their ideal, but had
lacked the force to put into practice. As early as 1844
the idea of a League found its exponent in the Serbian
statesman Ilija Garašanin; but his plans did not begin
to assume a concrete form till the accession of Prince
Michael Obrenović. In 1859 Michael had conferred
with the exiled Kossuth in London: "Fear of Russia
and hatred of Austria had brought together the Serb
prince and the Magyar patriot."[1] Kossuth, taking up
an early proposal of Mazzini,[2] advocated a Confederation of the Danubian states; and in his name General
Klapka carried on parallel negotiations with the new
Prince of Roumania, Alexander Couza.[3] The adher-
ence of Serb, Croat and Roumanian was to be paid for
by an abandonment of the Magyar racial policy of 1848

[1] Pinon, *L'Europe et La Jeune Turquie,* p. 448.
[2] *Scritti* (ed. 1847, Vol. III., p. 178).
[3] *Cf.* Kossuth, *Schriften aus der Emigration.*

and by the grant of linguistic concessions to all the nationalities of the future independent Hungary. Kossuth's day-dreams were rudely dispelled by the Peace of Villafranca and the disfavour of the Third Napoleon, which involved, among other things, the defection of Couza. But Michael and Garašanin quietly continued their propaganda, and early in the year 1868 concluded an agreement for joint action with the Bulgarian National Committee in Bucarest. To-day it is difficult to read their programme without a sigh of regret; for it proclaims the necessity of "a common existence" between "the two sister-nations," whose country shall in future be called "Serbo-Bulgaria" or "Bulgaro-Serbia," and whose national flag shall be formed of the combined colours of the two races. The same year witnessed the conclusion of a close treaty between Serbia and Montenegro, engaging the two peoples to work for the emancipation of their kinsmen, and the formation of an unitary Southern Slav state. If the struggle should be brought to a successful issue, Prince Nicholas undertook to abdicate in favour of Prince Michael, but in the event of the latter's death without issue, Nicholas was to be proclaimed King of Serbia. Meanwhile a Serbo-Greek alliance was already on the point of conclusion, and Michael, in the course of a visit to Bucarest, had won over to his projects Couza's successor, Prince Charles of Hohenzollern.

The assassination of Prince Michael in June, 1868, dashed the whole of this airy fabric to the ground at the very moment when it seemed about to assume definite form. The tragedy of Topčider is one of the decisive events of Balkan history during the past century; and without indulging in useless speculations, we may safely affirm that if Michael had been alive in 1876–7 the Russo-Turkish war and the great international crisis which it evoked would have taken an utterly different turn. Whether centripetal forces would have triumphed over the intrigues and interferences of the Great Powers and led to the formation of a single South Slavonic state, it is, of course, quite impossible to determine.

Michael's successor Milan, though by no means devoid of talents, lacked the mental and moral qualities of his cousin, and was too unstable and selfish to focus around him the aspirations of Balkan patriots. Close co-operation between Serbia and Montenegro was achieved during the war of 1876; but Milan was only saved from disaster by foreign intervention, and the prize for which the Serbs had fought fell to the share of the Dual Monarchy. During the war the Bulgarians gave no sign of their future military prowess, while the Roumanians, whose gallantry retrieved the situation of the Russian army before Plevna, were too fully occupied to assist their Western neighbours. The time was not yet ripe for a general combination against the Turks; all else was overshadowed by the Panslavonic ambitions of Russia.

After the settlement of Berlin the ex-Regent of Serbia, Jovan Ristić, attempted to revive the projects of Garašanin, and dreamt of a League which should include the constitutional Turkey of Midhat and his followers. But such an idea was still wholly premature. The vision of Balkan unity might haunt the dreams of a few far-sighted individuals, but public opinion, such as it then was, was too entirely dominated by the religious and racial feuds of centuries to permit of any real co-operation. As for Turkey, the brief era of Midhat gave place to the thirty years' terror of Abdul Hamid, who sought in Panislamic designs a counterpoise to the incurable disloyalty which his infamous *régime* had fostered among the Christian subjects of the Porte.

The next move towards Unity came from Bulgaria, which in 1884 tried to win Serbia for a customs union.

But these advances met with no response from the Government of King Milan, whose reckless and un-generous policy of war fixed in the following year a gulf of blood between the two Slavonic neighbours. While the endeavour to check Bulgaria's legitimate expansion ended in hideous failure, the Bulgarian *coup d'état* of 1886 produced a radical change in the Balkan policy of the Great Powers, Austria and Russia virtually changing swords in their perennial contest; and the uncertainty of the new situation was highly unfavourable to all plans of combination. In 1887 Alexander of Battenberg's vacant throne was offered by a group of Bulgarian statesmen to King Charles of Roumania, and his refusal seemed to many observers a fresh victory for centrifugal tendencies. But it may be doubted whether a union of the Crowns could ever have been permanent, so radically different are the political and social conditions of Roumania and Bulgaria, and indeed the whole character and outlook of the two peoples.

In 1891 the idea of a Balkan League was revived in another quarter. The foremost statesman of Greece, M. Tricoupis, visited Belgrade and Sofia and boldly advocated a joint campaign against the Turks and the partition of Macedonia among the allies in the event of success.[1] The existence of such a scheme had already become known to the Turkish Minister at Belgrade, when the masterful Stambulov betrayed the details to the Porte and thus effectually destroyed all hope of its realisation in the immediate future. His treachery was resented all the more because it earned for Bulgaria a number of special concessions to her kinsmen in Mace-donia; and the collapse of the idea of co-operation was

---

[1] As early as 1867 the Roumanian envoy at Athens had laid before M. Tricoupis a proposal of Prince Charles for joint action by the Balkan States. See *Aus dem Leben des König Karls*, vol. I., p. 478.

followed by a period of furious racial rivalry. When in 1897 Greece plunged into her ill-considered and ill-conducted war with Turkey, Serbia and Bulgaria were successfully held back by the Great Powers, and the despairing effort of the Greeks to stave off disaster by offering Bulgaria the partition of Macedonia and a port on the Ægean was promptly declined by the Government of Sofia. The divergence between Hellenic and Slavonic aspirations seemed insuperable, and in 1901 Greece tried to escape from her isolation by a short-lived entente with Roumania, who throughout this period had surrendered herself blindly to the guidance of Austria-Hungary.

The Macedonian insurrection of 1903 and the reprisals with which the Turks underlined its failure resulted, not in the expected torpor of exhaustion, but in an accentuation of racial strife, in which the hand of every race was against its neighbour. The excesses of Bulgarian komitadjis and above all the terrorism exercised by the desperadoes of the "External Organisation," roused the Greeks and Serbians to similar efforts. Greek illtreatment of the Vlachs provoked an open diplomatic rupture between Bucarest and Athens. Greek and Bulgar massacred each other, while the Turks favoured the weaker Serbs against the Bulgarians and simultaneously incited the Albanians in their onslaughts upon the Serbs. The one serious attempt at co-operation during this period, the projected Serbo-Bulgarian customs entente (1907), was foiled by the diplomatic pressure of Austria-Hungary, then engaged in the attempt to reduce Serbia to a state of economic vassalage.

The Young Turkish Revolution of 1908 rapidly transformed the Balkan situation. The sudden orgy of racial reconciliation which followed the revival of the Ottoman Constitution subsided as quickly as it had broken out. The Young Turks soon betrayed Chauvinistic sentiments such as the Hamidian *régime* had never known, and made little concealment of their intention to summon to the new Parliament in Constantinople the representatives of Crete, of Eastern Roumelia, and of Bosnia. From the moment that their ulterior aim, the Turkification of Turkey, began to emerge into prominence, a combination of all the Balkan nations against the common danger became inevitable. That events did not immediately take this course was due to the attitude of Europe towards the new *régime,* and to the international crisis evoked by the parallel action of Austria-Hungary and Bulgaria in the winter of 1908. The annexation of Bosnia and Herzegovina, though it was but the consummation of a ceremony performed thirty years before, aroused frantic protests from the two independent Serb states; and for the time it seemed as though they were even prepared to risk a conflict with the Dual Monarchy. Popular enthusiasm overbore the personal friction which had existed between the Karagjorgjević and Petrović dynasties; and the military convention then concluded for the contingency of war with Austria-Hungary may be regarded as the first germ of the later and more comprehensive League. The next step seemed to be a Slavonic Triple Alliance in the Balkans, which was rendered popular by the widespread belief—whether well founded or not can hardly be determined—that King Ferdinand had refused overtures from Baron Aehrenthal for a joint Austro-Bulgarian campaign of aggression against Serbia. While both in Bulgaria and in Serbia the jealousy engendered by rival propaganda was gradually subsiding, Russian initiative gave a fresh turn to the development of political thought in the Balkans. At the height of the Bosnian crisis M. Izvolsky, in his famous Christmas speech, had proclaimed as the latest aim of Russian policy a Balkan League which should unite Christian and Moslem "in defence of their national and economic development." Significantly enough, this league was to be confined to Turkey and the three Slavonic states. No mention was made of Roumania, which was treated as wholly in the orbit of Austria-Hungary, nor of Greece, whose Panhellenic aspirations were distasteful to the Chauvinists of St. Petersburg. Uninformed public opinion passed the same verdict upon the excessive self-effacement of Roumania and the internal instability of Greece, and thus these two states came to be regarded, save by a few far-sighted individuals, as negligible quantities in the politics of the Near East.

The undue emphasis laid by Russia upon the Slavonic elements in the peninsula merely represented a new phase in that attempt to oust Austrian influence, which had achieved a brilliant but fleeting success by the liquidation of Bulgaria's debt to Turkey. Two of the ablest Russian diplomats were entrusted with the special surveillance of the new policy, and the results achieved by M. Čarikov at Constantinople and M. Hartwig at Belgrade, though perhaps differing materially from the original intentions of the Government, were unquestionably of capital importance in the history of the Near East.

One of the first-fruits of the short-lived Turco-Christian *rapprochement* was the visit of Bulgarian officers to Constantinople on the occasion of the first anniversary of the restored Turkish Constitution (July, 1909). The intolerance of the Committee of Union and Progress soon led to a renewal of the old friction; but in the following January matters were smoothed over once more by a special mission of Dr. Danev, and the combined efforts of Bulgarian and Russian diplomacy secured from the Porte a temporary return to milder methods. Dr. Danev visited Constantinople to plead for an understanding, and paved the way for the state visits of King Ferdinand and King Peter to the Sultan

(March, 1910), which were followed three months later by return visits of the Turkish Heir-Apparent to Sofia and Belgrade. The circumstance that the meeting of the two monarchs with the representative of their countries' former overlord had been immediately preceded by their reception in St. Petersburg by the Tsar of All the Russias not unnaturally gave rise to fresh rumours of a Turco-Slavonic League. But though such a combination was undoubtedly favoured by a certain section of Turkish statesmen, the more masterful members of the Committee had other views. They realised that the policy of Turkification on which they were firmly resolved was wholly incompatible with cordial relations towards the Christian Balkan states; and arrogantly regarding a rupture as not only inevitable but desirable, they endeavoured to sow discord among the rival races, and to play off one against the other. Thus while King Ferdinand was prevented from returning home by Athos, full permission was accorded to King Peter to visit both the monasteries of the Holy Mountain and the Macedonian capital; and the ostentatious demonstrations of the Greeks of Pera in favour of the Serbian King seem to have been rather encouraged than repressed by the Turkish authorities.

In the summer of 1910 the old hatred between Moslem and Christian flamed up as fiercely as ever. The extreme brutality of the methods employed to disarm the Macedonian population was felt by Bulgar and Serb, by Greek and Albanian alike, and brought home to the former rivals the urgency of co-operation. The first sign of returning harmony had been the compact between Bulgars and Greeks regarding their relative representation in the Ottoman Parliament, and the acts of official violence which disfigured the second general election brought them still closer together. A growing number of refugees crossed the Bulgarian, Greek and Monte-

negrin frontiers and swelled the clamour of those who
opposed the official Turcophil policy. Nor did the
Christians stand alone; for nowhere did Young Turkish
tyranny encounter a more stubborn resistance than
among the Albanians, who had so long been regarded
as the surest bulwark of the Hamidian *régime*. It would
be unfair to suggest that the Balkan Governments were
not in earnest in their attempts to reach an understanding with the Turks. Serbia in particular had the
strongest reasons for cultivating the friendship of the
Porte. The tariff war with Austria-Hungary, the
annexation of Bosnia, the campaign inaugurated by
Aehrenthal and his Magyar allies against the Serbs of
Croatia and Bosnia, the grave scandals of the Agram
Treason Trial and of the Vasić-Forgách forgeries—all
this had convinced her that the true enemy of her race
was not so much Turkey as the Dual Monarchy. The
"pig war" having closed her northern frontier, Serbia
found her trade very largely dependent upon the goodwill of Turkey. Access to the port of Salonica was as
vital to her export of live stock as to her importation
of foreign war material. At the same time Serbia had
fewer racial grounds of complaint than any of her neighbours; for the Turks were openly favouring the Serbian
element in the vilayet of Kosovo at the expense of Bulgar
and Greek. Dr. Milovanović, then, had every reason to
work in favour of a Turco-Slavonic entente, though even
he appears to have felt sceptical as to the possibility
of permanent friendship with the Committee of Union
and Progress. In the meantime steps were taken to
promote further intimacy among the Balkan states and
their rulers; and for this the Montenegrin Jubilee and
the assumption of the royal title by Prince Nicholas
afforded a specially favourable occasion (August, 1910).
The presence of King Ferdinand and Crown Prince
Alexander in Cetinje, almost within sight of the moun-

tains where a Turkish army was ruthlessly crushing the insurgent Albanian tribes, was widely regarded as the forerunner of military action in favour of Macedonia and Albania. This surmise, however, rests upon as insufficient evidence as the sensational rumour launched in Paris a few months later, to the effect that Roumania had informed the Porte of her intention to mobilise in the event of a Turco-Bulgarian war. It is certain that Bulgarian aggression would have revived Roumania's old claim—long dormant, but never abandoned—to a revision of the Dobrudja frontier; but it is almost equally certain that active intervention in favour of the Crescent against the Cross was never seriously contemplated in Bucarest.

The winter months of 1910–11 witnessed important political changes in three out of the five Balkan capitals. In October the Cretan leader, M. Venizelos, became Premier of Greece; in January the Roumanian Liberals under M. Brătianu gave place to the Conservatives under M. Carp; in March the Russophile party of M. Gešov came into power at Sofia and acquired that complete command of the electorate which in Bulgaria always accompanies control of the executive. The new Greek and Bulgarian Premiers both favoured friendly relations with Turkey, and thus found themselves in full accord with their Serbian colleague, Dr. Milovanović. But the march of events rapidly committed them to a policy of which it may safely be assumed that none of them foresaw the issue. The person of M. Venizelos, despite his pacific leanings, was highly distasteful to the Chauvinists of the Committee, whose uncompromising attitude on the Cretan question coincided with an increasingly vexatious policy towards the Christians of Macedonia. The warnings of Count Aehrenthal to the Grand Vizier were disregarded, and, quite apart from the well-nigh inevitable racial troubles, the Young Turks wantonly alienated Greek and Bulgarian opinion by refusing to allow the concessions for the projected railway lines upon which Athens depended for her connection with Europe and Sofia for her connection with the Ægean.[1]   Thus while Milovanović and Hartwig continued with diminishing success to advocate a Turco-Slavonic league, Venizelos found himself rapidly driven to the conclusion that a Greco-Bulgarian entente was essential to Christian interests in the peninsula.   As early as April, 1911, therefore, cautious overtures were made in Sofia by the Greek Minister, M. Panas, who proposed in the name of his Government an entente for common action in defence of the privileges of the Macedonian Christians and a defensive alliance in the event of a Turkish attack upon either Greece or Bulgaria.[2]   At the same time Dr. Milovanović, probably acting in accord with the Russian Minister, M. Hartwig, made certain advances towards Bulgaria, but without putting forward any concrete suggestions or eliciting any definite response.   For the moment nothing seemed to have been effected, and the negotiations between Sofia and Athens were jealously concealed, not merely from Serbia and from the Great Powers, but even from most members of the Greek and Bulgarian Cabinets.   In August, 1911, the sessions of the Grand Sobranje at Tirnovo were marked by a highly significant incident. A revision of the Constitution was sanctioned, authorising the King to conclude secret treaties without consulting Parliament.   From this moment the plot began to ripen.   During the autumn both Venizelos and Milovanović gave public expression to their conviction that the adhesion of Turkey was an essential condition to the formation of a Balkan League.   But it is probable

[1] Kustendil to Kumanovo and Salonica to Larissa.
[2] Mr. Bourchier, the Balkan correspondent of the *Times*, had a direct share in these negotiations.

that by this time the orgies of Committee rule in Turkey had effectually cured both statesmen of all belief in their own professions, and that Russia, renouncing all hope of working with the Turks, was also beginning to devote her influence to furthering an entente among the Christian states of the peninsula. The part played by the Russian consuls in Macedonia in promoting harmony between Exarchists and Patriarchists—in other words, between Bulgars on the one hand, and Greeks, Serbs and Vlachs on the other—had already become very marked. It is, however, certain that at this stage there was still no idea of active intervention, for when on the outbreak of the Turco-Italian war Montenegro proposed a general order of mobilisation, Dr. Danev was dispatched to Constantinople to give pacific assurances to the Young Turks. Bulgaria realised her inability to enter the field alone, while both Serbia and Greece were still occupied in pushing forward their armaments. Indeed, the latter was engaged upon a drastic reform of her whole army system after the scandals of the Military League; and it was calculated that three years must elapse before her forces would be ready for full military action. The collapse of Turkey was already regarded as inevitable, but not even the most far-sighted of Balkan or Russian statesmen imagined it to be so near at hand. The policy which underlay all subsequent negotiations was a resolve to lay the basis of an enduring compromise, such as would enable the rival races to present an united front to the Turks when the final day of reckoning should arrive. But for the impetus imparted by the Tripolitan war to the internal process of decay in European Turkey, it is by no means impossible that this result would have been achieved.

Those who assign to Russian diplomacy the entire credit (or blame) for the creation of the Balkan League fall into the error of a colour-blind person who can only see the dominant colour in an Eastern carpet, and overlook the numerous threads of minor colours which give character to the whole design. There is every reason to believe that Greece's share in the alliance did not enter into Russian calculations at all, and that Russia's chief concern was to bring the Slav nations together. The manner in which Turkey was not merely eliminated from the scope of the League, but converted into the object of its attack, gave rise in some quarters to the belief that Russia had merely put forward proposals for the inclusion of the Turks as a "blind" which should include other and much more aggressive designs. What is more probable is that Russia's intentions towards the Turks were still of a mainly negative character, and that her statesmen would have been satisfied if they could neutralise German influence on the Bosphorus. But as has so often happened in Russian history, her diplomats were allowed (or, as hostile critics would suggest, were encouraged) to pursue a forward policy which far outstripped the more sober views of official St. Petersburg.

While the Greco-Bulgarian entente was in no sense the work of Russia, but may be traced to the initiative of M. Venizelos, the Serbo-Bulgarian entente—that other essential preliminary to a successful coalition— owes its origin very largely to the energy and skill of M. Hartwig. He it was who imparted to the proposed alliance that anti-Austrian tinge without which the statesmen of Belgrade would have been slow to jeopardise their relatively good understanding with Constantinople. Acting, then, in full accord with M. Hartwig, Dr. Milovanović in September, 1911, approached the Bulgarian Government with definite proposals which mark the turning-point in the history of the negotiations. A notable part was played in these, as also in the preparation of a Serbo-Bulgarian entente, by M. Spalajković, then Serbian Minister in Sofia, and formerly one of the decisive witnesses at the sensational Friedjung Trial in Vienna.

The celebrations which attended the coming-of-age of Prince Boris of Bulgaria (February, 1912) offered a favourable opportunity for friendly demonstrations among the Balkan peoples. The presence in Sofia of the Crown Princes of Roumania, Greece, Serbia and Montenegro was an unique incident which fired the imagination of their peoples and seemed of happy augury for the future. During the winter the negotiations had proceeded apace, and on March 13, 1912, a treaty of alliance was concluded between Bulgaria and Serbia. This was followed two months later (May 29) by a similar if less detailed treaty between Bulgaria and Greecè. The recall of M. Čarikov early in March may have been partially due, as was alleged at the time, to hostile intrigues in the Turkish capital; in reality it marks the final abandonment of the attempt to place Turkey at the head of a Balkan Confederation, and the conversion of the latter, with Russia's active connivance, into an instrument for the destruction of Ottoman rule in Europe.

Events in Turkey had contributed to hasten the formation of the League. The massacre at Istip in December, 1911, the system of assassination adopted by the Young Turks against their opponents, the widespread disorder throughout Macedonia, the economic stagnation produced by the Italian war, above all, the gross excesses of the Ottoman "elections," by which the Opposition was reduced to ten members—all this accentuated the general unrest and heralded an acute international crisis.

Once more the initiative came from the Albanians, who broke into open insurrection and, not content with putting forward various national and linguistic demands, clamoured for fresh elections and the impeachment of the late Cabinet. The efforts of the Young Turks to resist this movement resulted in a dangerous mutiny at their former stronghold of Monastir, followed by wholesale desertions and the formation of a hostile League of "Saviours of the Country." The gallant attempt of Mahmud Shevket Pasha to allay the storm by his own withdrawal from office proved unsuccessful, and on 17th July Said Pasha and his "Committee" Cabinet followed their most distinguished colleague into retirement. But even the appointment of Ghazi Mukhtar Pasha as Grand Vizier, with three such able men as Kiamil, Hilmi and Nazim as members of his Cabinet, failed to conciliate the Albanians; every fresh concession served only to embolden them still further. The tribesmen of the northern vilayets gathered in ever-increasing numbers, and after murdering several officers in Ipek and Mitrovica, marched upon Üsküb. By the middle of August, 1912, that town was occupied by at least 15,000 to 20,000 Albanians; the arsenal was plundered and thousands of rifles distributed. When at length the Porte, yielding to the inevitable, conceded the great majority of the insurgents' demands, a condition of complete anarchy already prevailed throughout Macedonia and Albania.

It would have been ridiculous to expect that Balkan statesmen should fail to take advantage of Turkey's difficulties, mainly due as they were to many generations of persistent misrule and neglect. Moreover, on 1st July the untimely death of Dr. Milovanović removed one of the chief restraining influences upon a policy of adventure. His successor, M. Pašić, combined with equal ability far more radical tendencies and the restless temperament born of Balkan unrest. But events had already passed the stage at which conservatism could have provided a solution. A series of outrages in different parts of Macedonia kindled racial passions to a white heat

and strengthened the hands of all those whose aim it
was to force intervention upon the Balkan Governments.
The gravest incidents took place at Berana on the
Montenegrin frontier, and at Kočana (1st August), where
a bomb explosion in the bazaar was followed by the
murder of 100 Bulgarians. The honest desire to avert
a conflict no longer existed, and the chief anxiety of the
new-fledged allies was to manœuvre themselves into a
favourable position for striking, and if possible to complete their preparations before Turkey could extricate
herself from the embarrassments of the Italian war.
The Serbo-Bulgar treaty had found its natural comple-
ment in a military convention (12th May) and the
summer months had been employed in negotiating a
parallel arrangement between Bulgaria and Greece,
which was finally signed on 23rd September. The
prospect of war with Turkey not later than the autumn
of 1912 was frankly accepted by all concerned as the
basis of discussion; the Angellic conviction that war is
never inevitable had not penetrated to the minds of
Balkan politicians. The earlier of the two conventions,
by which Bulgaria undertook to place at least 200,000,
Serbia at least 150,000, men in the field against Turkey,
clearly reflects the strategic needs of the moment. Serbia
held the key to the situation; for with Serbia merely
neutral, Bulgaria would be condemned to inactivity,
unless she was prepared to cope with a simultaneous
Turkish assault upon both flanks, from Adrianople and
from Üsküb. Moreover, Serbia was for the moment on
a relatively better footing with the Turks than were any
of her Christian neighbours, and keen as was her interest
in the Macedonian problem, it was wholly eclipsed by
her concern and resentment at the course of events on
her northern and western frontiers. The real motive
of Serbian armaments lay in what she regarded as the
Austrian menace, and she was not prepared to risk
bearing the brunt of a war in the south when her action

might involve her in complications on a still larger scale
elsewhere. Hence the military convention contained
the provisions that Bulgaria should send 100,000 men
to the support of the Serbian army in Macedonia, and
in the event of Austrian intervention, twice that number
against the Dual Monarchy. The first of these provisions is explained by the fact that the Bulgarian and
Serbian General Staffs agreed in anticipating the main
opposition of the Turks in Macedonia, the second by the
presumption that Austrian intervention would bring
Russia into the field. In that event a Russian invasion
of Armenia would compel the Turks to reduce their
forces in Thrace, thus serving as a necessary diversion in
favour of Bulgaria, while her armies were engaged in
helping their Serb kinsmen against Austria. It is highly
significant that the idea of Serbian co-operation in
Thrace is not even mentioned in the agreement—an
eloquent proof of the importance assigned by its framers
to the Vardar valley. According to the original plan
of campaign, which was mainly the work of General
Fičev, the Bulgarians were to have maintained a defensive attitude on the Thracian frontier, while their main
forces, in conjunction with their Serb and Greek allies,
vigorously pushed forward the conquest of Macedonia.
Late in the summer, however, a change of plan was
introduced by General Savov, and henceforth Thrace
was marked out as the scene of the main Bulgarian
offensive. On 5th September the Serbian General Staff
formally consented to the modifications in the general
plan which this involved, and though still adhering to
its view as to the relative importance of the two fields
of operation, consented to a reduction of the Bulgarian
contingent in Macedonia from 100,000 to 25,000 men.[1]
But the agreements which embodied this and other

[1] On these negotiations it is well to consult *Serbien und Bulgarien im Balkankriege* (pp. 60-65), by "Balcanicus," a prominent member of the then Serbian Cabinet.

less vital tactical changes differed essentially from the
original convention; for while this was a state document
to which the two Kings, the Premiers, the Ministers of
Foreign Affairs and War, and the Chiefs of the General
Staffs all appended their signatures, the later protocols
were merely friendly arrangements between the military
chiefs. This circumstance, though quite immaterial at
the time, acquired no little importance when events came
to centre round the exact fulfilment and literal interpretation of the various treaties between the Allies. The
Bulgarians, not content with the revised agreement,
endeavoured to reverse the whole position by securing
Serbian reinforcements for Thrace; but here they were
met by a friendly but firm refusal. It should be added
that this sudden change in the Bulgarian attitude was at
least partially due to persistent rumours of an impending
Turkish concentration round Adrianople.

Towards the end of September the Turkish Government did actually announce its intention of holding
grand manœuvres in Northern Thrace, in which 300,000
troops were to take part. But this decision was almost
immediately revoked at the instance of Great Britain
and Russia, who pointed out to the Porte the provo-
catory effect of such a step. At the outbreak of war,
as we shall see, the Turkish army in Thrace amounted
to less than half the contemplated number; but the
Bulgarian General Staff, despite the excellence of its
intelligence department, appears to have genuinely over-
estimated the enemy.

The Greco-Bulgarian convention of 23rd September
reveals the progress of opinion during the summer.
Bulgaria now pledges herself to place not less than
300,000 men in the field (an increase of one-third since
the convention with Serbia), while the Greek forces are
placed at a minimum of 120,000. The strength of the
Bulgarian contingent in Macedonia was to depend upon

that of the Serbian army[1]—a somewhat singular arrangement in view of the fact that Serbia was not a party to this agreement. By a strange irony of fate Sofia formed the connecting link between Serbia and Greece; for it must be remembered that no formal treaty bound the future allies of the second Balkan war.

The attitude of the Great Powers towards the growing crisis in the Near East had for some time past been compounded of despairing *laisser faire* and ill-concealed cynicism. The success of the Albanian movement, the growing anarchy throughout Macedonia, the frequent incidents on the Montenegrin and Bulgarian frontiers, and the weak attitude adopted by the new Turkish Cabinet under Ghazi Mukhtar Pasha, were steadily creating one of those political situations in which a snowball soon becomes an avalanche. On 20th August the Austro-Hungarian Foreign Minister, Count Berchtold, made a belated attempt to restore confidence, and his proposals for decentralisation and administrative reforms, adapted to local conditions, were sympathetically received by the other Great Powers, but never passed beyond the purely platonic stage.

Two days earlier a number of Turkish officers were murdered at Ipek and Mitrovica, and the Albanians assembled in thousands all over the vilayet of Kosovo, fraternised with the troops, and, marching upon Üsküb, broke into the military depots and distributed rifles and ammunition broadcast. The Central Government, finding itself powerless to cope with the movement, conceded the majority of the insurgents' claims—the opening of Albanian schools, the recognition of the Albanian language, the building of roads, fresh elections, and (in ambiguous terms) the impeachment of the Hakki Cabinet. But on two points—the localisation of military service

[1] See Mr. Bourchier, Article 4, in the *Times,* 11th June, 1913.

and the arming of all and sundry in Albania—the Porte
remained obdurate; and it was just on these two points
that the insurgents set especial value. A deadlock
ensued, and the authority of Stambul sank to zero
throughout the greater part of Macedonia.

Though at first unwilling to listen to Count Berchtold's advice, the Turkish statesmen afterwards modified
their views sufficiently to extend to the whole Empire
the inadequate privileges conceded to Albania (22nd September). But by this time the situation was rapidly
getting out of hand. The Balkan states were secretly
completing their preparations for war, and the Porte
stopped the passage of Serbian war material through
Salonica and decided, under pretext of holding grand
manœuvres, to mass 300,000 troops around Adrianople.

On the very day upon which the new Turkish reforms
were announced, the French Premier, M. Poincaré,[1] suggested to the British Government that the Powers should
urge a pacific attitude upon the Balkan states, pointing out
that in the event of war they need not hope for territorial
gains and that at the same time they should exercise further
pressure upon the Porte, in order to secure the necessary concessions in Macedonia. Before, however, the
views of all the Powers could be collated, the situation
had been gravely compromised by the almost simultaneous orders for the mobilisation of the Bulgarian,
Serbian, Greek and Turkish armies (1st October). The
ponderous machinery of the Concert rendered further
delays inevitable, and before any decisive step could
be taken in Constantinople, the Porte, hesitating to the
last between the two extremes of concession and sword-
rattling, had announced its resolve to put in force the
Vilayet Law of 1880, and thus, after an interval of a
generation, to carry out the provisions of the Treaty of
Berlin (6th October). It thus forestalled by a few days

[1] To-day President of the Republic.

the Collective Note of the five Great Powers,[1] which, in its endeavour to soothe Turkish susceptibilities, deprived its advocacy of reform of any such value as it might otherwise have possessed in the eyes of the Balkan Allies. Indeed, the chief concern of the Note seemed to be to safeguard the territorial integrity of Turkey and the sovereign rights of the Sultan, and only then to further the cause of reform. Meanwhile another Note was addressed by the Powers to the four Balkan states, strongly deprecating any hostile action, pledging themselves to enforce the Treaty of Berlin (after a lapse of thirty-four years), and adding the warning that no change in the territorial *status quo* would be tolerated, even in the event of war. When, however, the Russian and Austro-Hungarian Ministers at Cetinje, acting for themselves and their colleagues, presented the Note to King Nicholas, they were informed that he had only a few hours before declared war upon Turkey (8th October). This step, which was undoubtedly the result of collusion, greatly diminished the chances of a peaceful settlement, and at the same time gave the other three states an excuse for raising their demands. On 13th October Bulgaria, Serbia and Greece replied to the Powers that in such a situation far more drastic reforms were required than those included in the stillborn Law of Vilayets, and at the same time presented the Porte with a formidable list of demands, adding a request for their acceptance within a period of six weeks and for the demobilisation of the Turkish army in the meantime. The main points in this new programme were : racial autonomy for all the nationalities of the Ottoman Empire, and their proportional representation in Parliament; equality of Christian and Moslem schools; a pledge that the Christians would not be liable to military service outside their own province, and that no

[1] Italy, being still at war, naturally could not participate.

attempt would be made to alter the racial character of any district; the reorganisation of the gendarmerie under Swiss or Belgian chiefs; the appointment of Swiss or Belgian Valis, with elected councils to advise them; and the creation of a Supreme Council at Constantinople, composed equally of Christians and Moslems, whose duty it would be to watch over the execution of reforms and whose functions would be subject to the control of the Ambassadors of the Great Powers. Such demands far exceeded what any sovereign state could be expected to accept under the pressure of foreign dictation, and were probably not intended to be accepted. As a matter of fact, the Porte decided to ignore the Note altogether, and on 15th October requested the Ministers of Bulgaria, Serbia and Greece to apply for their passports. The diplomatic breach with Greece had already been rendered inevitable by the final admission of the Cretan deputies into the Greek Parliament; and Turkey found herself plunged into war with four new adversaries on the very day following the conclusion of peace with Italy.

CHAPTER XIII

THE TURCO-BALKAN WAR

No war of modern times has been conducted under conditions of such absolute secrecy as the two Balkan wars of 1912–13, and many incidents of both campaigns, especially of the second, are still shrouded in mystery. The railway, the telegraph and the telephone have transformed modern warfare, but instead of contributing to the elucidation of the real facts, they have actually rendered it more difficult. In time of war all channels of information are controlled by the military authorities to a degree even to-day not generally recognised, and nowhere was this more true than in the Balkans, where the interception of news was favoured by the backward state of the country and the lack of means of communication. The drastic measures adopted by the General Staffs of all the countries engaged ought not to have surprised anyone. During the Russo-Japanese War it had become apparent that the days of the war correspondent were numbered, and at the time of the Bosnian crisis no secret was made of the fact that in the event of war no journalist, of whatever nationality, would be allowed anywhere near the front. The hordes of journalists who, on the outbreak of war in October, 1912, flocked from all parts of Europe to the Balkans, reduced their profession *ad absurdum,* not merely by their often ludicrous lack of qualifications, but by the arrogance of their claims for assistance.[1] No army in the world would have tolerated their presence in such numbers, and it is only to be regretted that this was not made clear from the very first.[2]

At the outset, the complete absence of outside control of news enabled the rival General Staffs to supply Europe with false or misleading information regarding the progress of the campaign, and thus to impress or influence public opinion in the various capitals during a critical period when there was still danger of intervention. This was especially marked in the case of the Bulgarian Staff, which, in its extremely able reports for foreign consumption, appears to have invented or suppressed whole battles, according as the strategy of the moment seemed to recommend. For the time being this method was, of course, eminently successful, the more so as it coincided with the interests of the sensational Yellow Press; but it carried with it its own revenge. At first Europe imagined that Lüle Burgas was only the last of a series of mighty battles, that the Bulgars were close on the heels of the retreating Turks, and that Tchataldja might fall at any moment. When at last the truth began to trickle through, enthusiasm was succeeded by scepticism; and after the resumption of war in February, 1913, and still more during the Serbo-Bulgar campaign, sane foreign opinion was openly disinclined to credit any official information supplied from Sofia.

After what has been said, it would be extremely rash

[1] To this general rule there were, of course, certain brilliant exceptions, whose names will at once occur to many readers.

[2] I leave the above paragraph unaltered, as I wrote it in February, 1914. To-day it may seem obvious and even banal, but I do not feel ashamed of having written it six months before the bursting of the storm which has revolutionised all our military and civil standards. I may add that the whole of Chapters XIII. and XIV. were written during the winter of 1913–14.

for a mere civilian to attempt any detailed narrative of the Balkan campaigns; and, indeed, any adequate treatment would far exceed the limits of the present volume.[1] My aim is rather to supply the reader with a brief summary of the war as a connected whole, to show its component parts in their true perspective, and to indicate some at least of the underlying causes which decided the issue.

In meeting the onslaught of the four allies, the Turks were faced with the problem of defending simultaneously four widely separated theatres of war. Of these, the Montenegrin and Greek could for the moment be left out of account. The relatively small numbers of the Montenegrin and Greek armies, the acute crisis which the latter had so recently passed through, and above all the strength of the fortresses of Skutari and Janina, would, it was argued, neutralise all serious danger from these two sides. Even at the worst, a defensive attitude in Epirus and in the difficult passes behind Olympus ought to prevent the Greeks from threatening Salonica,

---

[1] Little wonder that there are so few books of any real value dealing with either war. The only *general* surveys that need be seriously considered are in German—Colonel Immanuel, *Der Balkankrieg,* 1912/13, in 5 parts, and Major Alfred Meyer, *Der Balkankrieg,* in 4 parts. For the Thracian campaign the most authoritative sources are the publication of the German General Staff, *Der Balkankrieg,* 1912/13 (No. 50 in the series, *Kriegsgeschichtliche Einzelschriften*), and the admirable treatise of Major P. Howell, *The Campaign in Thrace.* Lord Percy's article in the *National Review* for February, 1914, also deserves mention. On the Turkish side we have the books of Mr. Ashmead-Bartlett, Major James (slight), and especially Mahmud Mukhtar Pasha and Major von Hochwaechter (both in German). Colonel de Mondésir's monograph on the Siege of Adrianople (in French) is also valuable. On the Serbian campaign consult Taburno and Barby; on the Greek, Cassavetti and Nikolaides (all four eulogistic). For further details, see bibliography.

until a decisive action had been fought out elsewhere. In this calculation the Turks, like the rest of Europe, placed far too low a value upon the Greek army.

In theory, then, the Turks might be expected to assume the immediate offensive and to endeavour to force Bulgaria and Serbia to their knees before the two smaller states could join hands with them. In practice, however, the outbreak of war found the Turks extremely ill-prepared. Their contemptuous attitude towards the Balkan states had betrayed them into the fatal error of disbanding, as recently as August, 1912, the large army of 120,000 men which Mahmud Shevket Pasha had assembled at Smyrna to prevent an Italian landing in Asia Minor. Incidentally this action may be regarded as a conclusive proof that the Porte as yet knew nothing of the military conventions which already existed between the Balkan states.

The Turks rashly neglected the axiom that in time of war, and above all in the selection of the right moment, diplomacy and strategy must act in unison. Political motives—compounded of Chauvinism, false pride, over-confidence, and a desire to impress home and foreign opinion—led them to declare war on Bulgaria and Serbia (17th October). Such a step had absolutely no meaning unless it was to be followed by prompt aggression, and this was quite beyond the power of the Turks. Thus the fact that four days were allowed to elapse without any move on their part is in itself a proof that the necessary harmony and co-operation between the Ministries of War and Foreign Affairs were lacking from the very first. There were plenty of paper theories in Constantinople, but no serious attempt to carry them into practice, and this neglect of practical details was immensely aggravated by a radical divergence of opinion between the Commander-in-Chief and his higher officers in the field. To those acquainted with the true facts of the case it seemed that the Turks had everything to gain by delay. Their natural tactics would have been to remain on the defensive, "using the pivots Adrianople and Kirk Kilisse as breakwaters against the tide of Bulgarian invasion,"[1] until mobilisation was completed, and the raw Redifs at the front could be replaced by the seasoned troops of Asia Minor.[2] An even more effectual plan, according to some strategists, would have been to leave an adequate garrison in Adrianople and then withdraw to a strong position behind the river Ergene, until the army was ready for a vigorous offensive movement. That this second plan was never seriously considered was due partly to the over-confidence of the Turkish commanders, but above all to a much more cogent reason, namely, the effect which a withdrawal might have had upon the *moral* of the troops. But prestige and *moral,* always matters of the first importance in war, were in this case over-emphasised, the warnings of von der Goltz Pasha were ignored, and a plan was put into operation, the success of which was from the outset rendered more than doubtful by the inadequate numbers, inferior material and utterly faulty equipment of the Turkish army. The design of Nazim Pasha—imposed upon Abdullah Pasha against the latter's better judgment[3]—was to press home from Kirk Kilisse in a south-westerly direction, to drive the Bulgars back upon Adrianople, and thus hem them in between the main Turkish army and the garrison of the city. The Turks were well informed as to the movements of two of the three invading armies, but either failed to reckon with, or else under-estimated the strength of, the Bulgarian movement from the north

[1] *Cit.* Howell, p. 4 : *cf.* Immanuel, Heft II., p. 10.
[2] *Cf.* Hochwachter, p. 12.
[3] Immanuel, Heft II., p. 26.

against the Turkish right.[1] It has since transpired that
the Bulgarian Third Army (General Dimitriev) was
still more in the dark as to the movements and numbers
of the Turks opposed to it, and we may therefore conclude that in theory Nazim Pasha's scheme had a real
prospect of success and only broke down owing to the
complete lack of organisation.

While internal circumstances, then still unknown to
the outer world,[2] rendered a Turkish victory in Thrace
well-nigh impossible, the situation of the Turks in Macedonia, though by no means free from difficulty, was still
distinctly more favourable than farther east. In the
first place, their Serb and Greek opponents seemed far
less redoubtable than the Bulgarians, who had, it was
notorious, been preparing for the struggle for a whole
generation past; the Turkish army started upon its task
full of confidence and with a record of former victories.
Secondly, Zekki Pasha had succeeded in concentrating
the main body of the Macedonian army in the district
between Üsküb (Skoplje) and Ishtib (Štip) and thus
possessed an admirable base of operations against the
invaders. Finally, strange as it may seem, Macedonia
was, from a military point of view, relatively better
prepared for war than Thrace. It must be remembered
than Salonica and Monastir were the real strongholds

[1] *Cf.* the *Times* of 13th February, 1913, in which its correspondent in Thrace challenges the statement of Major Howell
that the Bulgarian screening operations were successful. He
was in a position to assert that the Turkish General Staff were
aware, "before the outbreak of hostilities," "of the concentration of the two Bulgarian armies at Jamboli." During a con-
versation with Nazim Pasha at the time, he was informed that
the main Bulgarian army of invasion was coming from the north.

[2] How far this applies to the allies, is a question which has
not as yet received any adequate answer, though both the Bulgarian and Serbian Intelligence Departments are known to have
been very well served.

of the Young Turkish movement and had received the
special attention of its leaders, both civil and military.
Even the casual traveller could not fail to notice the
evident stress laid by the new *régime* upon the military
defence of Old Serbia[1] and Macedonia. At every place
of importance the chief features in the landscape were
huge new or enlarged and reconstructed barracks, military schools and hospitals. The only roads which were
built were those which served a strategic purpose—
notably those which ran from Monastir through Prilep
to Veles, and from Veles across the Ovčepolje (the
Sheepdowns) to Ishtib; and it is significant that the
latter was in course of extension towards the Bulgarian
frontier, thus linking both Monastir and Salonica with
the shortest route of access to Sofia. It was to the
prompt action of the troops stationed in Macedonia that
the Committee owed its final triumph over Abdul Hamid
in April, 1909, and in the following three years the repeated risings in Albania had led to large concentrations
of troops in Monastir and Üsküb. That in the summer
of 1912 the Turks still had very considerable military
forces in Macedonia was due to two circumstances. On
the one hand, the war with Italy had deprived them of
the command of the Ægean and so had rendered the
transference of troops from Macedonia impossible, save
by the tortuous land route Salonica—Dedeagač—Constantinople—Anatolia. But quite apart from this tech-
nical difficulty, the Porte had the strongest reasons for
leaving them where they were. Albania was still full of
unrest, and it was feared that Italy might attempt to
bring matters to a climax by landing troops between

[1] It is necessary to point out that till the expulsion of the Turks
from Macedonia "Old Serbia" meant the territory inhabited by
Serbs, lying south of the Serbo-Turkish frontier.   Since 1912,
however, it has been applied to the original Kingdom of Serbia,
the newly acquired territory being described as "*New* Serbia."

Valona and Corfu. The design, if it had ever been seriously entertained in Rome, was abandoned from fear of international complications; but it found full credence in Constantinople, and amply justified the retention of strong forces in Macedonia. The growing rivalry of Committee and anti-Committee officers, nowhere so marked as in Monastir, supplied the Government with an additional motive for not moving these forces to the capital.

At the outbreak of war Zekki Pasha was in command of the Vardar Army, consisting of not less than 85,000 troops and 20,000 to 25,000 Albanian irregulars—in other words, of a force larger than that which Abdullah Pasha had at his disposal for aggression in Thrace, since the garrison of Adrianople, being bound to the defensive, has to be deducted from the Turkish total. Zekki's plan of campaign was obvious. He had to assume the aggressive against the First Serbian Army (Crown Prince Alexander), to defeat it before it could unite with the Third and Second Armies, advancing by Priština and Egri Palanka, and then to crush these two weaker units in detail. If this could be achieved (and it is clear that a decisive defeat of the Crown Prince would almost certainly have involved the other armies in ruin), the Serbs would be forced back upon Niš, the road to Sofia would be open, the Bulgarians would have to recall one of their Thracian armies to defend the capital, and the whole plan of campaign of the allies would fall to the ground. The potential value of the Vardar army as the means of creating a diversion in favour of the ill-prepared Thracian army can hardly be exaggerated; and it is remarkable that this point has been so little insisted upon. The very rapidity and completeness of the Serb success, in removing all fear of such a contingency, actually contributed to obscure the gravity of the issues involved, and at the same time removed the necessity of adjusting the focus for a general survey of the campaign.

Meanwhile, the task before the Allies was equally clear. Their ulterior aim, though at first concealed by vague diplomatic assurances, was unquestionably the expulsion of the Turks from Europe. This could only be effected as the result of a decisive and crushing defeat, and for various reasons this demanded great rapidity of action. Every day gained increased the chances of the Allies, since it lessened the danger of European intervention and reduced the time available to the Turks for bringing up reinforcements from Asia Minor. While, then, Montenegro endeavoured to " rush " Skutari, the main Serbian and Greek armies and a lesser Bulgarian force advanced simultaneously from the north, south and north-east, with Salonica as their objective. Meanwhile, the three principal Bulgarian armies concentrated their efforts upon Thrace, their plan of campaign being to mask Adrianople as rapidly as possible, to attack, and if necessary storm, Kirk Kilisse, and, this once accomplished, to mass against the main Turkish army, and force on a decisive combat before the raw levies at the front could be augmented by seasoned Anatolian troops.

The campaign was opened by Montenegro, who declared war as early as 8th October. Its action was determined alike by military and political reasons. The allies, having once embarked upon mobilisation, wished at all costs to frustrate the efforts of the Great Powers to preserve peace. That the challenge should come from the most insignificant of Turkey's opponents was a calculated insult which could not fail to infuriate the Porte, already irritable and excited after the events of the preceding summer. Montenegro, owing to its small area and the primitive basis of its military system, could collect its forces more rapidly than the other Balkan

states, and at the same time it ran less grave risks, both
in view of its remote geographical situation and of the
fact that the Turkish forces round Skutari, though adequate for the defence of that city, were far too weak to
assume the offensive against the almost impregnable
mountain fastnesses of King Nicholas. Moreover, the
best hope of the Montenegrins lay in surprising Skutari
by a rapid *coup de main*, their army being, despite its
heroic gallantry, lacking in the discipline and equipment
necessary for modern siege operations.

In the initial stages the Montenegrins had the assistance of the Mirdite and Malissori tribes of North Albania, and this proved invaluable during the advance along
the difficult country to the east of the Lake of Skutari.
On October 10 Dečić, and four days later Šipcanik, the
key to the Turkish frontier positions, were captured after
a stubborn resistance and heavy losses on both sides.
The issue was decided by the superior artillery fire of the
invaders; 3,500 men and 24 guns fell into their hands.
But though this victory brought the Montenegrins within
6,000 yards of Skutari (October 25), they were not
strong enough to reduce it to submission. The army of
Crown Prince Danilo, advancing from Antivari, succeeded in storming one of the western forts; but the
formidable hill of Taraboš prevented further progress on
that side. On 29th October a storming party, after
heroic efforts, ejected the Turks from the important position of Bardanjolt, but next day it was retaken, and the
exhausted Montenegrins were no further than before.
The Turks, under the able leadership of Hassan Riza
Pasha, made repeated sorties from the town and it was
not until the Serbs occupied Alessio (19th November)
and Medua (21st) that the investment of Skutari became
effective. The siege operations were still dragging on
indefinitely when the armistice was proclaimed; but
Hassan Riza, being cut off from all connection with Con-

stantinople, refused to recognise it, and a state of unofficial war ensued.

THRACE

For a whole generation past Bulgaria had regarded a war with Turkey as sooner or later inevitable, and had made her military preparations accordingly. While doubtless giving careful consideration to a number of alternative plans of campaign, whose adoption would depend upon the circumstances of the moment, the General Staff seems to have always realised that its chief aim must be to seek out and crush the main Turkish army, and that all else must be regarded as subordinate. That the reduction of Ardianople by siege had never seriously entered into the calculations of Bulgaria, is best shown by the fact that during her long and careful preparation for war she omitted to provide herself with the heavy siege guns necessary to reduce a strong modern fortress.[1]

It is an open secret that this omission was in deference to Russia, who had no desire that Adrianople, if it ceased to be Turkish, should pass into any hands but her own, and who only withdrew her veto as a result of the League's rapid triumph and of Austrian competition for Bulgarian favour. But Adrianople, if not captured, or stormed, must, owing to its geographical position, be isolated before any further advance into Thrace was possible. To the Second Army, therefore (about 90,000 men under General Ivanov), was assigned the task of "sealing up" Adrianople and digging itself into positions of sufficient strength to repel any serious sortie of the garrison.

The mountainous country lying to the west of Adrianople not permitting of any advance on a large scale,

[1] See *infra*.

the next problem before the Bulgarians was that of Kirk
Kilisse, separated from Adrianople by 30 miles of open
downland. Had the Turks carried out the projects of
their German advisers, Kirk Kilisse would have been a
modern fortress "capable of holding the Prussian army
at bay for three months"; in reality, its fortifications had
remained almost entirely on paper, and only fools can
regard its unopposed capture as a rebuff to German
strategy. It has not yet transpired to what extent the
Bulgarian plan of campaign was based upon a knowledge
of Turkish unpreparedness; but it may be assumed that
their information was detailed and accurate, for the advance from Jamboli would have been an extremely risky
undertaking if Kirk Kilisse had deserved its paper reputation.[1] It seems certain that General Savov hoped to
take the Turks unawares, and therefore made every effort
by a strict censorship of news and by elaborate screening
movements of his cavalry, to conceal from the enemy till
the last moment the direction from which his main attack was to come. As a matter of fact, the Turks were
better informed than Savov had imagined, and their complete failure to check the Bulgarian Third Army was due,
not to surprise or ignorance, but to other causes to which
we shall refer later.

The Second Army crossed the frontier on 18th October,
occupied Mustafa Pasha and its bridge, and advanced on
Adrianople virtually unopposed. It at once proceeded
to invest the city, first blocking the western access in the
Marica Valley, and then gradually extending its operations to the northern, eastern and southern sectors.
Meanwhile, the Third Army, numbering 70,000 to 80,000
men under General Dimitriev, advanced southwards
from Jamboli in Eastern Bulgaria, with definite instructions to take Kirk Kilisse, while the gap between Ivanov

[1] On the other hand, Savov's caution after the fall of Kirk
Kilisse suggests the contrary.

and Dimitriev was filled by the First Army under General Kutinčev ready to reinforce one or other according to necessity.   Savov's plan was to take no undue risks and to refrain from any direct aggression until the besiegers of Adrianople had time to "dig themselves in "[1] ; but in any case the First and Third Armies were delayed by difficulties of transport, due to the absence of real roads and the continuous heavy rain.   The dissensions among the Turkish commanders paralysed the execution of Nazim Pasha's plan[2] and it was not until 22nd October that the first contact was established.   On that day there was more or less serious fighting along the entire front.   The Adrianople garrison was repulsed by the First Army at Kaipa, to the north-east of the city, while further east, at Seliolu, the Turks were routed after a fierce encounter and pursued by the Bulgarian cavalry as far as Kavakli, on the new railway linking Kirk Kilisse with the Orient route.   This pursuit, in the course of which the baggage of the first Turkish Army Corps was captured, appears to have had a demoralising effect on the Turkish forces round Kirk Kilisse, which consisted to a large extent of undisciplined and ill-equipped Redifs, still further weakened by an admixture of unwilling Christians in the ranks.   On the following day (23rd October) the Bulgarians resumed the attack between Petra and Erekler, where the Turkish resistance, never very formidable, soon ended in a panic, which, despite all the efforts of the able Turkish General, Mahmud Mukhtar Pasha, degenerated into a disorderly retreat southwards.   This continued throughout the night, and on 24th October the Bulgars occupied Kirk Kilisse unopposed.   Unfortunately, they were exhausted by the fighting following on many days of strenuous marching, and were, moreover, unaware of

[1] Howell, *op. cit.*, p. 54.
[2] See *supra*, p. 170.

the completeness of their success. Dimitriev was anxious to push on without delay; but Savov was still determined to take no risks, "to locate the Turkish mass" before striking, and then "to strike with his full force, suitably disposed, reorganised, well-supplied and rested."[1] He therefore ordered a halt, and a pause of four days ensued.

Needless to say, this momentous decision affected the whole issue of the war. If Dimitriev had had his way, the remnants of the Turkish army might have been annihilated or cut off, and the lines of Tchataldja and with them Constantinople itself might have lain at the mercy of the invaders. It is easy to be wise after the event, and we now know that there would have been no risk involved in an immediate advance, the more so as the captured stores of Kirk Kilisse had solved the problem of supplies. But if we limit ourselves to the facts then at Savov's disposal, we must in all fairness admit that though he guessed wrong, all the probabilities were in favour of his guess. While, however, the military student will absolve him, the historian must regard his decision as mainly responsible for Bulgaria's subsequent failure to break down the last defences of the Turks.

Four days elapsed before hostilities were resumed, and this respite enabled the Turks to rally their broken columns and to concentrate their main forces along the Karagatch-dere river. But the dissensions among the Turkish Commanders continued, and prevented full advantage being taken of the natural strength of their new position.[2] On 28th October the Bulgarians resumed the offensive, and for five days a fierce battle raged along a front of almost 25 miles, from Lüle Burgas on the south as far as Bunar Hissar and Sirmos on the north. The

---

[1] cit., Howell, op. cit., p. 76.
[2] Immanuel, op. cit., p. 95.

Bulgarian plan consisted in a determined frontal attack, followed by an enveloping movement on the Turkish left, designed to drive the enemy off the railway and their lines of communication, and to direct their retreat towards the Istranja Balkan mountains—a geographical *cul de sac*. The most noteworthy feature of the battle is the poor leadership on both sides. In the case of the Turks, Abdullah Pasha was at variance both with headquarters at Constantinople and with his own chief officers in the field, and the Turkish machine broke down so utterly that each separate command virtually acted on its own responsibility. At one time the General Staff actually appears to have been without telephonic or even tele-graphic connection with the various units; in such cir-cumstances there could be nothing in the nature of a general plan. The Bulgarians, in their turn, were seriously handicapped by the remote position of the General Staff. For reasons of geography and weather, Savov had been forced either to remain at Kizilagatch or to lose touch with the front for two days, which would have involved too great a risk; he thus had to surrender tactical control to his second in command, Dimitriev, and thereby sacrificed unity of design. While the Bulgarian left, thanks mainly to "record" marching, came into action sooner than had been anticipated, the heavy rains had delayed the advance of the First Army on the right. Gaps arose in the Bulgarian line, for a time intercommunication practically ceased,[1] and on the evening of the second day of the battle (29th October) the situation of the Third Army would have been highly precarious, if it had been faced by troops still capable of taking the offensive. Meanwhile Shükri Pasha ordered a sortie from Adrianople, but made the fatal error of striking westwards along the Maritza valley. If instead of this he had moved upon Lüle Burgas—a

---

[1] Howell, *op. cit.*, p. 116.

distance of barely forty miles—his arrival might have decided the battle in favour of the Turks.[1] While, then, 29th October was a critical day for the Bulgarian centre, the left wing was held at bay by the spirited defence of Mahmud Mukhtar; desperate fighting took place, and Poryali changed hands at least four times. It was not till daylight on the fourth day (31st October) that the centre succeeded in storming the heights at Karagatch; but even then one division failed to cross the river. Towards afternoon the superior fire of the Bulgarian artillery finally crushed the resistance of the Turkish left, but no pursuit was attempted. Mahmud Mukhtar, now isolated on the Turkish right, still offered a gallant resistance on the fifth day (1st November), but the Bulgarian artillery fire directed against both flanks at last forced his troops into flight, and the Turkish retreat became general.

As at Kirk Kilisse, there was no pursuit. The Bulgarian army, though victorious, was at the last stage of exhaustion; there were no fresh troops available to take their place, and the cavalry division, instead of being held in reserve, had been worn out by constant reconnoitring, and at the critical moment when Dimitriev gave the order for pursuit was physically incapable of obeying. The torrents of rain which again set in on the night of 1st November finally settled the question. The Bulgarian general plan had failed, and the battle of Lüle Burgas cannot be described as truly decisive. The Turkish retreat became a panic, such as had no European parallel since the Borodino,[2] and a pitiless pursuit would have led to the annihilation of the beaten army and the occupation of the lines of Tchataldja.

[1] *Ibid.*, p. 119.
[2] On November 2, the artillery of the Third Army Corps actually fired on its own troops, mistaking them for the enemy. See Hochwaechter's Diary.

This would have been the turning-point of the war and might even have involved the final expulsion of the Turks from Europe. But this effort was beyond the power of the Bulgarians. Their victory was due, not to the superior strategy of the commanders, but to the heroism and enthusiasm of the rank and file and to the complete breakdown of the Turkish military system. A combination of high patriotic ideals with practical training gave to the Bulgarian peasant an irresistible *élan* such as was wholly lacking to the ill-led and half-starved Turkish army. The spade and the bayonet were used with equal effect, and their work was completed by superior artillery practice. But victory was paid for by enormous losses, and there can be no question that many lives were recklessly wasted in frontal attacks, and that the almost entire neglect of sanitary precautions[1] increased the mortality and added to the exhaustion which followed battle. The callousness to human life displayed by the Bulgarians in both these directions brought its own revenge at a later period.

On 1st November the Bulgarians were left in possession of the field; but five days of absolute rest elapsed before the advance was resumed, and even then the pace was far from rapid. Though the distance from Lüle Burgas to the lines of Tchataldja is only seventy miles, it was not till the 16th that the Bulgarians arrived within reach of the Turkish guns.[2] This interval of a fortnight had been employed to strengthen the defences of the capital, and to remove some at least of the worst deficiencies of the lines. Their desperate condition at the time of the retreat may be judged by the fact that on

---

[1] *Cf.* Pennenrun, *La Guerre des Balkans.* Openly admitted by the Foreign Minister, Genadiev, in his speech in Sofia on 16th November, 1913. ("Sanitary material was virtually non-existent.")

[2] Immanuel, II., p. 53.

4th November Major von Hochwaechter, as an active member of Mahmud Mukhtar's staff, recorded in his diary : "Indeed, on the whole, the Tchataldja line has been given up." This verdict was, of course, based upon purely military considerations; but it has since transpired that on the following day (5th November) the Turkish Government, through its diplomatic representatives, was assuring the Great Powers of its inability to defend the lines and was already relying upon external political pressure to prevent a Bulgarian occupation of Constantinople.[1] Full advantage, however, was taken of the respite offered by the invader; siege guns were hurriedly moved up to the lines, proper stores and ammunition were accumulated, drastic measures were adopted to stamp out the epidemic of cholera which had followed the retreat, and, above all, great efforts were expended on entrenchments and wire entanglements.

During this fortnight of preparation, Europe rang with the fictitious accounts of a great battle waged for three days (3rd, 4th, 5th November) at Tcherkeskoj, followed by a general assault on Tchataldja, also lasting three days (7th–9th November).[2] These stories, garnished with minute geographical and strategic details, were supplied by the Bulgarian General Staff to the correspondent of a prominent Viennese newspaper, whose knowledge of Balkan languages had already enabled him to outdistance his numerous journalistic rivals.

The real battle of Tchataldja commenced on 17th November with a heavy cannonade against the Turkish positions. This was followed up by a determined assault

---

[1] Cf. Roumanian Green Book.

[2] Cf. Reichspost, Nos. 512 (4th November), 575, 577 (7th November), 519–531 (8th–15th November). In a telegram dated from the Bulgarian Headquarters at 10 a.m. on 7th November, minute details (covering a column and a half) are given of these imaginary events.

upon the weakest spot of the defence, beside the Lake of Derkos, and during the night the Bulgarians succeeded in getting within 600 to 800 yards and digging themselves in. On the 18th, however, no further progress could be made, for the Turkish artillery fire gradually asserted its superiority. On the third day the battle was confined to an artillery duel, in which the Black Sea fleet took some part; and at nightfall the Bulgarians retired, after losses which have been estimated at 10,000 killed and wounded.[1] Their original *élan* had forsaken them;[2] their exhaustion had been completed by a temporary dislocation of the commissariat,[3] by shocking sanitary conditions, and the consequent outbreak of dysentery and cholera. On the other hand, the desperate efforts of the Turkish commanders had infused a new spirit into their troops; and the battle afforded a new proof that the Ottoman soldier is at his best in a defensive position. But the determining factor in the battle was the Turkish artillery, which disproved the alleged inferiority of German armaments.[4] The lines had proved too tough a nut for the Bulgars to crack, and they now withdrew to a defensive position some miles to the north of the lines, and definitely abandoned the idea of a triumphal entry into Constantinople. Thus both in a strategical and in a political sense the battle of Tchataldja was the decisive event

[1] Immanuel, II., p. 58. Pennenrun, p. 135.

[2] "Il a manqué aux Bulgares ce souffle, ce cœur qui les avait fait vainqueurs jusqu'ici."—Pennenrun, p. 114. "Ces gens-là n'ont pas l'air de vainqueurs," said someone to Pennenrun on 17th November, as they watched the Bulgarian columns moving to the front.

[3] The Third Army ran short of provisions for two days on the eve of Tchataldja (15th–16th November). See Pennenrun, pp. 19, 91.

[4] See Hochwaechter, p. 121, who described it as "ein glänzender Erfolg der Türken."

which preserved to the Turks the last and most vital
fragment of their European empire, and at the same time
denied to Bulgaria the coveted *rôle* of the Prussia of
the Balkans.

While their main armies had been concentrated in
Thrace, the Bulgarians had not been idle further west.
One division had been posted at Küstendil, to co-operate
with the Serbs and if necessary screen Sofia from attack.
The decisive battle of Kumanovo removed all danger
from this quarter; and not merely this division, but
also the greater part of the Second Serbian Army under
General Stepanović were promptly transferred to
Adrianople to reinforce the besieging army. To another
Bulgarian group had been assigned the task of occupying the country south of the Rhodope range and of
"cutting" the railway between Constantinople and
Salonica. The advance took place in two parallel
columns down the valleys of the Mestra and Struma,
Kavala and Seres being occupied without serious resistance within a couple of days of each other; but it was
not till 9th November that the main force succeeded
in reaching Salonica, which had already capitulated on
the previous day to the Greek Crown Prince.

Meanwhile, the investment of Adrianople was steadily
pushed forward. Shükri Pasha had 40,000 to 50,000
men under his command, while General Ivanov's forces
considerably exceeded 100,000. On 7th November the
Bulgarians stormed two positions on the south-west of
the city, which secured to them the command of the
railway along the Marica. But this progress was handicapped by lack of heavy siege-guns and by the outbreak
of disease and epidemics; while the Turkish garrison,
well supplied with stores and courageously led, showed
a fighting spirit, and made at least four determined
sorties during November. The Turkish headquarters,
encouraged by their success at Tchataldja, began to

concert measures for the relief of Adrianople, and with this end in view sent considerable reinforcements to Gallipoli and Bulair, on the isthmus behind the Dardanelles. If at this stage the Turks had been really capable of an offensive stroke, they might by an advance upon Dimotika have cut the communications of the Bulgarian army before Tchataldja. The Bulgarian General Staff took steps to avert this danger. The 2nd Division was moved against Dimotika, and on 28th November, at Merhumli, surrounded and took prisoners the last remnants of the Turkish forces in the Marica valley.[1] At the same time most of the 7th Division had been transferred on Greek transports from Salonica to Dedeagač, and by 1st December a compact Bulgarian force was advancing towards Bulair to forestall any Turkish attempt to assume the offensive. Towards the close of November the operations before Adrianople were resumed with fresh vigour, and after a continuous bombardment of three days an attempt was made on the night of 3rd December to storm the eastern sectors. Its failure was the last incident in this stage of the Balkan war, for on the following day the pourparlers which had been conducted between the Allies and the Turks for nearly a fortnight past reached a successful issue, and on 4th December an armistice was concluded.

MACEDONIA.

The Porte had declared war upon Bulgaria and Serbia simultaneously, and the armies of the two Slav allies crossed the frontier on the same day (18th October). In Serbia mobilisation was carried out with the same speed and smoothness as in Bulgaria. Within three days 95

[1] According to Immanuel (II., p. 70), 9,000 men with 10 guns.

per cent. of the reservists had presented themselves,[1] and before the opening of hostilities the number of men available is said to have exceeded by no fewer than 90,000 the estimate of the authorities.

The Turkish plan of campaign, as has already been pointed out, was to assume the aggressive against the main Serbian army, to crush it before it could unite with the auxiliary Serb and Bulgar columns to the north and east, and having thus driven it back to Serbian territory, to march upon Sofia. The main Bulgarian forces in Thrace would thus have been taken in the rear and probably forced to abandon the offensive.

The Serbian plan of campaign was directed in the first instance upon Üsküb (Skoplje), with the double object of recovering the ancient Serb capital and of acquiring a strategic centre whose capture would render Turkish aggression against Serbia or Bulgaria impossible. The Serbian forces advanced in four sections, disposed in *échelon* formation. The First Army, over 90,000 strong, under the Crown Prince and General Bojević, followed the valley of the Morava and the main railway line to Salonica. The Third Army, 34,000, under General Janković, crossed the Prepolac Pass to Priština, with the object of occupying the plain of Kosovo, and threatening Üsküb from the north. To a smaller group of 16,000 men under General Živković, starting from western Serbia, was assigned the task of occupying the Sandjak of Novibazar and joining hands with the eastern Montenegrin army; while the Second Army, consisting of 25,000 men under General Stepanović, advanced from Bulgarian territory by Egri Palanka, in co-operation with a similar Bulgarian force.

[1] It is worth noting that Serbia and Bulgaria had relatively but few emigrants. In the case of Montenegro and Greece, on the contrary, many thousands returned from America to fulfil their military obligations.

The Serbian operations were seriously delayed by heavy rains, which turned such roads as there were into mere quagmires, and by the activity of the Turkish advance posts and swarms of Albanian irregulars. Thus the First Army took four days to advance 36 kilometres,[1] and on 22nd October the General Staff, over-estimating the opposing forces, was virtually acting on the defensive. At the battle of Kumanovo (23rd–24th October) it was the Turks who first assumed the offensive. During the first day the Serbs were much inferior in numbers and had the greatest difficulty in holding their ground. Indeed, but for the possession of three curious rock-crowned hillocks some miles to the east of the town of Kumanovo, the Serb resistance would inevitably have been overpowered; the village of Nagoričano, the weak spot in the Serb defences, was the scene of desperate fighting all day and till far into the night, and changed hands at least four times. Djavid Pasha, the commander of the Turkish right, aimed at turning the left flank of the Serbs and thus threatening their line of advance upon Kumanovo. Reinforcements came up slowly on both sides during the night, and early next morning the two armies took the offensive almost simultaneously. The issue was finally decided towards afternoon on 24th October, by the accurate and deadly fire of the Serbian artillery, which only came into action on the second day. The Albanian irregulars on the Turkish left were stricken with panic and fled in wild disorder westwards, thus exposing the centre to the attack of fresh Serb columns advancing from the north. Thus the panic spread and soon became general; only the right under Djavid Pasha held its ground till 4 p.m. and then withdrew in fair order towards Ishtib. While the losses of the victors amounted to 1,000 killed and 3,200 wounded, those of the Turks have been estimated

---

[1] Immanuel, p. 74.

at 12,000 men, including 2,000 prisoners. Sixty-five
guns and large military stores fell into the hands of the
Serbs; indeed, by 25th November the number of captured cannon had risen to 150.[1]   But even these figures
do not reveal the full extent of the Turkish collapse.
So dire a disaster, following close upon overweening
self-confidence, completely demoralised the remains of
Zekki Pasha's army; thousands melted away during the
retreat and stormed the trains for Salonica.   Privates
and even officers threw off their uniforms, and when the
Serbs entered Üsküb, were found in disguises of a
strange and sometimes ludicrous nature.

Kumanovo, like Lüle Burgas, was pre-eminently a
soldier's battle.   On neither side was any brilliant
generalship shown, and both armies seem to have been
surprised at finding the enemy where they did.   The
dashing qualities of the Serbian infantry and the excellence of their artillery gave a brilliant foretaste of subsequent achievements.

The Serbian General Staff, misled by a false report
that the Sixth Turkish Army Corps was advancing from
Veles, refrained from any active pursuit and did not
enter the town of Kumanovo until the following day.
Their excessive caution, which offers an exact parallel
to Savov's attitude at Kirk Kilisse, was based upon a
general over-estimate of the Turks, but suggests the
possibility that the allies were still reckoning with international complications.

In Üsküb chaos reigned for forty-eight hours, and the
foreign consuls found it necessary to assume the direction of affairs until the Serbs arrived.   Some idea of
the prevailing panic may be obtained from a single
incident.   The Vali, while crossing the old bridge on

[1] This number is given by Zekki Pasha in his telegram announcing the defeat to Ali Riza Pasha in Salonica (reproduced
in Barby, *Les Victoires Serbes,* p. 82).

his way to the station and to safety, was fired upon by an Albanian volunteer. No one was hit, but the cry of "The Serbs!" was raised, and a wild *sauve qui peut* followed. Four batteries were abandoned in the main street, their gunners cutting the traces and riding off; and thirty hours later, when the Serbian army entered Üsküb, the guns were still there! Under such dramatic circumstances did the Serbs resume possession of the capital of their long-vanished Empire. The dreams of five hundred years of poetic lamentation were at length fulfilled, and the armies of King Peter had avenged the fatal defeat of Kosovo. Üsküb had become Skoplje once more.

At this point it is interesting to compare the psychology of the allied forces. Bulgars and Serbs, fired by equal enthusiasm, were at first held back by the over-anxiety of their leaders; then, as victory crowned their arms, the *élan* of the former slowly decreased, while that of the latter became more and more marked—a contrast which is largely accounted for by their respective attitude to problems of commissariat and sanitation. It was the Greeks who from the very first day displayed the most dashing qualities; and even though this may be partly due to the relative ease of their task and to the fact that they are "good winners," we must not withhold our recognition of the admirable spirit displayed by the Greek army.

The elation which this event aroused throughout the entire Serbo-Croat race did not betray the Serbian General Staff into undue haste; as at Kirk Kilisse, reasons of geography and strategy combined to enforce a slight pause in the operations. Four days were spent in a redistribution of the Serbian forces. The Third Army, which had occupied Priština on 22nd October and reached Skoplje from the north only two days later than the main army, was now considerably reduced in numbers and left to cope with the Albanian irregulars. The Second Army, which could now be safely spared, was promptly dispatched to the aid of the Bulgarians before Adrianople, where it arrived on 5th November. The Crown Prince and his Generals were thus left with 85,000 men to cope with the remainder of the Turkish forces, which had abandoned the Vardar Valley and fallen back upon Monastir as their base. On 1st November the Serbs advanced in three columns, the weakest of which, passing through Ishtib and Kavadar, met with no serious opposition whatever. The right occupied Tetovo (Kalkandelen) on 1st November and marched upon Krčevo, where the pass was defended by Fethi Pasha; on 6th November the Serbs succeeded in dislodging the enemy and driving them back towards Monastir, but a further advance had to be postponed, owing to the need of co-operation with the main army.

More serious resistance was encountered by the central column in its advance from Veles. On 5th November the Serbs attacked the Turks in a strong mountainous position at the pass of Prisat; owing to the lie of the ground it was found impossible to bring the Serbian artillery into action, and the battle was decided by a resolute flanking movement of the 1st Drina division, pushed home with the bayonet. That evening the town of Prilep was occupied without further opposition; but the Turks had merely withdrawn to a strong position on the low hills of Bakurna Gumna to the south of the town, and on the following morning they opened fire from their entrenchments. The Serbian commander, while directing a flanking movement against the Turkish left, supported it by an audacious frontal attack across five miles of open plain on which there was literally not cover enough for a dog. Simultaneously the Serb artillery, also without cover, poured a deadly fire upon the Turks, whose gunnery practice proved itself altogether inferior. The invincible spirit which animated the Serb army throughout the war is best illustrated by a single anecdote. Overlooking the plain of Prilep stands the ruined fortress of Marko Kraljević, the redoubtable hero round whose name many generations of Southern Slavs have woven a splendid garland of ballad poetry; and now, as the Serbs advanced to redeem the region which their ancestors had lost, more than one soldier in the ranks fancied that he saw King Marko on his piebald steed splashing through the mud and waving them on to victory. Such exaltation produced a corresponding depression among the Turks. Captured Ottoman officers confessed some months later in Belgrade that their men were infected by the doubt whether ordinary bullets could harm a Serbian soldier! Thus in Europe of the twentieth century do we recapture the atmosphere of Lake Regillus.

These two minor battles near Prilep had cost the Serbs over 3,000 killed and wounded. The Turkish losses may have been less heavy; they withdrew towards Monastir, leaving no prisoners, but over forty cannon. On the evening of the second fight heavy snow fell, and the floods which followed, coupled with scarcity of supplies and transport difficulties, rendered a fresh pause in the Serbian operations inevitable and gave the Turks time to place themselves on the defensive outside Monastir. It was not till 13th November that the advance was resumed and two more days passed before contact was restored.

In the interval Djavid Pasha had hurried southwards from Monastir and defeated the Greek army at Banica with a loss of twelve guns. Djavid, who alone of the Turkish generals in Macedonia showed high military capacity, now urged upon headquarters a plan for concentrating the entire Turkish forces against the Greeks, crushing their armies piecemeal, and only turning back against the Serbs after Greece had been brought to her knees. Such a result, if it could be attained, would, he argued, force Greece to withdraw from the League, thus restoring Turkey's control of the Ægean and enabling her to dispatch reinforcements to Salonica. We need not stop to consider what prospect of success such a plan may have had; for his arguments, though rendered highly plausible by the fact that for political reasons (see page 198) the Greek forces were at this very juncture scattered over a wide area, were never seriously entertained at Constantinople. For sentimental, if for no other reasons, Monastir must be defended at all costs. Hence the small Greek army was left to recover from its reverse at Banica and await the approach of the Crown Prince's army; while Djavid Pasha rejoined the main Turkish army outside Monastir.

The defensive position taken up by the Turks was one of great natural strength, resting against the range of hills which sheltered the city from the north, and extending over a front of about sixteen miles. The wide Pelagonian plain, upon the Turkish right wing, would in summer have favoured a flanking movement in that direction; but the heavy rains and consequent floods seriously hampered the invaders. Thus the Serbs, while endeavouring to envelop the enemy and intercept his main lines of retreat to Florina and to Resna, found it necessary to concentrate their efforts on the Turkish left. While the attack of the Serbian right was developing in the difficult country west of Monastir, the heavy artillery took up its position behind the ridge facing the Turkish centre, and later on other guns were posted in a deliberately exposed position on the flat ground further east, in order to keep the Turkish right fully occupied. The turning movement met with desperate resistance from Djavid Pasha and his troops; Oblakovo (1450 m.), the key to the Turkish position, was taken and retaken, and on the second day of the battle (16th November) the issue was still undecided. Next day, in order to prevent the Turks from concentrating still further on their left flank, the Serbs undertook a frontal attack upon the Turkish centre. Supported by heavy artillery fire and taking advantage of the misty weather, portions of the 1st Morava and Drina Divisions advanced across the flooded valley of the Sevnica and towards night managed to ensconce themselves along the raised causeway of the public road. Many of the troops were several hours in the water, sometimes up to their shoulders, and within full range of the Turkish rifle fire. After spending the night in this precarious position they were able early next morning (18th November) to force their way right up to the Turkish trenches, the Serbian artillery, by its superior fire and remarkable precision, having utterly crushed the resistance of the Turkish batteries. Meanwhile pontoons had been erected on the Serbian left, and the right had at length stormed Oblakovo at the point of the bayonet. On the afternoon of 18th November the victorious army occupied Monastir, capturing 8000 prisoners, 95 guns (including the 12 pieces taken from the Greeks), and enormous military stores. The Turkish losses were estimated at 7000 killed and wounded, those of the Serbs at 4000 to 5000.[1] Both from a strategic point of view and as an example of prowess, endurance and efficiency, the German critic, Colonel Immanuel, is probably justified in describing the battle of Monastir as " the best performance of the entire Balkan War."[2] The Turks were beaten not only by superior numbers,[3] but by better leadership and tactical skill ; the Serbian plan was carefully thought out and succeeded in every particular.

[1] Barby, p. 124.   [2] *Op cit.,* II., p. 88.
[3] The Turks had 65,000 troops and a good many thousand irregulars, whose numbers cannot be determined; the Serbs, 80,000.

The battle of Monastir finally decided the Macedonian campaign in favour of the allies. Henceforward the best which the Turks could hope for was to prolong operations by guerilla warfare and if possible to retain their hold upon the fortresses of Skutari and Janina, as subjects of bargaining at the peace negotiations. Some broken fragments of the Turkish army survived the battle. Zekki Pasha, with at least 15,000 men, effected his retreat to Janina, though pursued by both Serbs and Greeks, and brought a most welcome addition to the forces of the garrison. Fethi Pasha, with barely 4000 men, retreated westwards upon Resna, but was overtaken by the Serbs and routed outside the town; the unfortunate general was killed, and his troops scattered in all directions. Meanwhile Djavid Pasha, finding his retreat by Resna cut off, made his way along the western slopes of Mt. Perister, and withdrew into central Albania with about 16,000 men. Here the allies wisely refrained from following him; and the presence of a Turkish general in the district of Berat, acting in nominal agreement with the new "government" at Valona, deprived the Great Powers of any excuse for military intervention in favour of Albania.

It remains for us to consider the minor operations of the Serbs in the northern theatre of war. The Third Army, under General Janković, had, as we have seen, occupied without much difficulty Priština and the historic plain of Kosóvo. Meanwhile General Živković invaded the Sandjak from western Serbia (22nd October), occupied Sjenica and Novibazar after a brief but sharp resistance (24th October), and joined hands with a Montenegrin detachment at Plevlje, whose garrison withdrew into Bosnian territory and was disarmed by the Austrians. The Sandjak being thus cleared of Turkish troops, and the two independent Serb States being united for the first time in history, a simultaneous advance was made against the Albanian irregulars, and before the close of the month Živković had occupied Djakovo, the Montenegrins, Ipek, and Janković, Prizren (30th-31st October). But a further task awaited the Serbs—that of securing that outlet to the sea to which they had so long aspired and which to them was the most valuable prize of war. Their natural access through Bosnia and Dalmatia, provinces inhabited by their own race, is in the hands of the Dual Monarchy, and thus they were of necessity led to seek it at the expense of a neighbouring race's independence.

After the fall of Prizren ten days were spent in measures of precaution and transport arrangements. To the troops of General Živković was assigned the task of policing the thinly-peopled and mountainous Sandjak, disarming the native Albanians and raising new regiments from the Serb population; while General Janković was left to supervise the advance to the coast. Two entirely separate expeditions were sent. The first, consisting of 8,700 men of the 2nd Drina Division, 10 mountain guns, and 10 machine-guns, left Djakovo on 10th November, and crossing the river Drin at Spas, made its way through the wild Mirdite country to Puka and Alessio, whose garrison, astounded at the appearance of a Serb army, surrendered after a short passage of arms (19th November). The second, composed of 7,000 men of the 1st Šumadia Division, with 4 guns and 10 machine-guns, left Prizren one day earlier and followed an even more difficult course to Kroja and Tirana, only reaching their goal at Durazzo after a fortnight of continual danger and privation. In both cases the march lay for many days through wild and trackless mountains; deep snow and swollen rivers were among the obstacles encountered. Provisions were often not obtainable on the way, and it was difficult to carry much with them. Sometimes their rations were reduced

to uncooked maize, grass, and roots. Weakened by
hunger and cold, they had to find a passage for their
guns and ammunition. With very imperfect maps, and
permanently exposed to the attack of guerilla bands, they
dared not leave their wounded or sick comrades behind
them. An English military critic has compared their
achievement to Pizarro's passage of the Andes, and it
certainly has no parallel in Europe since Napoleon
crossed into Italy.[1] It deserves special prominence, not
only as the most adventurous incident of the whole war,
but as one to which full justice has not hitherto been
done.[2]

Finally, after the battle of Monastir, columns were
pushed forward from Ochrida down the valley of the
White Drin to Dibra and westwards to Elbasan. Before
the conclusion of the armistice the whole of northern
Albania was in effective possession of the Serbian army.
Their arms had been crowned with unbroken success.
Unaided they had crushed the western Turkish army,
and now, after occupying more territory than their
wildest dreams had bade them hope for, they were free
to send large contingents to the aid of their allies before
Adrianople and Skutari. The position envisaged by the
treaty of alliance had been strikingly reversed; instead
of Bulgaria aiding Serbia with 100,000 men, she was
herself accepting the assistance of 50,000 Serbian troops.

THESSALY AND EPIRUS.

The Turkish declaration of war against Bulgaria and
Serbia had been immediately followed by the Greek
declaration of war against Turkey; and on 18th October

---

[1] Granville Baker, *Passing of the Turkish Empire*, p. 290.
[2] Even the well-informed and accurate Colonel Immanuel has
failed to realise that there were two distinct expeditions. *Cf.
op. cit.*, pp. 100-102. The numbers and route are based on information supplied me at headquarters in Skoplje in May, 1913.

Crown Prince Constantine crossed the frontier at the head of 60,000 men. His opponent, Hassan Tahsim Pasha, has been credited with the design of marching upon Larissa by the coast route and thus cutting off the Greek army from its base; but not the slightest attempt was made to execute such a move. The Turkish forces at this point cannot have exceeded 40,000 men, but their inferiority in numbers was compensated by the great strength of the mountain passes through which the Greeks were obliged to advance. Yet Elassona was occupied on the very first day, and every skirmish resulted in a fresh Turkish withdrawal. On 22nd October a battle took place at Serfidje, which ended in the rout of the Turks and the capture of 22 guns; the losses on both sides amounted to about 3,000 killed and wounded. The whole northern slopes of Olympos thus fell into Greek hands; Veria and Vodena were occupied unopposed and the railway between Monastir and Salonica was cut. The Turks fell back in two main bodies, the one towards Monastir, the other towards Salonica, and therefore the pursuing Greeks also divided their forces. On 1st November a second battle opened at Jenidje-Vardar, Tahsim Pasha holding an entrenched position between the mountains and the marshes. The Greeks were again completely successful, and, without sustaining any very serious losses, drove the Turks back upon Salonica in disorderly flight. In the city itself all discipline was at an end, its fortifications were old and worthless, and the problem of defence was complicated by the presence of 50,000 Moslem refugees. For a few days the Greek advance was checked by the Vardar river, but on 7th November, through the mediation of the foreign consuls, negotiations were opened between the Crown Prince and the Turkish commander. Two days later the victorious Greek army occupied Salonica. The bloodless surrender of Tahsim Pasha, with 26,000 men and 100 guns, gave

rise to unproved rumours that money had completed
what force of arms began.   The truth is that fortune
greatly favoured the Greek arms, but this does not
detract from the fine leadership of the Crown Prince or
from the bravery of his troops.

On the very evening after the surrender the 7th Bulgarian Division, under General Todorov, entered from the
north, and was assigned the church of St. George and
the eastern section of the city.   Next day there also
arrived a Serb cavalry regiment, which had pushed down
the valley of the Vardar after Kumanovo; but finding its
presence unnecessary, it retraced its steps a few days
later to Veles, and after rapid marching arrived before
Monastir in time for the battle.

From the very first there was serious friction between
the Greeks and Bulgars at Salonica, the latter even proclaiming themselves as the first-comers until the full facts
became known, and reproaching the Turks for not sur-
rendering to them as the strongest of the allies.   Regarding themselves as the natural reversionaries of Macedonia, they claimed Salonica as a necessary appendage
to its hinterland.   But the fortune of war had given
priority to a nation whose acquisitiveness throws even
that of the Bulgars into the shade, and as the two momentary allies had embarked upon the war without any
agreement with regard to sharing the spoils, the Greeks
were fully within their rights in acting upon the motto
" *J'y suis, j'y reste.*"

The Greeks, having thus accomplished their main
object, at once offered to send four divisions to the aid
of the Bulgarians in Thrace : but the offer was not
unnaturally declined, from the fear lest it might provide
Greece with an opportunity of pegging out a further
claim in what Bulgaria regarded as her exclusive sphere
of influence.   Greek transports were supplied for the
conveyance of 13,000 Bulgarian troops from Salonica to

Dedeagač; but under the circumstances no credit accrues to the Greeks for this service, since they were thereby ridding themselves of a dangerous rival.

After the battle of Serfidje one section of the beaten Turkish army had retreated in the direction of Florina and Monastir. Tahsim Pasha's troops being utterly demoralised and no longer capable of taking the offensive, the Greeks ought, from a purely strategic point of view, to have concentrated against the western Turkish column and driven it back upon Monastir, thus opening the way for active co-operation with the Serbs and placing Zekki Pasha and the main Turkish army between two fires. The final defeat of Zekki would at once render hopeless all further resistance on the part of Tahsim. But political considerations were for the moment more urgent than reasons of strategy, and the Crown Prince decided to make sure of Salonica before all else. Hence the column dispatched northwards from Serfidje towards the Lake of Ostrovo only consisted of 11,000 men, under Colonel Matthiopoulos. On 29th October this little army met with unexpected resistance at the village of Nalbandkoj, but drove back the Turks, who were still inferior in numbers, with a loss of over 1,000 men and 4 guns. On 1st November the Greeks occupied the passes and village of Banica almost unopposed, and the road to Monastir already seemed open, when the tables were turned with dramatic suddenness. Djavid Pasha, though not allowed to carry out his plan of campaign in its entirety, hastened southwards with greatly superior forces, and, fiercely attacking the Greeks at Banica, drove them back upon Sorović with the loss of 500 men and 12 guns (2nd November). Here fighting was resumed on the two following days, but the Greeks, though hard pressed by a flanking movement of the Young Turk leader Niazi Bey, were able to hold their own in entrenched positions. Djavid Pasha's initiative was thus brought to a standstill, and the threatened Serb advance from the north forced him to return, with most of his troops, to Monastir. But the Greek advance had been effectually checked, and Turkish and Albanian bands wreaked their vengeance upon the Greek and Vlach peasantry in the mountainous district lying to the west of the Greek occupation.[1] It is only fair to add that the behaviour of the Turkish troops, as distinguished from the irregular forces employed, appears to have been exemplary throughout the war.

On 14th November Crown Prince Constantine left Salonica at the head of four divisions, and advanced by forced marches. After several sharp skirmishes with the Turks near the Lake of Ostrovo (17th-18th November), Banica was reoccupied by the Greeks, and on 20th November the allied Greek and Serb forces met at Florina. But despite every effort the Greeks arrived two days too late; for after his defeat at Monastir Zekki Pasha, with 15,000 men, had effected his escape through Florina in a south-westerly direction. On 21st November the pursuing Greeks fought a rearguard action with him at Pissoderi, but failed to bring him to a halt; and he eventually made his way to Janina, thus greatly strengthening the garrison's powers of resistance. Zekki's escape reflects no discredit upon the Greeks, for the consequences fell not upon their allies, but upon themselves alone, and subsequent events have proved that they would have paid for a too rapid concentration against Monastir by the loss of Salonica to the Bulgarians.

Parallel with the main advance from the Thessalian frontier, General Sapundzakis had invaded Epirus with 10,000 regular troops and numerous bands. Advancing slowly from the south, he had a violent encounter with the Turks under Essad Pasha at Gribovo (24th October)

[1] Especially below Kastoria and Grevena.

and drove them back upon Janina. Prevesa fell on 1st November, but the Greeks were not strong enough for further offensive action until a fresh detachment of 4,000 men, crossing the passes of the Pindus, occupied Metsovon (14th November) and thus began to turn the Turkish flank. By 25th November Janina was invested from three sides, but the great natural strength of its position and the inferior forces at the command of the Greeks made it impossible for them to complete the circle on the northern side. Thus the way was open to Zekki Pasha, whose arrival with 15,000 fresh troops placed the Turks in a position of marked superiority,[1] and destroyed all hope of capturing the town until the arrival of considerable reinforcements. It was above all this consideration which led Greece to decline the armistice now about to be concluded by her three allies, and to continue with renewed vigour the campaign in Epirus.

Though the land forces of Greece did not, as we have seen, exercise any decisive influence upon the early course of the war, the strategic importance of the Greek navy cannot easily be exaggerated. Such naval engagements as took place[2] were not of a very serious character, though the Greek sailors showed great gallantry. But the essential fact remains that the Greeks were able to retain the mastery of the Ægean and thus to prevent the possibility of Turkish reinforcements being sent by sea to the western area. The tortuous Dedeagač-Salonica railway was thus the only available connection with Macedonia, and as this not merely proved to be quite unequal to the severe strain put upon it, but was much

[1] Probably not fewer than 36,000, including 7,000 to 8,000 Albanians. The Greeks only had 24,000 men, exclusive of bands. Cf. Immanuel, II., p. 100-2.

[2] A useful account will be found in Cassavetti, *Hellas and the Balkan Wars*; those who wish to study the naval operations in detail, may be referred to Hans Rohde, *Die Ereignisse zur See und das Zusammenwirken von Heer und Flotte im Balkankrieg*."

exposed to raids from the north, Macedonia was almost from the first isolated and left to its own resources. It must, however, be remembered that the Greek command of the sea was hardly less serviceable to Bulgaria than to Greece and Serbia; for it prevented the Turks from shipping their troops from Smyrna to Dedeagač and Gallipoli as well as to Salonika, and thus limited them to the devious course of the Anatolian railway. A reference to the map of Asia Minor will render superfluous any commentary upon this fact. During the decisive weeks of the war all reinforcements for Thrace had to pass through the capital, and the flagrant disorganisation of the Turkish railway system effectually prevented the transport of large masses of troops to the front. Command of the sea would have solved the whole problem of transport. To take only two instances, the Bulgarian right wing, which decided the issue of the battle of Lüle Burgas, could not have acted as it did if Dedeagač and Enos had been available for the landing of Turkish reinforcements, while in the second stage of the war the Bulgarian operations against Bulair could never even have been attempted, if the Gulf of Xeres had been accessible to the Turkish fleet. Seldom in history has there been so striking an object-lesson of the value of sea-power, and when we consider the very inadequate equipment of the Greek fleet, the far-reaching consequences of its superiority seem all the more remarkable.

CHAPTER XIV

THE SECOND PHASE OF THE WAR

On 4th December, 1912, the armistice came into force between Turkey on the one hand and Bulgaria, Serbia, and Montenegro on the other. Outside Skutari, however, hostilities did not cease, since the Turkish commander refused to be bound by an arrangement of which he had no official intimation from headquarters. Meanwhile Greece declined to accept the armistice and continued the war. This decision was prompted by her obvious desire to reduce Janina and to complete her occupation of the Ægean islands. But it is possible that there were other contributory motives, and that Greece was secretly encouraged by her allies in a step which would effectually prevent the Turks from moving up fresh troops by sea.

On the Turkish side, the armistice gave the authorities a welcome opportunity of strengthening still further the lines of Tchataldja, stamping out the cholera, restoring discipline to the army, and augmenting it by Asiatic levies. The Fabian tactics so dear to Turkish diplomacy might be employed with the reasonable hope that international complications would enable the Porte to extricate itself from an otherwise hopeless situation. Meanwhile the Bulgarians were far nearer the end of their resources than they cared to admit; the exhaustion following upon heavy losses had been increased by a serious outbreak of cholera. They had reached the

utmost limit of territorial expansion and might reason-
ably hope to reduce Adrianople without a costly assault.
The Serbs, for their part, had achieved complete success
and had nothing further left to fight for; while the
Montenegrins looked to the Great Powers to secure for
them what they had failed to win by force of arms.

The conditions of the truce fall under three main heads.
The armies were to remain in their positions; the
besieged towns were not to be revictualled; and the terms
of peace were referred to a Conference in London. On
16th December the delegates of the five States met at
St. James's Palace, Turkey being represented by Mustafa
Reshid Pasha, a former Ambassador in Rome and
Vienna, and Osman Nizami Pasha, the acting Ambassa-
dor in Berlin; Bulgaria by the President of the Sobranje
Dr. Danev, General Paprikov, and the Minister in
London, M. Madjarov; Serbia by the historian and
former Premier Dr. Novaković, the President of the
Skupština M. Nikolič, and the Minister in Paris, M.
Vesnić; Greece by her distinguished Premier Mr.
Venizelos, and the Greek Ministers in London and
Vienna, MM. Gennadius and Streit; Montenegro by the
ex-Premier Mr. Miušković and the Croat historian Count
Lujo Vojnović.   No such representative meeting of
Balkan statesmen had taken place since the Christian
states of the peninsula first came into being.

The allies at once laid claim to the whole of European
Turkey, except the Dardanelles and the immediate
neighbourhood of Constantinople, Bulgaria in particular
insisting upon access to the Sea of Marmora at Rodosto.
The Turks met these uncompromising demands with
delay and prevarication and relied upon the support of
the Great Powers in a matter which affected the delicate
question of the Straits. The persistence with which
the Roumanian Government urged upon Bulgaria its
claim   for   territorial   compensation   still   further

strengthened the Turks in their *non possumus*
attitude. The meetings of the conference soon
became a mere formality, while the real negotiations
took the shape of elaborate intrigues behind the scenes.
At length, when a month had been wasted in
truly Byzantine methods of diplomacy, the Great
Powers, showing quite unexpected unanimity, presented a Joint Note to the Porte (18th January, 1913)
advising the cession of Adrianople to Bulgaria, and
adding the outspoken warning that a resumption of the
war might involve the loss of Constantinople itself. The
bitter pill thus offered to the Turks was gilded by the
somewhat equivocal promise to reserve the questions of
the Ægean islands and of a war indemnity for the decision of the European Concert, and considerable loans
were held in prospect, should Turkey show herself amenable to reason. The veteran Grand Vizier, Kiamil
Pasha, unable of himself to assume so grave a responsibility, laid the proposals of the Powers before a specially
convoked Council of Notables, which, in sanctioning
compliance, implicitly recognised Europe's right of
mediation between Turkey and the Balkan League (22nd
January). But this complete surrender roused the Chauvinist forces of the Turkish capital to a final effort, and
on the following day the Young Turk leader, Enver Bey,
and his adherents forced their way into the presence of
the Cabinet, dictated to Kiamil his resignation, and shot
down the Commander-in-Chief, Nazim Pasha, in the
ante-room. This murder, like that of the Mexican
President, Madero, a few months later, was lightly
passed off as a regrettable misunderstanding, and the
spoils of power were once more in the hands of the Committee of Union and Progress. But though the new
Cabinet raised the cry that the national honour was in
danger and that Adrianople must be held to the bitter
end, there is good reason to suspect that motives of

personal ambition were the dominant factor in the revolution. No one was better aware than Mahmud Shevket
Pasha, the new Vizier, of the hopelessness of further
aggressive action; and though repudiating his predecessor's answer to the Powers, his Government only five
days later put forward the relatively moderate proposal
that the river Marica should form the new frontier. In
view of the united front presented by the Great Powers,
there can be little doubt that the Turks would soon have
made further concessions and that a renewal of the war
might have been avoided. Unfortunately, the Balkan
delegates in London took the protestations of the Young
Turks at their face value, and immediately broke off the
negotiations (28th January). This result was due, above
all, to the arrogance of the Bulgarian delegates, who, not
content with displaying an absolute rigidity in their
dealings with the Turks, intrigued with Austria-Hungary behind the backs of their Serbian colleagues and
steadily repelled all the overtures of the Greek Premier
in favour of the amicable discussion of disputed points
between Greece and Bulgaria.

On 3rd February hostilities were resumed, but their
character was widely different from that of the war in
its earlier stages. Rapid advance and fiery onslaught
were, except on rare occasions, replaced by slow and
deliberate move and counter-move. The only hope of
the Turks lay in assuming the offensive, but such a task
was altogether beyond their powers, despite all the
improvements which had been effected during the seven
weeks' truce. The cholera had been stamped out, the commissariat reorganised, discipline restored, and new troops
assembled; but the spirit of initiative, the soul of the
army, was lacking. On the Bulgarian side all idea of
occupying Constantinople had been finally abandoned,
and every effort was concentrated upon the reduction of
Adrianople. The First and Third Armies, amounting

to 132,000 men, were still left outside Tchataldja, but in order to avoid needless skirmishes and bloodshed, were withdrawn before the middle of February to a strong position on the Ergene, from whence any fresh movement on the part of the Turks could be at once observed and checked.

The Turks, recognising that an advance from Tchataldja could only end in failure, conceived the idea of moving upon Adrianople from the Dardanelles, and for this purpose began to strengthen their forces on the isthmus of Gallipoli. Shortly before the conclusion of the armistice the Bulgarians, foreseeing the possibility of such a move, had pushed the Fourth Army, under General Kovačev, southwards from Dimotika towards Bulair. On the resumption of hostilities Bulair at once became the centre of sharp fighting (4th-7th February). The Turks, under the command of Hurshid Pasha and his chief of staff, Enver Bey, laid their plans for a general attack from the isthmus, to be supported by a landing of the Tenth Army Corps in the rear of the Bulgarian position, under cover of the fleet. The battle began in earnest on 8th February, but as both the Turkish wings, advancing from Gallipoli, received a very decided check, their co-operation with Hurshid Pasha completely broke down, and those troops which had already landed had to be hastily re-embarked and withdrawn to Gallipoli. Severe weather put an end to further action, and the last danger of a serious Turkish initiative vanished. Coast batteries were erected by the Bulgarians to prevent any further landing. The battle of Bulair proved that the Bulgarians had lost none of their original valour and endurance, and definitely sealed the fate of Adrianople. As in the earlier stages of the war, false reports were spread abroad regarding the aims and intentions of the Bulgarians, and Western public opinion seriously credited them with the design of seizing the Dardanelles

for themselves and admitting the Greek fleet into the
Sea of Marmora.   In reality their sole aim was to hold
back the Turks from the beleaguered city, and when this
object had once been attained, fighting virtually ceased
outside Bulair, as outside Tchataldja.

Meanwhile the siege of Adrianople was resumed with
fresh vigour, but Shükri Pasha had employed the period
of the armistice in strengthening his defences and in
erecting an elaborate system of wire entanglements.   The
city's food supply was quite adequate.   The besieging
army, under General Ivanov, consisted of 60,000 Bulgarians and 47,000 Serbs, while the garrison did not greatly
exceed 40,000 men.   The Bulgarians, however, were
handicapped by the lack of heavy siege guns, and it was
not until the arrival of the Serb siege train, consisting
of 38 guns (12 and 15 centimetre) on 14th February that
the bombardment could be entirely effective.   Moreover,
operations were hampered by terrible snowstorms during
the second half of February; and the troops suffered
severely from lack of shelter, from bad water, and even
from a partial breakdown of the commissariat.   On 11th
February the rations of the Bulgarian troops were reduced from 300 to 150 grammes;[1] and this doubtless
accounts both for General Ivanov's refusal to admit correspondents to the lines and also for the circumstance that
his Serb allies were left to provide their own supplies from
distant Serbia.   Privation bred disease, and the Bulgarians
lost heavily from dysentery, typhus, and even cholera.

From the end of February the exposed sectors of the
fortress, especially those on the north-east and east, were
repeatedly bombarded, and the besiegers crept steadily
nearer.   At length, on 24th March, the order was given
for a general assault, and after an artillery duel lasting
eight hours several of the advanced positions were
stormed at dead of night by the Bulgarians, who in some

[1] *Cf.* Barby, p. 224.

cases got within 100 yards unchallenged. Once more they displayed their prowess with the bayonet, and under cover of a thick fog were able to move their artillery into the captured positions. Meanwhile the garrison held its own against the Serbs and Bulgars in the west and south; but on the north-west the First Timok Division of the Serbs stormed the forts and repelled a strong counter-attack, though supported by nothing more than field artillery. On the following night (25th–26th March) the assault was resumed with even greater success; the Turkish resistance was broken, and an entrance was effected almost simultaneously by the Bulgarians on the east and south and by the Serbs on the west. Shükri Pasha, with 12 Pashas, 1000 officers, 38,500 men, and 600 guns, fell into the hands of the allies. On examination it transpired that the much-vaunted fortifications of Adrianople fell far short of modern scientific requirements, and that an assault might have been hazarded three months earlier with reasonable prospects of success. While the Turkish resistance cannot be compared to that offered by Osman Pasha at Plevna, it worthily vindicated the honour of the Turkish army and earned for Shükri the coveted epithet of "Ghazi."

Unhappily, this splendid victory was marred by an undignified dispute between the allies, each claiming the distinction of having captured the Turkish Commander-in-Chief. It is not easy to reconcile the rival versions of this affair, but there is no reason to doubt the good faith of all parties concerned. In the absence of detailed information, we are limited to the following facts :—that the Bulgarian Colonel Markolev accepted Shükri Pasha's *parole* about 10 a.m. on 26th March, but subsequently withdrew and left him unguarded; that at 1 p.m. the 20th Serb Regiment, on entering Fort Haderluk, found Shükri Pasha, attended by 2 generals and 216 officers, but not a single Bulgarian soldier; that its commander,

Colonel Gavrilović, in his turn, accepted Shükri's surrender; and that an official written receipt was given by General Ivanov to his Serb colleague, General Stepanović, when Shükri Pasha was handed over to the Bulgarians next day.[1]

It would have been well to draw a veil over this quarrel but for the light which it throws upon the psychology of the two allied peoples during the second war. The cordial telegram of Ivanov :—" This work will show the enemies of the Slavs what a sincere alliance and union among them can accomplish "—was soon to receive a melancholy commentary; for there can be no doubt that the five months of co-operation outside Adrianople, instead of cementing the alliance, actually increased the estrangement which political differences were evoking. The Bulgar combines with many admirable qualities an extreme frugality which his neighbours regard as niggardly and mean; his immobile and unadaptable nature betrays him into an arrogant self-confidence which distrusts the warnings of his friends and minimises the strength of his opponents. The faults of the Serb are far more suggestive of the Celtic temperament. A certain lack of balance leads him into alternate extremes of self-depreciation and megalomania. Ever the plaything of sentiment, he is easily roused to anger and as easily reconciled. The Serb, when a favour is asked of him, is too proud to exact his price; the Bulgar, to whom an offer is made, is too canny to refuse it, and assuming from his own experience that nothing is given for nothing, is only too ready to exact his pound of flesh and haggle with his dearest friend. The risk of a misunderstanding between two such different natures increased in proportion to the length of the war. The Bulgarians, belittling the

---

[1] *Cf.* Barby, p. 249; Balcanicus, *Serben und Bulgaren,* and General Ivanov's published statement.

achievements of the Serbs in Macedonia, treated their
ready assistance before Adrianople as a matter of course
and nursed a grievance against the Voivode Putnik for
only sending two instead of three divisions. This army,
which Serbia was under no treaty obligation to provide,
was not merely expected to supply all its wants from
home, but was charged freight for all that it transported
on the Bulgarian railways, and on its return to Serbia
in April, 1913, a bill was presented by Sofia for transport expenses. Though the coinage of both countries
belongs to the Latin Union and the credit of Belgrade
was no worse at the outbreak of war than that
of Sofia, yet the Government of the latter imposed an agio of 10 per cent. on all Serbian money
circulating in Bulgaria, and this was rigorously
exacted even from the Serb soldiers outside the
besieged city. Not content with charging customs
dues on the Red Cross material so freely supplied by
Russia for the benefit of their own troops, the Bulgarians
actually refused to allow the remains of fallen Serb soldiers to be sent home to Serbia until the representative
of the dead man had deposited a sum of 200 francs to
defray expenses. The indignant resentment on the part
of poor Serbian peasants at such meanness on the part
of their " brothers " can easily be imagined. After the
fall of Adrianople the Serbs were not invited to share in
the triumphal entry, and on their homeward passage
through Bulgaria they were not the objects of a single
demonstration of friendship or gratitude. When
General Stepanovič—himself a pronounced Bulgaro-
phile—passed through Sofia, the Bulgarian authorities
did not even send an official representative to greet him
at the station ! The effect of such incidents upon the
temper of the Serbian private soldier was only too
apparent when, in May, 1913, I visited near Kumanovo
the camps of some regiments which had then recently
returned from Adrianople.

EPIRUS.

For very obvious reasons Greece had declined to enter upon the armistice with her three allies, and during December and January proceeded steadily with the occupation of the Ægean Islands. On 2nd January the Turkish garrison of Chios surrendered, and soon afterwards Lesbos and the autonomous island of Samos followed their example.

In Epirus operations moved much more slowly. The garrison of Janina, as reinforced by the fragments of the Vardar army, was numerically much superior to the Greek forces, and held one of the strongest natural positions in the peninsula. Thus no real aggression was possible until four fresh Greek divisions could be transferred by sea to Prevesa and Santi Quaranta; and it was not till 23rd January that the Crown Prince assumed command before Janina and organised the attack with great vigour. The bad weather which prevailed throughout February gave rise to further delays; but in the first week of March a heavy bombardment was opened on the south and east, while the Greek left stormed several of the heights commanding the western portion of the town (1st–5th March). A fresh assault had already been ordered, when negotiations were opened by Essad Pasha, and on 6th March Janina surrendered unconditionally to Crown Prince Constantine. Hunger and lack of ammunition rendered further resistance useless, and the Greek losses were relatively immaterial. Nearly 23,000 Turks became prisoners of war, but Essad Pasha, with at least 7000 men, took advantage of the interval between the opening of pourparlers and the actual surrender to escape northwards into Albania.[1] The capture of Janina

---

[1] He is not to be confused with the well-known Albanian leader of the same name, who succeeded Hassan Riza in the command of Skutari.

was due in great part to previous neglect of its fortifications, the indifferent quality of its garrison, and the shortage of supplies; but this in no way detracts from the achievement of the Greek Crown Prince, who finally and completely revindicated his military reputation.

Skutari.

We have already seen that the Turkish commandant, Hassan Riza, declined to recognise the existence of the armistice, under the pretext of having received no instructions from his Government. In reality his object was to maintain the irregular connection with the northern Albanian tribes, to which he owed the replenishing of his stores and ammunition; and he cleverly reckoned that the continuance of hostilities with Montenegro would increase the chances of European intervention in favour of Albania, without adding materially to the risk of capture. Thus throughout December and January there were repeated encounters, but no operations on a large scale. After the official resumption of the war in February, the Montenegrins strained every nerve to reduce Skutari to submission, and King Nicholas appealed to Serbia for help. The Voivode Putnik placed three divisions and some heavy guns at his disposal, and on 7th February a general assault was directed by the two allies against the main positions of Tárabóš and Brdica. But once more the garrison held its own, and the attack was beaten off with terribly heavy losses. A fresh pause was ordered, while further Serbian reinforcements and siege guns were shipped from Salonica to Medua on Greek transports; but early in March the Montenegrins resumed the bombardment. With every fresh delay the political difficulties increased; for the Great Powers, yielding to the importunity of Austria-Hungary and Italy, had definitely decided upon the inclusion of Skutari

in the new Albanian state, and Austrian troops were
being steadily massed along the Dalmatian and Bosnian
frontiers, with a view to enforcing the nominal wishes
of Europe upon recalcitrant Montenegro. On 31st March
the general assault was resumed, this time under the
supervision of the Serbian general Bojević, but again
without success. At this stage Hassan Riza, who steadily
declined to sanction the departure of the civil population,
was treacherously murdered by an Albanian; but his
successor, Essad Pasha, in answer to a summons of the
besiegers, proclaimed his resolve to defend the town till
the last man had fallen. Meanwhile the pressure of the
Powers assumed a new form, and it was only the
unwearying mediation of Sir Edward Grey that prevented the keen divergence of opinion between Vienna
and St. Petersburg from leading to an open rupture.
Isolated Austrian intervention could only be averted by
the clumsy expedient of a combined naval demonstration. On 10th April there opened the farcical spectacle
of the fleets of the five Great Powers (Russia held aloof)
defying a persistent scirocco along the unfriendly Montenegrin coast, in order, forsooth, to blockade Antivari
and Dulcigno, two ports whose commercial importance
may be compared to that of Mallaig or Tobermory!
From his mountain eyrie King Nicholas scoffed at the
distant fleet and declined to suspend operations against
Skutari. A thick veil of mystery still shrouds the subsequent proceedings; but enough has transpired to show
that the actual combatants were mere pawns in an elaborate game of intrigue between Skutari, Cetinje, Belgrade,
Constantinople, Vienna, and Rome. Vienna had been
prepared to acquiesce in the cession of Skutari to Montenegro; but the price demanded was nothing less than
the mountain peak of Lovčen, which dominates the Austrian naval base in the Bocche di Cattaro. It is just possible that King Nicholas might have thrown poetic

tradition to the winds and ceded a position upon which the defensibility of Cetinje depends, in return for a new and far better situated capital at Skutari. The hostility of Italy had hitherto been regarded as the chief obstacle to an arrangement which would have rendered Austria supreme on the eastern Adriatic; but this, though serious, could probably have been overcome by concessions farther down the coast. The decisive factor in the situation was the attitude of Russia, who left the Ballplatz in no doubt that the acquisition of Lovčen by Austria would be regarded as a hostile act. Russian public opinion approved of this attitude as the defence of a small kinsman against a powerful bully; but Austrian statesmen, of course, treated it as a further proof that the Panslav designs of Russia reach far beyond the Dardanelles and include even the Adriatic within their aggressive sphere. The exact date of this veto is not easily determined; but from a fact within the knowledge of the present writer it would be possible to infer that up to the very last moment Austria was prepared for a bargain. Within a week of the actual fall of Skutari military supplies, unshipped from Austrian or Hungarian vessels, were finding their way from southern Dalmatia to Cetinje! This involves either direct connivance on the part of the authorities or a combination of treachery and corruption which there are no adequate grounds for assuming.

Meanwhile the Cabinet of Belgrade, afraid of jeopardising the result of previous victories, saw itself obliged to yield to the urgent representations of Vienna and to order the withdrawal of the Serbian army from before Skutari. But here again the facts belied appearances, and though General Bojević countermanded an assault which was to have taken place within three hours of the actual receipt of his new orders, the Serbian artillery was left in position and the Serbian troops which now began to re-embark under the eyes of the international fleet were those which could best be spared from the siege. With the utmost secrecy negotiations were opened between King Nicholas and Essad Pasha, who conferred with some high Montenegrin officers regarding possible terms of surrender. Both Belgrade and Constantinople had a hand in the game, and a plot of truly Oriental ingenuity was concocted. When at the critical moment the Austro-Hungarian Legation at Cetinje got wind of the affair and dispatched its military attaché to Cattaro with the news, the Montenegrin Government did not scruple to declare the frontier closed and to delay his exit by rendering the only road impassable for motor traffic. On 23rd April Essad Pasha formally surrendered Skutari to the Montenegrins; the garrison marched out with the honours of war, carrying with them the greater part of their military stores. As in the case of Djavid Pasha at Berat in the previous December, the presence of a Turkish general and army in northern Albania deprived the interested Powers of all excuse for armed intervention. Neither Austria-Hungary nor Italy was entitled to be more Turcophil than the Turks. Essad Pasha, himself a powerful Albanian feudal chief, returned to his estates at Tirana, a prosperous little town lying to the east of Durazzo, and devoted his time to consolidating his influence in the northern and central districts and intriguing against the phantom Government of Valona. There can be no doubt that his proclamation as King of Albania was seriously contemplated, that the Governments of Cetinje and Belgrade, realising that the veto of the Powers upon their own territorial designs must be obeyed, would have welcomed the candidature of a native Moslem chief for the new throne, and that the scheme was secretly aided and abetted from Constantinople. The various foreign candidates would thus be forestalled and Essad Pasha would obviously, from the necessities of the case, be a more complaisant neighbour in questions of frontier regulation. The numerous cross-currents which contributed to the conception and failure of this design will perhaps never be known, but it may confidently be described as one of the prettiest intrigues in recent European history.

The triumph of the Montenegrins was short-lived. In view of the continued insistence of the Great Powers, their troops were withdrawn from Skutari early in May, and the maintenance of order was assigned to detachments of bluejackets from the international fleet, under the command of Admiral Burney. Meanwhile the Serbs had evacuated Durazzo and withdrawn their troops behind the artificial frontier laid down by the Ambassadors' Conference in London. Only in the wild Ljuma district between Dibra and Prizren did they still maintain advance posts, in the vain hope that a revision of frontier might be secured in accordance with the natural geographical boundaries. The final withdrawal of the Serbs in the autumn of 1913, at the peremptory summons of Austria-Hungary, was the signal for a formidable Albanian raid against Dibra and Tetovo, which of course in its turn led to severe reprisals by the Serbs.

The fall of Skutari was the last incident of the war. On 16th April the armistice had been renewed between Turkey and Bulgaria, and it was soon afterwards extended to the three other combatants. Peace negotiations were then resumed in London, but progress was as slow as ever. The allies, after the additional sacrifices of the past three months, were naturally disinclined to abate any of their original demands, while the successors of Kiamil Pasha could not decently sanction terms which a short time before had formed their excuse for a revolution. Moreover, the growing dissensions among the allies regarding the division of the spoils encouraged the Turks to hope for complications such as might assign to them the *rôle* of *tertius gaudens*. Before the delegates could be brought to business, it was necessary for Sir Edward Grey to abandon for once his suave reserve and bluntly to inform them that unless they were prepared to conclude peace without further delay, they had better leave London altogether. This intimation, combined with diplomatic pressure behind the scenes, at last produced the desired effect, and on 30th May, 1913, the Treaty of London was concluded between Turkey and the Balkan League, still regarded as a unit. Only in one particular did its terms differ very materially from those accepted by Kiamil Pasha. Bulgaria renounced her claim to a port upon the Sea of Marmora and contented herself with a frontier running from Enos, near the outlet of the Marica into the Ægean, to Midia, on the Black Sea. The details were to be settled later by a special commission. Crete was definitely ceded to the allies, but the future status of the other Turkish islands in the Ægean and of the peninsula of Mt. Athos was left to the decision of the Powers, to whom also was assigned the task of prescribing the frontiers and constitutional position of the new-born Albanian state. The financial questions arising from the war, notably the apportionment of liability for the Ottoman Debt, were referred to a special conference in Paris, at which the belligerent states and the Great Powers were all to be represented. Special conventions were to regulate the exchange of prisoners and both commercial and religious disputes arising out of the war.

From the very first the Treaty of London was regarded as a mere *provisorium*. The allies had shown remarkable restraint and unity of purpose during the long campaign, and had resolutely postponed their internal jealousies until the enemy could be completely crushed. But this very postponement, following upon the terri-

torial surprises of November and December and the long
strain of the spring, had crystallised the rival claims,
whetted the appetites of the claimants and rendered
mutual concession infinitely more difficult.   The unexpected creation of Albania had fatally disturbed the
balance upon which the intended partition rested, and
vital economic interests combined with reasons of race
and sentiment to stiffen the unyielding attitude of the
rivals and to accentuate the mutual charges of treachery
and intolerance.   This must form the subject of a subsequent chapter; for the moment it only remains for us
to direct attention to some of the underlying factors
of a war which revolutionised South-Eastern Europe
and directly paved the way to the far greater conflict
of 1914.

Many causes contributed to the defeat of the Turkish
arms. It has become the fashion to throw all the blame
upon the recklessness and Chauvinism of the Young
Turk *régime,* and it is certainly true that their internal
policy, combined with weak diplomacy, brought about a
political conjuncture more unfavourable to the Ottoman
state than any which it had faced for generations. Both
good and bad elements in the new *régime* had their
share in this result. The promises of universal brother-
hood which were so liberally made after the Revolution
of 1908 caused serious alarm among the Christian states
of the peninsula, and for a time seemed seriously to
threaten their position as reversionary legatees to the
Sick Man's inheritance. Their selfish political interests
ran directly counter to any genuine Turkish revival,
and the exiles with whom thirty years of Hamidian misrule had crowded every Balkan capital set their whole
propaganda in action to complicate the issue. When
all too soon the Committee's liberal promises were
superseded by a policy of violent Turkification, racial
passions were revived with greater intensity than ever,

Balkan public opinion clamoured for action in favour of the victims, and acute friction between the Christian states and Turkey became inevitable. The evil influences which emanated from the Salonican lodges and the secret international forces which lurked in the background rapidly overpowered whatever idealism had possessed the Turkish reformers.

If from the political side the Young Turks are unquestionably responsible for the *débâcle* of 1912, the blame from a military point of view must rest above all with the Hamidian *régime*. The late Sultan relied less upon the force of arms than upon his own mastery of the art of diplomacy and upon the prestige of the Khalifate; and the splendid army which he had received from his brother, defeated but crowned with the laurels of Plevna, was ruined by thirty years of inaction and inquisition. The system of espionage which Abdul Hamid introduced into all branches of the public service exercised its corroding influence upon both officers and men. To such lengths was it carried that officers dared not meet together, whether for study or pleasure; that army manœuvres were abandoned for a whole generation; that military science and rifle practice alike were neglected; that the men's training was confined to the barrack square and all intercourse between officers and men virtually ceased.[1] When the Revolution came, the Turkish army had to be recreated from the very foundations—a labour of Hercules which required ten years of peace.[2] The fatal weakening of authority which resulted from the upheaval of 1908 became even more marked after the military revolt of the following year. A whole generation of incompetent officers had been passed over to make way for the young Committee plotters, and the

[1] Von der Goltz, *Der jungen Türkei Niederlage*, p. 9. It was exceptional for the men to know even the names of the higher officers, often even of the battalion commanders.

[2] *Ibid.*, p. 10.

countless feuds and intrigues to which this gave rise were multiplied tenfold by the arrogance of the new-comers and by the Court favouritism which too often determined appointments and promotions.[1] This, in its turn, engendered a factious spirit within the ranks of the Committee, and neutralised every effort of Mahmud Shevket Pasha and a few genuine army re-formers to divert all energies into purely military chan-nels. Politics and doctrinaire theories played havoc in ground already poisoned by a repudiation of the tradi-tions and tenets of Islam. While Mahmud Shevket remained at the War Office, much was done to repair the errors and omissions of the past. New instructors were summoned from abroad, large sums were spent on ammunition and equipments, the military schools were extended, new courses of training were opened and manœuvres were held near Adrianople and on a smaller scale in Macedonia. But the need for repressing the continual revolts which broke out in various parts of the Empire—in Arabia, Syria, Albania—and the further complications caused by the Tripolitan War, proved fatal to the maintenance of a steadfast policy at the War Office. Continual changes were made to meet the demands of the moment and reviving efficiency was undermined once more.

The famous German instructor, Baron von der Goltz Pasha, sums up in two brief sentences the prime secret of the Turkish defeat. " A modern army of a million men cannot be created out of nothing in three years." "Europe, in passing sentence, completely overlooked the fact that the beaten army was only three years old."[2]

[1] This is emphasised by von der Goltz, *ibid.,* p. 33.

[2] *Ibid.,* pp. 18 and 20. I leave these quotations exactly as I wrote them down in April, 1914. Every reader is to-day in a position to judge how far the military upheaval of the last two years in our own country justifies the views of the great German strategist.

The administrative chaos, the deterioration of the officers' corps, the loss of all zeal for efficiency as an end in
itself—all this could not fail to exercise a fatal influence
upon the Turkish soldier, whose peculiar psychology
has always lain at the root of Turkish military triumphs.
The new catchword of a constitution, utterly meaningless to the Anatolian or Thracian peasant, effaced the
old ideals—blind faith in the Padishah's commands and
the zest of fighting against the unbeliever.   The decay
of religious sentiment,[1] already promoted by the unortho-
doxy of the Young Turk officers, was still further
affected by the admission of Christians to the ranks.
These were, of course, quite unreliable against their
Christian kinsmen and generally took the first opportunity to desert.[2]

Such, briefly, were the antecedents of the beaten army.
The more immediate causes were faulty strategy and
overhaste, a tendency to undervalue the enemy, the lack
of good officers, and a complete breakdown of the
administration and the commissariat.   Both at Kirk
Kilisse and at Lüle Burgas many of the troops were
without food for forty-eight hours, or even longer; the
stubbornness of their resistance under such conditions
can only be described as heroic.   There were no field
kitchens or bakeries, a hopeless shortage of cloaks and
mantles, no proper protection against cold and rain,
hardly any doctors, no first-aid appliances, no attempt
at sanitary precautions, no water fit either for drinking
or for washing wounds, very often even a lack of cart-
ridges.   The railway system broke down under the strain,
and frequent collisions added to the confusion and panic.

---

[1] Cf. Sir Edwin Pears, "Turkey, Present and Future" (Contemporary Review, June, 1913).

[2] Cf. Noel Buxton, With the Bulgarian Staff.   At Lüle Burgas, however, not a single Christian soldier remained on the
Turkish side.   See Mahmud Mukhtar Pasha, op. cit., p. 164.

The roads were appalling, the bridges were often impassable or non-existent. The field telegraphs and telephones did not break down, for the simple reason that they were never in working order. The telegraph clerks could not always be relied upon, and messages were sometimes transmitted in German, because spies were suspected among them. At Kirk Kilisse—in other words at a critical point in the scheme of defence adopted—the earthworks and fortifications designed by the German advisers of the Porte seem to have remained almost entirely on paper, and the defences of Salonica, Janina, even Adrianople, had suffered from a similar neglect. The majority of the Turkish troops who first met the Bulgar attack were not regulars, but Redifs, wretchedly equipped and undisciplined, without spirit or initiative, and with incompetent officers to lead them. Indeed, many of the men did not even know how to load a rifle! In addition to all these fatal errors and omissions, the Turks, in defiance of the good advice offered by German strategists, adopted a plan of campaign which was neither truly aggressive nor truly defensive, but combined the defects of either method. In short, the leaders were at variance among themselves, and the men were altogether unequal to the task imposed upon them. In the words of one of their ablest generals, the Turks were, above all, "the victims of their own mistakes."[1]

All this may seem at first sight to belittle the achievement of Bulgaria, and, indeed, it does detract from the absurdly exaggerated accounts which filled the European Press. Public opinion, which before the war had formed far too high an estimate of the Turkish army, soon atoned for this error by a corresponding overestimate of the victorious Bulgarians. But in emphasising the absurdity of loose talk about "the new

[1] Mahmud Mukhtar Pasha, *op. cit.*, p. 180.

Napoleon " and the " Japanese of the West " we must not be accused of depreciating the splendid qualities of the Bulgarian army. War in the twentieth century, as in all past history, is decided by two main factors— leadership and *moral*. In the former the Bulgarians, without displaying any real military genius, showed themselves markedly superior to the Turks. But it is in the latter respect that they deserve the most unstinted praise. The patriotic fervour which inspired the whole nation found expression in countless acts of self-sacrifice and heroism, and imparted to the somewhat unemotional and phlegmatic Bulgarian peasant an *élan* which in the earlier stages of the war was almost irresistible. In feats of marching, in simple and uncomplaining endurance of fatigue, exposure, and pain, in their equally effective use of the bayonet and of the spade, the Bulgarians established a record of which any nation might be proud.

On the other hand, the course of the war revealed certain grave defects on the part of the Bulgarian authorities. Their sheer disregard for human life, which explains many a frontal attack that could easily have been avoided, finds its most striking illustration in the almost total neglect of sanitary arrangements. While every Serbian soldier carried two packets of first-aid appliances and knew how to use them in case of need, this simple measure had been neglected by the Bulgarians, with the result that cases of mortification and gangrene were about four times as numerous among the latter as among their allies. The strict rules of cleanliness and disinfecting precautions enforced in the Serbian camps before Adrianople account for the fact that their casualties were not merely absolutely but also relatively far lower than those of the Bulgarians. Neglect soon brought its own punishment, and the disease which sapped the vigour of the advancing army may be regarded as the main reason why their attack was not overwhelming.

A further grave error, from a national point of view, lay in their absolute refusal to differentiate. In a citizen army there can be no exemptions, but the Bulgarian system represents democracy run wild. Instead of employing the members of their all too scanty educated and professional class upon tasks of administration and organisation at the rear of the army, the authorities allowed them to follow their own natural inclination and take their chance at the front. The result has been the decimation of the *élite* of Bulgaria. At the very moment when schoolmasters and trained officials are needed in greater numbers than ever, their ranks have been terribly thinned by war. I was informed from a reliable source in Sofia that the first war cost Bulgaria no fewer than 300 officials in the judicial branch alone. The National Theatre lost its two leading actors—a terrible blow to a country whose drama is still in its infancy. The Serbs showed greater wisdom in this respect, and I shall long remember the disgust of a Serbian poet, who, instead of serving in the fighting line, had been entrusted for many months with the task of organising the supplies of fodder for the bullocks on which the whole transport system of the army depended. It had not occurred to him to write an ode to the Balkan ox, in some respects the true hero of the war ![1]

When we turn from a comparison of Turk and Bulgar to consider the relative value of the allies themselves, we at once find ourselves on extremely delicate ground. In the foregoing narrative we have attempted to place the various incidents of the war in their true perspective and to make it clear that public opinion in the West, in

---

[1] If these remarks were true when written in the spring of 1914, they have been accentuated tenfold by the events of 1914-1916.

concentrating its attention upon Bulgaria and ignoring or slurring over the achievement of her allies, was not only guilty of an injustice, but was replacing one false estimate by another and rendering itself incapable of forecasting the outcome of the second war. Several causes contributed to this mistake. The proximity of the Turkish capital invested the battlefields of Thrace with a special interest and glamour of their own. The sterling merits of Bulgaria and her army had been consistently advertised for many years, and their sudden victory seemed to prove all that had been asserted in their favour. But, above all, the ill-repute of a distant past hung over the Serbian and Greek armies, and it was rashly assumed that nothing had changed since the defeat of Slivnica in 1885 or the Thessalian rout of 1897. For at least a generation past it has been the custom of the Western Press to report nothing from Belgrade save some tit-bit of sensational scandal, nothing from Athens save the harmless chronicle of the Royal family. The revival of Serbia had remained unnoticed, and the dark shadow of the regicide obscured the country's reputation abroad. In reality great changes had taken place in the Serbian army in the years preceding the war. Perhaps in no other country are the relations between officers and men characterised by such a delightful blend of bonhomie and discipline; and competent military critics are of opinion that the fighting qualities of the Serb soldier, combining alertness and intelligence with fire and endurance, make him the equal of any soldier in Europe.[1]

The Greeks had a much easier task than any of their allies, but this fact does not detract from what was in every way a very fine performance for an army still in the course of radical reorganisation. Their peculiar

---

[1] Here again the Great War has amply vindicated what was written before its outbreak.

temperament was specially favoured by the initial successes, and in dash and enterprise they were unsurpassed
throughout the war. The best proof of the extraordinary
enthusiasm which prevailed throughout the Greek race
is the fact that over 40,000 emigrants returned from
America and other parts of the world to serve against
the hereditary enemy.

A few words must be devoted to the vexed question
of armaments. In certain quarters the Turkish *débâcle*
was acclaimed as a victory of Creusot over Krupp and
as a condemnation of the German instructors of the
Turkish army. This parrot cry, repeated by so many
superficial journalists, has not the slightest foundation
in real fact. The fault lay, not with German methods,
but with those who neglected to translate them from
theory into practice,[1] not with German guns, but with
those who were incapable of working them. A saying
ascribed to Marshal von der Goltz Pasha—that Kirk
Kilisse could hold the Prussian army at bay for three
months—was skilfully exploited as a means of extolling
the Bulgarians, who occupied it on the sixth day of the
war; but nothing was said of those premises on which
his remark was based, and in the absence of which it
simply becomes meaningless. As for the Krupp guns,
their excellence was amply demonstrated at Tchataldja,
when at last they had competent gunners behind them;
the repulse of the Bulgarians was due above all to the
superiority of the Turkish artillery.[2]

[1] *Cf.* Hochwaechter, *op. cit.,* p. 121.
[2] Even so well-informed a correspondent as M. Barby, of *Le
Journal,* who remained concealed for some weeks at the siege
of Adrianople as a Serb volunteer, seems to be firmly persuaded of
the myth of Krupp's inferiority and to have been encouraged in
this by Serbian officers. Personally, I had opportunities during
May and June, 1913, of questioning a number of Serbian line

It would be mere audacity on my part to draw military lessons from the Balkan war. But one fact has emerged with absolute certainty and cannot be emphasised too strongly—the supreme importance of psychology in war. Just as bravery is of little avail without discipline and training, so, on the other hand, even the highest efficiency depends for its effect upon the spirit of the troops. It was their superior *moral* and national enthusiasm that carried the forces of the allies to victory. The Balkan war was essentially a soldiers' war.

and artillery officers (including members of the General Staff) on this very point; but I never found a single one who would admit any inferiority on the part of Krupp. My own opinion, as that of a civilian, is, of course, worthless on this point. But the reader may be referred to Major Howell (*op. cit.*, p. 162), who found among the Bulgarian General Staff the same opinion as I elicited from their Serbian colleagues. The truth is that the products of Creusot-Schneider and of Krupp both belong to the very first class, and that each has its own special points of excellence.

CHAPTER XV

THE DISPUTE AMONG THE ALLIES

THE Treaty of London was from the very first regarded as a temporary makeshift. For the moment Turkey could withdraw into the background, but with the scarcely concealed intention of assuming the *rôle* of *tertius gaudens* in the approaching conflict between the allies. The origin of this conflict, and the various causes which actuated it, must form the subject of the present chapter.

History offers few examples of a military campaign conducted by four allies in a spirit of such loyal and harmonious co-operation as the first Balkan war. In the period preceding the first armistice the only apparent friction was that which characterised the race for Salonica and the partially successful effort of General Hasapčev to peg out a Bulgarian claim in the Macedonian capital. But though the occupation of the city was marked by several ominous incidents, an open breach was averted by the personal influence of King George and King Ferdinand; and European public opinion, which still nursed the happy illusion that Salonica was to become an international free port, overlooked for a time amid the excitements of the Prochaska affair, the dangers involved in a division of the spoils.

The dispute assumed a two-fold form : on the one hand Bulgaria's claims against Serbia, and on the other her claims against Greece. From a legal point of view the former were infinitely stronger than the latter, for they were based upon a definite treaty of partition. By it all territories occupied by the allies were to be regarded as a condominium, but a division of the spoils was to take place within three months of the final conclusion of peace, in accordance with a very clearly defined plan. The two contracting states recognised all the territory east of the river Struma as within the Bulgarian, all territory north and west of the Šar Mountains as within the Serbian, sphere of interest. The remainder, as the wording of the Agreement clearly implied, was expected to form an autonomous Macedonia; but it is expressly laid down that in event of this solution proving impossible, Serbia shall not lay claim to anything situated beyond a line drawn from a point on the Old Turco-Bulgarian frontier near Egri Palanka as far as the lake of Ochrida. The adoption of this line as the new frontier between the allies would have involved Serbia's evacuation of Ochrida, Monastir, Prilep, Veles, and Štip, but would have left her in possession of Struga, Tetovo, Skoplje (Usküb), and Kumanovo. In case of disagreement both Governments pledged themselves to accept the arbitration of the Tsar. By the secret military convention which formed a natural corollary to this treaty Bulgaria and Serbia undertook to place in the field a force of not fewer than 200,000 and 150,000 regular troops respectively.

A whole series of clauses was included to guard against various eventualities. If either Roumania or Turkey should attack Bulgaria, Serbia was bound to send 100,000 men to the latter's assistance, while Bulgaria in her turn was to render similar aid in the event of an attack upon Serbia. Above all, if Austria-Hungary should attack Serbia, Bulgaria pledged herself to supply as many as 200,000 troops in aid of the Serbs, and this was also to apply in the event of an Austrian invasion of the Sandjak, whether with or without Turkish consent. Finally, in the event of Bulgaria and Serbia simultaneously declaring war upon Turkey (as actually occurred), each of the two states was bound to dispatch an army of at least 100,000 men to the Vardar valley.

It is thus clear that a literal interpretation of the treaty must inevitably result in Bulgaria's favour. And if the first conference in London had been successful the Serbian Government would probably have had no alternative but to withdraw its troops from Monastir and Prilep. But the negotiations were broken off, and during the four weary months of hostilities which followed an entirely new situation arose. On the one hand the pæans of praise with which Europe greeted the Thracian victories completely turned the heads of the Bulgarians and betrayed them into an exaggerated estimate of their own powers and a corresponding contempt for their allies. On the other, the Serbians, having found it necessary to establish some kind of administration in the territory which they had occupied, soon began to develop that appetite which comes with eating and to show a growing reluctance to disgorge any of the spoils of war. The old controversies with regard to the racial composition of the Macedonian population were revived by the rival Chauvinists and professional statisticians of Sofia, Belgrade, and Athens, and ill-feeling was aggravated by a series of incidents in which neither the Serbian authorities nor the Bulgarian propagandists showed to advantage. The strength of the military party in Serbia, which strenuously opposed all serious concessions, found its counterpart in the influence of the Macedonian *émigrés* in Sofia, which stiffened the back of the Government and acted as an irritant upon public opinion.

The longer the war lasted, the more steadily dwindled all inclinations towards concession on either side, and by the month of June it had become clear that the only hope of averting a conflict lay in the imposition of a settlement from without. Unhappily, what little energy the Concert of Europe still possessed had been expended upon the creation of Albania and the concession of Silistria to Roumania. A really effective demonstration on the part of all the Great Powers was not to be expected, for of the two whose interests seemed most vitally affected, Austria-Hungary was openly relieved at the prospect of a dissolution of the Balkan League, while Russia, though genuinely alarmed and distressed by the dissensions of her *protégés,* was also highly reluctant to exercise the privilege of arbiter, which seemed to forecast the certain resentment of one or other of the claimants.

The difficulties of a peaceful solution may best be realised if we consider the dominant motives of the combatants in entering upon the war against the Turks. While dynastic ambition, the greed of territory, and many other reasons undoubtedly played their part, there can be no doubt that the Bulgarian nation as a whole believed itself to have embarked upon a war of liberation on behalf of their oppressed kinsmen under the Turkish yoke. To every subject of King Ferdinand Macedonia was a Bulgarian province, whose historic associations, civil and religious alike, were intimately bound up with the ancient Tsardom of Boris and Samuel. Towards Macedonia had been directed forty years of sacrifice and propaganda. The boundaries which the Tsar Liberator had proclaimed at San Stefano, but which Europe had unjustly annulled, were the watchword of a Big Bulgaria : and after a war of unexampled success nothing less could satisfy the nation.

The motives which underlay Serbia's initiative were

somewhat different. There was, of course, the same popular enthusiasm for the liberation of the Balkan Christians and for the expulsion of the Turks from Europe. But beside and beyond this was the intolerable geographical situation of the little kingdom, her imperative need for a direct connection with Montenegro, and, above all, for free access to the sea. The events of the previous eight years—the tariff war with Austria-Hungary, the Bosnian crisis, Turkey's absolute control of the introduction of war material, and a hundred minor incidents—rendered this a question of life and death for Serbia; and in concluding the Balkan alliance the calculations of her statesmen centred upon the acquisition, first, of the Sandjak and Kosovo as the means to an end, and, secondly, of a port in northern Albania as a final objective. Even before the first conference met in London, the intervention of Austria-Hungary in favour of an independent Albania had rendered the realisation of Serbia's dream in the highest degree precarious. Yielding to earnest representations from more than one quarter, her statesmen consented in principle to the evacuation of Durazzo and Medua, and refrained from exacting from Bulgaria the fulfilment of her pledge of assistance against Austrian interference. But, once shut out from the Adriatic, they were forced to look elsewhere for an outlet; and a glance at the map shows that the sole possible alternative to an outlet in northern Albania is an outlet along the valley of the Vardar. Thus southern Macedonia assumed at once an importance which it had not hitherto possessed. When once the creation of Albania had been ordained, Bulgaria's possession of Monastir and Ochrida would have destroyed the possibility of a joint Serbo-Greek frontier, such as had been contemplated by the allied Cabinets.

If, then, Salonica should remain in Greek hands, Serbia's position would be worse than before the war, for she would no longer have one, but two, customs frontiers between her and her main access to the sea, and the two countries which would block her way would no longer be moribund Turkey, with its lack of commercial enterprise and its free trade principles, but two virile and expanding national states, each with an aggressive commercial policy and a protective tariff of its own.

The conditions under which the original treaty had been concluded having thus been radically altered by the course of events, Serbia decided to put forward the plea *rebus sic stantibus* and to claim a revision of the territorial settlement.   As, however, it was not to be expected that Bulgaria would give her consent without very material compensation, Serbia endeavoured to find this in the Eastern theatre of war.

It is an open secret that Bulgaria, when entering upon the war, never contemplated the retention of any portions of the vilayet of Adrianople, Russia having, ever since San Stefano, inculcated in Sofia the doctrine that Adrianople, as a strategic key to Constantinople, lay within her sphere of influence, just as the Sandjak lay within that of Austria-Hungary till the winter of 1908. Here, too, the Turkish *débâcle* created a new situation. The Bulgarians openly claimed the Midia-Enos line as a minimum, and began to regard even Rodosto as a permanent conquest; while King Ferdinand, for once losing his grip of realities, was occupied with plans for his state entry into Constantinople, and even his proclamation as Emperor of the East.   When, then, under stress of Austrian diplomatic competition in Sofia, Russia withdrew her veto upon the cession of Adrianople to Bulgaria, her action only served to increase the arrogance and inelasticity of the Bulgarian claims.   The statesmen of Sofia were unable or unwilling to realise that Petrograd regarded this as a more than generous compensation for concessions to Serbia in Macedonia.

They stubbornly insisted upon a literal fulfilment of the treaty of alliance, and declined to admit the argument that circumstances alter cases.

During the negotiations relative to Albania, Serbia was offered from Vienna the whole valley of the Vardar, with Salonica itself, if only she would abandon her pretensions on the Adriatic.[1] But so far from being impressed by her loyal rejection of this offer, the Bulgarian delegates in London bluntly warned their Serbian colleagues that they must not expect Bulgaria's support of their Adriatic claims, and, indeed, made it clear that Bulgaria was not prepared to fulfil her treaty obligations in the event of Austrian intervention. Much may be said in favour of such an attitude, for at that moment Tchataldja and Adrianople were straining Bulgaria's entire resources, and it would not have been easy to withdraw so large a body of troops from Thrace. But this circumstance, while absolving Bulgaria from the charge of bad faith, immensely weakens her position as the vindicator of a literal interpretation of the treaty.

Not content, however, with withholding their diplomatic support, the Bulgarian delegates intrigued actively behind the backs of their colleagues at the conference. They endeavoured to induce the Ambassadors of the Great Powers to exclude the town of Dibra from the new Albania, whose frontiers were then under consideration—not that it might be incorporated with Serbia, but that it might form an outpost of Greater Bulgaria, and perhaps even supply a point of contact between Bulgaria and Montenegro.[2] The unscrupulous nature of

[1] Cf. the speech of Mr. Pašić in the Skupština, 28th May, 1914.

[2] This incident, a knowledge of which is by no means confined to Serbian diplomatic circles, received an interesting confirmation in the indiscreet interview published by Slovenec (organ of the Slovene Clericals in Laibach) in the last week of May, 1913, with a secretary of the Bulgarian Legation in London. This young diplomat, speaking in the name of his chief, expressly declared

this intrigue is best illustrated by the fact that according to the treaty which Bulgaria proclaimed as so inviolable, Dibra lies within the territory which is recognised as indisputably Serbian! As a well-known Bulgarian diplomat, M. Rizov, has since publicly admitted, the statesmen of Sofia knew from the first that they could not hope to attain their end alone, and consequently Serbian aid was essential to success. They were also very well aware that their objective, the erection of a Big Bulgaria in the widest sense of that term, would be fatal to Serbia's continued existence as an independent state, and despite that knowledge they deliberately attempted to commit Serbia to acquiescence in a Bulgarian hegemony in the peninsula. There is no longer any room for doubt that in this policy they were secretly encouraged by Austria-Hungary, who, perhaps not unnaturally, in view of the anti-Austrian clauses of the alliance, held herself to be justified in playing the part of Mephistopheles in the duel of the allies.

Meanwhile, despite growing friction, the allies were unanimous in postponing any settlement of their disputes until the close of hostilities against the common enemy. The demands of Bulgaria proved inacceptable to the Turks, and the London conference came to an abrupt close. The Serbian Government lent its unqualified support to these demands, partly from a desire to convince its ally of its loyal intentions, partly in the belief that the larger the spoils of war might be, the greater was the prospect of an amicable agreement for their division As a pledge of goodwill it had already sent a contingent of 50,000 troops to Adrianople, though no such assistance had been contemplated by the treaty;

that one of Bulgaria's special ambitions was to acquire a joint frontier with Montenegro across the Šar Mts. Incidentally, he expounded the view that the Greek Navy had injured rather than assisted Bulgaria!

and this freewill offering, in return for which the Pašić Cabinet, in opposition to the urgent advice of Marshal Putnik, refused to exact any equivalent, was now continued till the fall of the besieged city. Of equal value was the loan of Serbia's heavy siege guns, which supplied a very serious want on the part of the Bulgarians. Incidentally, it may be pointed out that the fact that a country which had been preparing for war against the Turks for a whole generation past possessed no adequate siege guns for the reduction of the chief fortress which blocked their advance, goes far towards proving the contention that Bulgaria, even in her wildest dreams, never expected to retain Adrianople. Unhappily, this assistance, as we have already seen, actually increased instead of diminished the friction.[1] The Bulgarian censor rigorously " cut " any references to the two Serbian divisions in the telegrams of foreign correspondents,[2] and public opinion in Sofia either failed to realise, or declined to admit, the sterling services which Serbia had so freely rendered to the common cause. In short, Bulgaria held out stubbornly for the treaty, the whole treaty, and nothing but the treaty.

Many further arguments have been adduced on both sides. The Serbians, for instance, point out that Bulgaria never fulfilled that clause of the treaty which pledged her to send 100,000 men to the Vardar valley; while the Bulgars reply that this provision was modified by a subsequent agreement between the Bulgarian and Serbian General Staffs on 23rd August, 1912, on the ground that further reinforcements were required for the Thracian campaign. The Serbs point out that they sent two divisions to Adrianople, and this in order to win for Bulgaria territory the acquisition of which had never been foreseen by the treaty; the Bulgarians reply

[1] See page 212.
[2] See Barby, *Bregalnitza*, p. 2.

that such works of supererogation on the part of an ally do not in any way affect the question, and that a bargain is a bargain. Such pleas, however, are of purely controversial value. The really decisive arguments lie far deeper. On the one side the possession of the Vardar valley was to Serbia a vital economic necessity : its loss would have endangered her whole future prospects of economic independence and undone all the advantages which accrued to her from victory. Bulgaria, on the other side, was intoxicated by the dream of national unity, but in her zeal allowed herself to interpret it as a right to unrestrained hegemony over the whole peninsula.

CHAPTER XVI

THE BREAK-UP OF THE BALKAN LEAGUE

THE sudden victories of the Balkan League had taken Europe completely by surprise; and the effect on public opinion in the West was heightened still further by the cordial co-operation of the four allies. By the beginning of December Europe, as voiced by her responsible statesmen, had abandoned the long-cherished principle of the *status quo,* and established in its place the more convenient formula that the allies must not be robbed of the fruits of their victories. Yet among the Great Powers there was one to whom Turkey's defeat seemed equivalent to her own. Austria-Hungary, still under the evil influence of the Aehrenthal tradition, hampered at every turn by Magyar racial policy, both in Hungary proper and, above all, in Croatia and the Southern Slav provinces of the Monarchy, proved herself incapable of modifying her Slavophobe attitude, and thus, renouncing the confidence and approval of the Slav majority among her population, gravitated slowly but surely towards a position of vassalage to Berlin. After an initial period of irresolution, following on the unexpected collapse of Turkey, Count Berchtold quite definitely rejected the overtures of the Pašić Cabinet for a commercial understanding and ordered an extensive mobilisation on the southern frontier. The notorious Prochaska

Affair and the sudden prohibition of all demonstrations in favour of the Balkan allies were outward signs of the growth of acute friction between Austria-Hungary and Serbia, whose increased prestige with her Serbo-Croat and Slovene kinsmen was intensely distasteful to Vienna and Budapest. Having based her calculations upon a Turkish victory, Austria-Hungary had to choose between one of two alternatives—either a complete and prompt reversal of her whole anti-Slav policy or the encouragement at all costs of discord between the Balkan allies. With this latter end in view—for the rival policy was never seriously considered—Austria-Hungary imposed an emphatic veto upon Serbia's access to the Adriatic. Baulked in her efforts to escape from the economic orbit of the Monarchy, the little landlocked kingdom would, it was rightly argued, look eastwards for her outlet, and thus speedily embroil herself with Bulgaria. The plot succeeded only too well. The Serbs, whose motives in going to war were almost equally national and economic, were absolutely bent upon securing an access to the sea, and Austria-Hungary's very insistence served to reveal to them the gravity of their danger. It soon became obvious that, in view of the attitude of the Great Powers, their hopes of an Adriatic port were illusory. Even Russia did not back Serbia, and on 9th November Mr. Sazonov invited the Bulgarian Government to restrain Serbia from her Adriatic designs.[1] As early as 16th December Mr. Novaković, the chief Serbian delegate to the London Peace Conference, informed the Russian Ambassador in Paris, Mr. Izvolsky, that if the Serbian claim to a port were disallowed Serbia would be forced to look for compensation beyond the frontiers fixed by the Serbo-Bulgar treaty. At an early stage in the conference the Serbian delegates were seriously perturbed by the unfriendly attitude of Mr.

---

[1] Gešov, *Balkan League,* p. 63.

Danev, who behind their backs attempted to win the Great Powers to a settlement by which Bulgaria and Montenegro would secure a common frontier, at Serbia's expense, and in defiance of that treaty which he was so ready to treat as sacrosanct when it suited his purpose. His action in stopping at Budapest to confer with leading Austrian and Hungarian statesmen, but passing through Belgrade without even exchanging greetings with his allies, was something more than mere tactlessness; indeed, there are some grounds for believing that the visit marked a fresh stage in the Austro-Bulgarian understanding which began in 1908 and reached completion in 1915.

The Bulgarians did nothing whatever to back the Serbian claim to a port,[1] and at the same time preserved an evasive silence when Mr. Venizelos pressed for an amicable discussion of the respective claims of Greece and Bulgaria, with the view of avoiding the growth of doubt and misunderstanding. The arrogance and angularity of the chief Bulgarian delegate, Mr. Danev, did much to widen the growing breach at a time when every week's delay increased the dangers to the alliance. But for Bulgaria peace might have been attained early in January; yet Serbia, whose military task was over, loyally continued the war and contributed very materially to winding up the Thracian campaign. But as the year advanced, it became obvious that the decisions of the Conference of Ambassadors had radically transformed the situation and that the treaty could not fail to be affected by the change. As a matter of fact, it was not till 1st March that Mr. Pašić officially raised the question of revision by a letter addressed to the Bulgarian Government. This step led to lengthy discussions between the latter and Mr. Spalajković, the Serbian Minister in Sofia,

[1] Mr. Gešov denies this, but produces no evidence to support his denial (*op. cit.*, p. 64).

who eventually suggested that the whole matter should be referred to arbitration.[1]

From the first the statesmen of Bulgaria displayed the same *intransigeant* spirit which had already earned Dr. Danev so unenviable a reputation in London; and the best indication of their outlook lies in the fact that as early as 5th April, 1913, a Cabinet Council held at Adrianople under the presidency of King Ferdinand resolved to negotiate secretly with the Turks for an armistice and to transfer the army as soon as possible against the Serbs and Greeks.[2]

It is not clear whether this was known at the time to Belgrade and Athens, but the uncompromising attitude of the Bulgars was patent even to the most superficial observer; and it is difficult to blame the Serbian and Greek Governments for discussing precautionary measures. The first germ of an arrangement may be traced to informal conversations in London, when Mr. Venizelos, alarmed at Dr. Danev's abrupt rejection of his overtures, discussed the future with the Serbian delegates. A further stage was reached on 23rd January, when Prince Alexander paid a visit to Prince Nicholas of Greece at Salonica. The visit had been prompted by a disquieting rumour that Greece had made a secret bargain with Bulgaria, by which she was to retain Salonica in return for ejecting the Serbs from Monastir. The two princes having traced the origin of the story in a flimsy intrigue to set Greece and Serbia at loggerheads, passed on to a general discussion of the situation and were soon able to convince each other of their common interests.[3] On 10th March a second meeting

---

[1] Gešov, *op. cit.*, p. 74.

[2] General Savov in *Dnevnik* of 29th May, 1914, *cit.* Balcanicus, *op. cit.*, p. 3.

[3] Crawfurd Price, *The Balkan Cockpit*, p. 237. Mr. Price played a part in these negotiations not altogether dissimilar to

took place between the two princes, and this time serious negotiations were entered upon, which ended in an agreement with regard to the future Serbo-Greek frontier and foreshadowed joint action in the event of a Bulgarian attack upon either of her neighbours.[1] The assassination of King George on 18th March undoubtedly removed a real bulwark of peace and strengthened the hands of the Greek military party. George I., a monarch of experience and moderation, was succeeded by his son, Constantine, a man of obstinate temper and limited political intelligence, unreasonably jealous of the great statesman whom he found at the head of affairs, and, above all, eager to increase his own military prestige.

The growing tension between the allies and the clandestine efforts of Austro-Hungarian diplomacy to accentuate it still further, were viewed with growing alarm by Mr. Sazonov, who at first made no secret of his regret that the Serbian Government should have raised the question of revision, and on 17th April definitely expressed disapproval of the Serbo-Greek negotiations, as bound to lead to a disruption of the Balkan alliance. That the Russian Foreign Minister was fully alive to both sides of the question was shown by the warning which his representative conveyed to the Government of Sofia on 28th April, to the effect that an armed conflict would not merely expose Bulgaria to real danger from Roumania, but would tend to alienate public opinion in Russia itself, and would render the Treaty of 1912 null and void.[2] It was further suggested that the Balkan Premiers would do well to meet for an amicable discussion of the whole question. On 30th April Mr. Nekljudov and Mr. Hartwig,[3] acting upon

that played by Mr. Bourchier at an earlier stage between Sofia and Athens.   [1] *Ibid.*, pp. 240–1.

[2] Balcanicus, *The Aspirations of Bulgaria*, p. 2.

[3] The Russian Ministers at Sofia and Belgrade.

identical instructions, intimated the regret of Russia at the budding quarrel, and pointedly reminded the allies of the stipulation by which "every dispute concerning the interpretation and application of the treaty and the military convention must be submitted to the arbitration of Russia."[1] A week earlier Russia had proposed simultaneous demobilisation by the rival claimants, and on the 29th both General Savov and his Chief of Staff, General Fičev, appear to have advised the Cabinet to comply, though in point of fact with the object of postponing the attack upon their allies until the autumn.

As at this moment the Skutari crisis was at its height and Austria-Hungary seemed likely to proceed to extreme measures against the two Serbian kingdoms, it is by no means impossible that Sofia reckoned upon securing Macedonia peacefully, after they had been reduced to impotence by an attack from the north. On 2nd May that able exponent of the extreme Bulgarian view, Mr. Bourchier, telegraphed the inspired warning that a Serbo-Bulgarian collision could only redound to the advantage of Austria-Hungary and " might bring about the final liquidation of Serbia, who would find herself encompassed by enemies on both sides." He even hinted that "circumstances might bring into existence " a compact between Austria-Hungary and Bulgaria.[2]

During the first half of May the attitude of Bulgaria appears to have stiffened still further. General Savov, who had hitherto opposed war both on strategic grounds and owing to the increasing discontent in the army,

---

[1] Russian Orange Book, No. 141, cit., Gešov, op. cit., p. 77.

[2] Times, 3rd May. His telegrams contain much the best presentment of the Bulgarian point of view throughout the critical period of May-August, 1913. Their animus against Serbia and Roumania is too patent to require any comment. (See especially Times of 14th, 17th, 18th, and 21st July, 1913.)

abandoned his opposition as a result of the intrigues which were undermining his position at Court. The settlement of the Bulgaro-Roumanian frontier dispute at Petrograd on terms highly favourable to Sofia, so far from rendering the Bulgarians more amenable, was treated by them as removing all danger of interference from the north of the Danube; and the extreme dissatisfaction of Roumania at these terms was wholly disregarded. General Savov, with all the zeal of a convert, urged upon Gešov that, as war was now inevitable, peace must be concluded with the Turks without delay. The true issue, he argued, was the hegemony of the peninsula, and a bold onslaught would swiftly settle this in favour of Bulgaria; four days of hostilities ought to suffice to separate the Greeks from the Serbs and force them to sue for peace.[1] Obviously it was essential to force a decision before the harvest,[2] and as the bulk of the Bulgarian army had to be transported from Thrace to the new western front, not a moment was to be lost in reaching such an agreement with Turkey as would permit of their transference. It was this underlying strategic factor, in this case compounded of geography and economics, which accounts for the eager impatience displayed by the Bulgarian peace delegates in London and the corresponding reluctance and dilatoriness of the Serbs and Greeks. From a theoretical standpoint Sir Edward Grey was unquestionably right in issuing his abrupt advice to sign or leave London; but in practice it cannot be denied that the effect was to encourage Bulgaria in her warlike designs and in the fatal illusion that the Powers, in guaranteeing the Treaty of London, were really freeing Bulgaria from the necessity of guarding her eastern frontier against the Turks.[3]

---

[1] Balcanicus, op. cit., p. 19.   [2] Times, 16th May.
[3] This view is shared by the anonymous author of Nationalism and War in the Near East, who writes (p. 250): "It is a melan-

Henceforth the breach between Bulgaria and Russia widens perceptibly. In Petrograd and Moscow the recalcitrant attitude of Sofia began to be regarded as a betrayal of the cause of Slav solidarity; while the inspired Press of Vienna and Budapest steadily fanned the quarrel of the two Slav peoples and magnified local frontier incidents into the opening stages of a new war.[1] The encouragement of Chauvinist feeling in any Balkan state is always an easy task, and the hotheads of Belgrade vied with the Macedonian agitators of Sofia in inflaming public opinion. In spite of Russian efforts to secure general demobilisation, even so wise a statesman as Mr. Paču, the Serbian Minister of Finance, publicly declared that Serbia could not think of such a step until the frontier question had been settled; and a few days later his colleague, the Minister of War, gave great offence in Sofia by repeating the same statement in a much more aggressive form.

But far more important than either utterance was the speech of the Serbian Premier Mr. Pašić, on 27th May, which certainly had the effect of posing the question for the first time publicly before Europe. It was unquestionably due to internal difficulties and to the persistent demand of the Opposition leaders for information, but is also to be explained partly by the fact that a defensive

choly probability that but for the success of the Powers in making a partial peace for Bulgaria with Turkey and Roumania, there would have been no war made by Bulgaria against Greece and Serbia. For even Bulgars swollen with success would not have attacked Greece and Serbia, unless they had supposed they were safe from Turkey and Roumania."

[1] See leader in *Pester Lloyd* of 25th May, which openly espouses the Bulgarian cause and speaks of 60,000 Bulgars beating the Greeks at Nigrita and marching on Salonica. There are believed to have been 13,000 Bulgars engaged, which is bad enough, but a very different matter. With the organ of the Hungarian Government the wish was obviously the father to the thought.

military convention with Greece had been signed on 14th May, and that the final Serbo-Greek Treaty was on the very point of signature.[1]

Mr. Pašić quite openly insisted upon a revision of the treaty, proclaimed it as the cardinal point in Serbian policy, and then went on to justify the demand, not merely by a long array of historical, political, and sentimental arguments, but, above all, by laying emphasis on the altered situation since the conclusion of the treaty. In order to demonstrate still further Serbia's loyal attitude towards her allies, he made known the fact that in the previous winter Austria-Hungary—whom he did not, of course, mention by name—had directly encouraged Serbia to compensate herself for her impending eviction from Albania by retaining the Vardar valley, and in that event had actually offered her support to a Serbian occupation of Salonica.

This sensational entrance of Mr. Pašić into the arena was undoubtedly one of the causes which led the pacific Mr. Gešov to place his resignation in the hands of King Ferdinand (30th May). But the main reason was the consciousness that his views conflicted with those of the King, of the General Staff, and of a powerful section of public opinion. Within two days of Gešov's acceptance of the Russian proposal for parallel demobilisation (26th May), King Ferdinand had himself ordered Savov to hasten the transport of the army westwards (28th); and the army chief had wired back next day that between twenty-five and thirty-five days would be required to transfer the troops from Bulair to Macedonia, and that if negotiations with Serbia could only be prolonged for this period, all military danger from the Ser-

---

[1] It was actually signed at Salonica on 1st June by MM. Alexandropoulos and Bošković for their respective Governments. Crawfurd Price, *op. cit.,* p. 241.

bian side would have disappeared.[1] What finally decided Mr. Gešov's attitude was the fact that on the
receipt of General Savov's wire King Ferdinand pri-
vately called together a meeting of all the Bulgarian
party leaders except the Premier himself, and that the
latter first learnt of this next day from the King's private
secretary, who then informed him that all the others
favoured a warlike policy.[2] In his own laconic phrase,
which reveals for an instant the existence of a whole
array of sinister secrets, "I was not in unity with the
Crown."[3] His resignation, which was timed to coincide
with the signature of the Treaty of London, was not
made public for the moment, and in response to urgent
representations from Petrograd he met Mr. Pašić at
Tsaribrod on 1st June, and joined the latter in accepting
the further Russian proposal that the Balkan Premiers
should meet and confer at Petrograd. While remaining for the whole of the next week *in statu demissionis,*
Mr. Gešov appears to have resigned himself to swim-
ming with the current. Mr. Sazanov's suggestion for the
reduction of the allied armies to one-third of their
strength, coupled with the announcement that both
Greece and Serbia had given their consent, was meekly
referred by Gešov to Savov for his opinion. The
general's reply was to impose three conditions—that the
Serbs should evacuate the disputed territory, or, failing
this, that the Great Powers should guarantee Serbia's
fulfilment of the treaty, and that in that event Bulgaria

[1] See Balcanicus, *op. cit.,* pp. 30-1. The position of the Serbs,
knowing that an attack was pending, but knowing also that by
forestalling it they would put themselves in the wrong before
Europe, has an interesting parallel in their position in October,
1915, when they knew of Bulgaria's impending attack, but were
not allowed to forestall it owing to the virtual veto of Entente
diplomacy.

[2] Balcanicus, *op. cit.,* p. 40.

[3] Gešov, *op. cit.,* p. 91.

should be allowed to send as many troops to Macedonia as the combined Serb and Greek forces already there. Obviously such proposals were acceptable neither to Bulgaria's allies nor to the Russian arbiter, and were never meant to be accepted. The general attitude in Sofia at this moment is clearly reflected in the *Times* telegrams of Mr. Bourchier, who on 1st June announces with evident approval :—" The Bulgarian character is singularly undemonstrative, but the national spirit is thoroughly aroused, and war with Serbia is not only eagerly desired, but is generally regarded as inevitable." Nor was he alone in pouring fresh oil upon the flames. A Bulgarian ex-Premier, General Petrov, interviewed by the *Neue Freie Presse* on 2nd June, declared that war could not be avoided unless Serbia observed every detail of the treaty and unless Greece evacuated Salonica; while the Serbian War Minister, General Bojanović, spoke of the possibility of "a short but bloody war," if Bulgaria persisted in claiming Veles and Monastir. An interview with the Serbian Crown Prince, published in the Belgrade *Politika* of 7th June, struck an equally uncompromising note; and the patent truth of his assertion that Bulgaria was really aiming at the hegemony of the Balkans only served to make it more unpalatable to Sofia.

The Russian Government continued untiringly in its efforts to promote an accord, but was met by growing suspicion and even hostility on the part of the Bulgarians, who contended that Russia had already prejudged the case by even considering the question of revision. Thus in the same breath they professed to accept arbitration and insisted upon limiting the sphere of the arbitration in such a way as to prejudge the case against Serbia in her turn. The bare idea of compromise was spurned : it must be the treaty, the whole treaty, and nothing but the treaty. On 8th June Mr. Bourchier announced that " the statement that Bulgaria has agreed to accept revision of the treaty with Serbia had no foundation whatever."[1]

On the same day the Tsar of Russia took the momentous step of directing a personal telegraphic appeal to the Kings of Serbia and Bulgaria, reminding them of their engagement to refer disputes to him as arbiter. " A war between the allies would not leave me indifferent. In fact, I should like to make it clear that the state which commences war will be held responsible before the Slav cause, and that I reserve to myself full liberty concerning the attitude which Russia will adopt at the end of such a criminal war." The publication of such a message from the acknowledged head of the Slavonic world, and its dispatch from the historic Kremlin, served to emphasise Russia's view of the gravity of the situation. The reply of King Peter has never been published, but its general terms are known. After expressions of respect and gratitude for Russia's untiring interest in the Slavonic cause, he emphasised the danger to which Serbia would be exposed by the realisation of Bulgaria's full claims, and the certainty that this would involve, not merely the fall of the Serbian Government, but serious internal convulsions and perhaps even the destruction of the dynasty. Meanwhile King Ferdinand did not show the same restraint, and his reply, couched in most acrid and unconciliatory terms, was immediately made public. After throwing the entire blame upon Serbia, and defining the functions of the arbiter in their narrowest sense, he proceeded to enlarge upon the unanimity of the Bulgarian nation and its duties towards the population of Macedonia, and closed upon a note which seemed to render further discussion hopeless :—
" And your Majesty will deign to remember that these duties have for many years past been recognised by

[1] *Times,* 10th June, 1913.

Russia herself." Such an answer was an open rebuff for the friends of peace, and there was only one quarter in which it was well received. The Press of Vienna and Budapest, which had hailed the Tsar's telegram as " a reprimand addressed to vassals " and an attempt to establish " a new Slav apostolate," could not conceal its satisfaction at Ferdinand's defiant attitude.

On the very eve of its dispatch a new Bulgarian Cabinet was formed under Dr. Danev as Premier (10th June); but any hopes which might have rested upon his Russophil tendencies had already been discounted by the rigid Jingoism which he had displayed at the two conferences in London. It is only fair to add that the responsibility for King Ferdinand's answer to the Tsar probably rests with the monarch himself and not with his newly appointed Minister. The special Slavonic appeal of Russia having failed, the clumsier apparatus of the European Concert was now set in motion. On 13th June a joint *démarche* of the Powers at Sofia and Belgrade urging the demobilisation of the two armies elicited the fact that Mr. Pašić had already made a similar proposal to Bulgaria, but that it, like his earlier notes in favour of revision and a conference of Premiers, had remained unanswered. When at last, on 15th June, the reply came, it consisted of a refusal to discuss revision and a long catalogue of the crimes of Greece and Serbia as the justification for precautionary measures on the part of Bulgaria.[1] At this moment the internal difficulties of the Pašić Cabinet reached an acute stage, as the result of sharp criticism in the Skupština: and though their resignation was not accepted by King Peter, they found themselves between a strong and restive opposition and the steady pressure of six Great

[1] See *Times,* 16th June. Wire of Mr. Bourchier, dated Sofia, 15th June, and summarising the points of a document which it suited the Bulgarian game to place at his disposal.

Powers, whose predominant feeling was annoyance at the persistence of a quarrel which their own secular jealousies had done so much to create.

On 17th June General Savov came from the army headquarters to the capital and reported to the King the growing symptoms of unrest among his troops.[1] He warned Dr. Danev that if they remained inactive more than ten days longer, it would become virtually impossible to retain them with the colours; and both appear to have accepted this period as a respite before the final decision need be made. Next day a secret circular was issued to the five army commanders, urging them to unity and warning them of the possibility of immediate operations.[2] Probably as the result of Savov's visit, Bulgaria proposed to Serbia, as a preliminary to demobilisation, the joint occupation of the disputed area, and in a further Note, handed in on 19th June, replied at considerable length to the Serbian arguments for revision. This pedantic insistence upon the letter of the law, and the parallel attempt to strengthen their case by allowing Mr. Bourchier to publish the first summary of the provisions of the much-cited but mysteriously guarded secret treaty, was not calculated, and probably not intended, to advance the cause of peace. On a literal interpretation of the treaty the Bulgarian case was unanswerable; but, of course, the whole contention of the Serbs was that equity demanded an observance of the spirit rather than the letter of the agreement.

On 19th June an event occurred which gave a fatal turn to the crisis and more than counteracted all the efforts of Russia. Count Stephen Tisza, who had succeeded only a week earlier to the Hungarian Premiership after the scandals of the Lukács-Désy trial, made an important pronouncement in Parliament on the

---

[1] *Times*, 17th, 18th June.
[2] Balcanicus, *op. cit.*, p. 52.

foreign policy of the Dual Monarchy. Opening with
the unfounded assertion that Austria-Hungary had been
the first state to declare that the Balkan people must not
be robbed of the fruits of victory, he pointed out that
their free development and complete independence was
her foremost aim. Disinterestedness he defined as "no
protectorate, privileged position, or plans of expansion,"
but also as not meaning lack of interest in Balkan affairs.
Passing finally to Russia's separate action, he added:
"Here also the Balkan states are independent, and consequently free to choose their own method of settling
their differences. They may—and we should deplore
it if they did so, but they are entitled to do so—choose
the method of war, or they may choose mediation or a
tribunal of arbitration. But it is self-evident that the
latter methods can only be applied on the basis of the
untrammelled decision of the independent states in question, and within the limits they may establish."[1] Austria-
Hungary could not allow any other state to acquire
special prerogatives in the Balkans.

Short of open hostility, it would have been difficult to
convey a plainer hint to Russia; and the Opposition
leader, Count Andrássy, hastened to endorse his rival's
view. Indeed, it was freely hinted in Vienna and Budapest that the Monarchy would be able to prevent Roumania's intervention on the Serbian side by promising
her a portion of Serbian territory in the event of
Bulgaria's victory; while if the improbable should
happen and Bulgaria should be defeated, Austria-
Hungary would immediately intervene to crush the
Serbs.

The stiffening effect of the speech became at once
apparent. On 22nd June Dr. Danev, in answer to fresh
Russian appeals for a conference of the four Premiers
at Petrograd, insisted on a preliminary guarantee from

[1] *Pester Lloyd*, and *Times* of 20th June.

the Serbs "that they will accept arbitration and the joint occupation of Macedonia." He ended his telegram to Mr. Sazonov with the truculent phrase : "Let the Imperial Government entertain no illusions on that subject."[1] A Crown Council, held the same day at King Ferdinand's summer palace outside Sofia, was influenced by urgent telegrams from General Savov, insisting that further delays would demoralise the army and make it unfit for action; but though some members favoured immediate war, it was finally decided to offer to Russia a week's delay, in which to pronounce her verdict as arbiter. If this offer should be accepted within forty-eight hours, Dr. Danev would be prepared to come to Petrograd.[2] It can hardly be wondered at that a message of this kind gave extreme offence in Russia. Through the medium of the Bulgarian Minister, Mr. Sazonov transmitted a stiff message to Dr. Danev, ascribing this "ultimatum" to Austrian influence and telling him to expect nothing more from Russia and to forget the existence of any engagements undertaken since 1902.[3] While the Russophil Premier, by his tactlessness, thus cut the ground from under his feet at Petrograd, the Austrian Minister in Sofia, Count Tarnowski, completed his ascendency over the political counsels of King Ferdinand and pulled the secret wires which were to lead to disaster.

Meanwhile the uncompromising attitude of the Serbian officers' corps and dissensions within the Cabinet had led Mr. Pašić to resign (22nd); but although three of his colleagues were believed to favour immediate

---

[1] This wire was afterwards copied from the Foreign Office archives in Sofia by Mr. Genadiev, Foreign Minister in the Radoslavov Cabinet, and read aloud during a debate in the Sobranje. See Balcanicus, *op. cit.,* p. 54.

[2] Mr. Venizelos and Mr. Pašić had given their unqualified consent on 17th June. See *Times,* 18th June.

[3] Balcanicus, *op. cit.,* p. 62.

annexation of the disputed territory, as a means of creating a *fait accompli,* this extreme step was avoided, and the Serbian Government consented to place its case unreservedly in the hands of Russia. After a stormy secret session of the Skupština, the Pašić Cabinet remained in office (26th). There followed a brief calm before the storm burst. Serbia had rejected the Bulgarian proposal for joint occupation (22nd), while Bulgaria refused the Greek suggestion for a reduction of effectives, unless immediate joint occupation was agreed upon (20th). The deadlock was complete. On 28th June the Roumanian Government, which had at an earlier stage given more than one informal indication of its attitude, officially informed Bulgaria that it would not remain neutral in the event of war.[1]

---

[1] When shortly afterwards Roumania did actually intervene, certain Bulgarophil organs in London bitterly attacked her as a "hyæna Power," and "an assassin treacherously stabbing in the back." Yet such an attitude on their part betrayed complete ignorance of the true situation, above all of the capital fact that Roumania had given Bulgaria fair warning, and that this warning was arrogantly disregarded. As I pointed out in a letter to the *Nation* (18th July, 1913) I was myself assured with great frankness on 20th June—*i.e.,* nine days before the night attack—in Bucarest by two prominent members of the Maiorescu Cabinet that Roumania would never allow Bulgaria to crush the Serbs, and that it had been made abundantly clear to the Bulgars that "if they move, we move also."

CHAPTER XVII

THE SECOND BALKAN WAR

PSYCHOLOGY is always an important factor in war, and in the critical period when war and peace hang in the balance the psychology of the governing class in each country may not unfairly be regarded as the decisive fact. Nowhere was this more certainly the case than in Bulgaria during the Balkan wars. In Sofia both the Court and the highest political and military circles were dominated by an arrogant sense of superiority to their rivals, which led them to despise and ignore the most obvious dangers and obstacles. General Savov is credibly reported to have expressed the opinion that the Bulgarian army would cut through the Serbs like a knife through rotten cheese,[1] while Dr. Danev on 1st July warned the Roumanian Minister that Serbian resistance would be at an end before Roumania could possibly hope to complete her mobilisation. Nothing proves the overweening self-confidence of the Bulgarians more glaringly than the fact that they seriously thought that General Hasapčev's little garrison of 1,500 men could hold all the Greeks of Salonica at bay until General Ivanov's triumphal entry into the town !

The second Balkan war was essentially a political war, alike in the manner of its outbreak and in the course

[1] A similar phrase was used by a prominent Macedo-Bulgar on 10th July to the Vienna correspondent of the *Times* (see *Times,* 11th July, 1913).

which it pursued. Its authors, soldiers and statesmen alike, allowed both strategy and tactics to be subordinated to purely political considerations. Long before the conclusion of peace with Turkey the Bulgarian General Staff had begun to work out an elaborate plan of campaign.[1] On 2nd July five army groups were to be deployed against the Serbs and Greeks along the whole front from the Danube to the Ægean. While the First Army under Kutinčev (45 battalions) moved on Knjaževac, the Third under Dimitriev (36 battalions) on Slivnica, and the Second under Ivanov (57 battalions) dealt with the Greeks, the main attack was to be directed by the Fourth Army under Kovačev against the Kočana-Štip-Strumnica front, and the Fifth Army (20 battalions) under Tošev was to be ready to supplement Kovačev's efforts from the neighbourhood of Kustendil.

Owing to the mutal recriminations which followed failure, far more of the secrets of these eventful days have transpired than is usual in contemporary history; but it is not yet clear what were the exact reasons which led to the execution of this plan in a premature and incomplete form. Absurd as it may seem, the aim of the Bulgarian authorities was to take forcible possession of the coveted territory without a declaration of war and then, having placed their quondam allies and Europe before a sudden *fait accompli,* to present themselves at the conference table in Petrograd in the guise of *beati possidentes.* This crudely naïve method had already been employed on several occasions with varying success. As early as 5th March, 1913, the Bulgars attempted to eject the Greeks from their positions at Nigrita, selecting

[1] The French military critic in the *Revue Bleue,* whose five articles are much the most authoritative account of the second war, has had this plan in his hands, and maintains that only a military expert can duly appreciate the length of time which it must have taken to prepare.

the day on which the latter were celebrating the news of the fall of Janina and the Romanov Tercentenary,[1] and only desisted after a two days' assault. This incident gave rise to an acrimonious correspondence between Prince Nicholas of Greece and General Hasapčev, and for two months there was no further disturbance of the peace. Early in May, however, there were fresh skirmishes, and on the 21st a large Bulgarian column[2] made a determined effort to drive the Greeks out of the Panghaion district, and were only repulsed after several days' fighting.

On 17th June an order was issued by General Kovačev at Radovište to the officers of his command, announcing that the concentration of troops would be completed within the next week, and that events would then be ripe for a decision. He instructed them to explain to their men the reasons which made an attack on their perfidious allies necessary, to rouse them by bringing them into contact with the Macedonian refugees, and to represent the Serbian and Greek soldiers as mere cowards, whose *moral* was at zero and who were deserting freely. The best proof of their rottenness, he argued, was their complete passivity in face of the Bulgarian concentration along their whole front.[3]

As a matter of fact the Serbian Commander-in-Chief, General Putnik, had ever since the beginning of June been aware that the Bulgarian forces round Kočana were being daily reinforced. At first he organised strong

---

[1] Celebrated throughout Greece in honour of Queen Olga, a Russian Princess.

[2] According to a telegram in *Pester Lloyd* of the 28th, 13,000 men with 24 cannon were involved. In a leader on 25th May in the same paper, 60,000 Bulgars were said to be marching on Salonica.

[3] *Revue Bleue,* 13th December, 1913. For the present this may be regarded as the chief authority on the strategy of the second war.

defensive positions and awaited events, but on 20th June, having received certain proofs that the enemy was less numerous than he had hitherto supposed, he revised his plans in such a way as to be able to counter any attack. Already on the 17th he had been warned by Mr. Pašić to take all necessary measures against the possibility of a Bulgarian surprise onslaught. He, therefore, made Skoplje his headquarters, and concentrated the First and Third Armies under the Crown Prince and General Janković, between Egri Palanka on the old Turko-Bulgarian frontier, and Veles, in the Vardar valley, leaving the weaker Second Army under General Stepanović to guard Serbia proper against invasion. In due course Serbian outposts were attacked by the Bulgars at Zletovo (25th June), and Putnik promptly gave orders to the First and Third Armies to concentrate in view of a general attack in the direction of Štip, and at the same time requested the Greek General Staff to send three divisions to Gjevgjeli to co-operate with the Serbian right wing in an attack upon Strumnica. The Greeks were able to adduce valid reasons for not complying with this request, and as the Bulgars had meanwhile withdrawn behind the Zletovska river, Putnik counter-manded the attack at the last moment.

By this time only extreme arrogance could have blinded the Bulgarian commanders to the fact that Putnik was fully alive to the danger which threatened him and ready to repay with interest any blow. How accurately he had gauged the enemy's intentions may be seen from the confidential instructions which he issued to his commanding officers. "The Bulgars," he said, "will use their amicable relations with us and will attack us by surprise. It is thus that they attacked the Greeks, and there is no doubt that they will do the same with us as soon as they find a favourable occasion. Consequently you must always be on your guard, above all at nights,

and be ready not only to repel the Bulgars, but above all
to take the offensive instantly and punish the Bulgars
by beating them and pursuing them mercilessly." [1]   In
point of fact, on certain sections of the front Serbian and
Bulgarian officers dined together on the evening preceding the final "stab in the back," and the very men
who a few hours before, with the fatal orders in their
pockets, had been clinking glasses with their Serbian
comrades, crept back at the dead of night in the hope of
slaughtering them unawares.   In all the grim story of
modern Balkan warfare this repulsive incident stands out
above all the rest and remains as an indelible stain upon
the Bulgarian scutcheon.

At 11.30 p.m. on 26th June the dispositions of the
various Bulgarian armies were issued by General Savov
to their respective commanders.[2]   Finally at 8 p.m. on
28th June the following order was dispatched by Savov
to Kovačev, the commander of the Fourth Army at
Radovište.   "In order to prevent our silence in presence
of the Serb attacks reacting unfavourably upon our
soldiers, and in order that the enemy should not be
further encouraged, I order you to attack the enemy as
energetically as possible, along the whole line, without
unmasking all your forces and without letting yourself be
drawn into a long engagement.   You will make an effort
to establish yourself securely at Krivolak, on the right
bank of the Bregalnica, on the height of Bogoslav, on
the ridge 550, and on the ridge near the village of
Dobrovo.   It is preferable for you to open hostilities in
the evening, and during the night, under cover of dark-

---

[1] *Revue Bleue, ibid.*

[2] This order (23) is quoted entire by Balcanicus, *op. cit.*,
p. 64-5 (reproduced from the Sofiote newspaper *Dnevnik*, where
Savov himself published it on 15th June, 1914, No. 4236).   More
detailed instructions (24) were prepared at the same time, but not
actually communicated till 30th June, the day following the night
attack.   No. 24 has not as yet been published.

ness, to deliver an impetuous attack along the whole line. This operation is to take place to-morrow evening, 29th June." [1] At the same time a shorter telegram was sent to General Ivanov, in command of the Second Army, informing him that the Fourth Army was about to attack the "entire Serbian line," and ordering him meanwhile to attack the Greeks " most energetically " at Leftera and Tsaigesi and to fortify himself well in those positions. [2]

The crisis found the Serbian Third Army ready for instant action. Its centre held the Ovčepolje (the Sheep Plain), wide grassy downs which form the strategic key of Macedonia; while its two flanks were protected by more mountainous country. The First Army further north was faced by a more difficult problem; for reasons of geography exposed it to attack from two different directions—from Kustendil on the old Serbo-Bulgar frontier, and from the Zletovska, on the extreme left of the sister army. While the former suffered from blazing heat, the latter, at no great distance from it but on far higher ground, was exposed to extreme cold, for which its summer outfit was ill-suited.

The Bulgarian attack opened on the night of 29th June, along a front of 100 kilometres. Between midnight and 2 a.m. the Bulgarians crossed the river Zletovska, while two hours later the strong fort of Redki-Buki fell into the hands of the Macedo-Adrianople division. It appears to be certain that if after this initial check Putnik had withdrawn his troops to defensive positions nearer Skoplje, the Bulgars would have made no attempt to follow him, but would have contented themselves with occupying the disputed territory. In brief, their aim was to overrun Ovčepolje by a rapid surprise movement, to

[1] Reproduced by Balcanicus, p. 66, *Revue Bleue* (first article), and *Nationalism and War*, p. 265.

[2] *Cit.*, Balcanicus, p. 67.

seize the bridge-head of Krivolak on the Vardar, and having thus cut the communications between the Serbs and Greeks, to move rapidly upon Monastir. The Greeks were regarded as almost a negligible quantity, and it was assumed that Salonica would fall an easy prey to General Ivanov.[1] But the whole of this calculation, reared upon a fixed theory of Serbian cowardice and incapacity, collapsed under the rude shock of General Putnik's counter-offensive. Leaving an adequate force on the defensive at Kustendil, and renouncing for the moment the idea of recapturing Redki-Buki, he launched a strong attack against the dominant position of Car Vrh (Sultan Tepe). The rashness of the Bulgarian design at once became apparent. The Fourth Army, 104 battalions strong, attacked along a front of 110 kilometres, with the result that its force was unduly scattered. *Qui trop embrasse, mal étreint.* Moreover, Bulgarian strategy fell between two stools. Savov, whose aim was not war but a sudden forcible seizure of the spoils, fully realised that to employ the First and Third Armies against Serbia proper in accordance with the original plan (see above, p. 258) would involve a definite rupture between the two countries; and yet he left them in position, instead of throwing all but a containing force into the Macedonian scales. Nay more, he did not even make use of the Fifth Army at Kustendil. Its commander, General Tošev, hearing the sound of the cannon to the south, wired to Sofia for instructions, but only received the order to attack on the evening of 30th June, when the psychological moment was already lost.[2] Worst of all, Kovačev's army was allowed to attack without any reserves save a single brigade at Radovište. Thus everything depended upon the enemy yielding at the first push or at least remaining upon the defensive, and it was precisely this

---

[1] Immanuel, *Der Balkankrieg,* Heft V., p. 37.
[2] *Revue Bleue,* I.

which Putnik avoided, thus showing a moral courage
and soundness of judgment which deserve the highest
praise. A further telegram dispatched by Savov to
Kovačev on the afternoon of 30th June, very strikingly
illustrates the degree to which he allowed politics to
outweigh military considerations. A declaration of war,
he explains, had been dispensed with for four reasons :
to raise the *moral* of the the troops and convince them
that their former allies had become enemies; to force
Russian diplomacy, by the danger of a declaration of
war, to make a speedy decision; to render the allies more
amenable by dealing smashing blows; and to seize and
hold the disputed territory until the intervention of the
Powers, which already seemed imminent. "Swift and
strong action" was thus essential, and the Fourth Army
was, therefore, ordered to continue the attack and occupy
Veles at all costs, while the Second Army, in event of
these operations being successful and the Vardar valley
strongly held, was to attack Salonica.[1] By the time this
order had arrived at the front the whole situation was
already transformed. Bulgaria's "stab in the back"
had glanced off the Serbian armour, and the Serbs were
in their turn assuming the offensive. Putnik's orders to
the First Army were to hold the left flank towards
Kustendil and to concentrate all other available forces
on the Redki-Buki-Račani front; while the Third Army
was told to check at all costs the enemy's offensive and
as soon as possible to counter with an offensive movement

[1] Quoted *in extenso* in *Revue Bleue*, first article, and in
Nationalism and War, p. 266. The *Times* of 12th July, 1913,
published a translation of the Order sent out by Colonel Enčev,
a brigadier of the 4th Bulgarian Division, at 8 p.m. on 29th June,
to the sectional commanders under him, for the attack on the
Serbs next day. This document was captured from the defeated
Bulgars, and, reproduced in facsimile, was the first piece of
evidence published in Western Europe, to show that the Bulgars
were the aggressors.

against Štip. That evening General Janković announced
that he was holding his own, but asked urgently for
reinforcements.   Putnik received his appeal philoso-
phically, and ordered him to hold his ground till next
day, when fresh troops would be brought up.

On 30th June the Bulgarian Fourth Army succeeded
in occupying Krivolak, while the Second, under Ivanov,
drove the Greeks out of Gjevgjeli.   But though the two
allies were thus separated by a wedge of Bulgarian troops
along the Vardar, the great gamble initiated by Savov
and his master had already signally failed.   Then came
perhaps the most incredible incident in a long series
of surprises.   On the morning of 1st July, Savov,
realising that the Serbs, so far from being intimidated,
were ready and eager for the fray, telegraphed the order
to stop hostilities.[1]   Thus for some hours there was a
pause along the entire front, and it is not altogether
clear at what point and on which side fighting recom-
menced. After the long strain passions had reached fever
heat in both armies and could no longer be restrained.
But the essential factor in the situation was that the Serbs
were thoroughly tired of Bulgarian methods, and determined to put the matter to a final and decisive test.

On 1st July a proclamation of King Peter was issued
to the Serbian troops, bidding them defend their
conquests shoulder to shoulder with the Greeks against
the greed of Bulgaria.   There is no reference to the night
attack, for the simple reason that the document had been
prepared some time previously in Belgrade and held in
readiness with a blank space for the insertion of the date.[2]
That afternoon the Serbian counter-offensive began in

---

[1] The *Revue Bleue* critic's terse but adequate comment upon
this *volte-face* is : "C'est à n'y pas croire."

[2] Published in facsimile in *Mir* (Mr. Gešov's organ) on 8th July,
1913, and reproduced in Gešov, *Balkan League*, p. 102.   It
affords an interesting proof of Serbia's "preparedness,"

real earnest. While the First Army attacked vigorously from Car Vrh in the direction of Kočana, the Third was ordered to remain on the defensive until the effect of the sister army's operation, and notably of the first Šumadia Division, should make itself felt, and then to assume the offensive without a moment's delay along the Zletovska front. Putnik's plan was brilliantly conceived, and if carried out in every detail would probably have ended in the complete destruction of Kovačev's army : for it took full advantage of the dangerous strategical position of the Bulgarians.   Immediately behind the latter's front and at right angles to it lay the Plaškovica Planina, a tract of lofty, inaccessible and pathless mountains, which, in the event of their complete lack of reserves forcing them to retreat, might become a solid wedge cutting their army into two halves, preventing all communication between the two and exposing the southern section to a Greek attack. Only two explanations of Savov's action are possible—complete military incompetence or an over-confidence so great as to accept altogether excessive risks : and it is to the latter explanation that all the evidence points.

On 2nd July, after fierce and prolonged fighting, the Bulgarians were thrown back across the Zletovska and ejected from the strong fortified position of Redki-Buki. All efforts of the Bulgarians to recover it next day were unsuccessful, and after nightfall they evacuated the right bank of the Zletovska. On the 4th, the Serbs, who had been growing steadily stronger, captured Račjanski Rid, one of the keys to the whole position, and drove the Bulgarians back in confusion in the direction of Kočana. The situation of the Third Army, however, still remained critical : the Bulgarians more than held their ground at Krivolak, and General Janković appears to have wavered and lost the power of initiative.[1] Thus on the night of

---

[1] *Revue Bleue,* fifth article.

the 4th, Putnik found it necessary to divert to Janković's aid a portion of the victorious First Army, with the result that the remainder was not able to follow up the pursuit, and what might have been a Bulgarian rout was merely a hurried retreat. Even after these reinforcements had reached him, and in spite of orders to attack the enemy "with the utmost energy," Janković still delayed, not realising that his own situation at Krivolak was infinitely less precarious than that of Kovačev on the Bregalnica. Between the 4th and 7th the Bulgarians withdrew their convoys and artillery, clinging the while desperately to the heights east of Egri Palanka and Car Vrh. Thus when at last the Serbs advanced in earnest on the afternoon of the 8th, contact with the enemy had already been lost, and Janković's army, in the words of a French critic, "*tomba dans le vide*."[1] On 9th July the whole Serbian Army was on the move, and occupied both Štip and Kočana, and on the next day Radovište.

In spite of the numerous "revelations" which prominent Bulgarian statesmen and generals have bandied at each other's heads ever since the final disaster, it is still too soon to apportion responsibility for the events of 29th June; but it is already clear that the lion's share must be assigned to King Ferdinand himself and to his close connections with Vienna and Budapest. In defending himself after the war against the savage attacks of his critics, Mr. Danev declared that during his premiership there was another irresponsible Cabinet behind the scenes, which without his knowledge reached the most momentous decisions, as the result of secret conferences with Count Tarnowsky. Two of Danev's colleagues, Mr. Todorov and Mr. Burov, also assured the Sobranje that as late as nine o'clock on the following evening they were still in ignorance of the attack[2]; and Mr. Gešov, though

---

[1] *Revue Bleue, ibid.*
[2] Balcanicus, *op. cit.* p. 72.

too discreet to lift the veil from the events concerning
which he unquestionably knows the truth, quite definitely
asserts in his recent book on the genesis of the Balkan
League, that the attack took place without the knowledge
of the Danev Cabinet and contrary to its unanimous
decision.[1] The mere fact that the Cabinet did not meet at
all on that eventful day is in itself highly significant.
If Dr. Danev and the author of certain sensational articles
in *Dnevnik*, presumably inspired by him and never
controverted officially, are to be believed, Tarnowsky had
already given verbal assurances to King Ferdinand that
Austro-Hungarian troops would reoccupy the Sandjak in
the event of a Serbo-Bulgar war, and on 26th June a
treaty was signed between Austria-Hungary and Bulgaria, by which the latter bound herself, in the event of
an Austro-Serbian or an Austro-Russian war, to mobilise
enough troops to paralyse Serbia's action, while Austria-
Hungary in her turn undertook to prevent, either by
diplomatic or military action, any attack of Roumania
upon Bulgaria in the event of the latter becoming involved in war with the allies, and even to intervene herself, should the war take a turn unfavourable to Bulgaria.
In any case, there can be no doubt that throughout the
summer of 1913 Austria-Hungary was seriously con-
templating an attack upon Serbia. In May the Austro-
Hungarian Minister in Bucarest, Prince Fürstenberg,
communicated to Mr. Take Ionescu, the Minister of the
Interior in the Maiorescu Cabinet, a long telegram which
he had received from Count Berchtold, and which instructed him to inform the Roumanian Government that
Austria-Hungary was ready to defend Bulgaria by force
of arms. Mr. Ionescu's attitude was so discouraging

[1] Gešov, *op. cit.*, p. 92. Evidence pointing in this direction
was produced at a political libel action in January, 1915, in the
form of a certificate from the secretary of the Ministerial Council,
stating that the Council's minutes contain no order for the opening of hostilities against Greece and Serbia.

that the Minister refrained from approaching Mr. Maiorescu, and warned his Government not to proceed. Henceforth Vienna concentrated its attention upon Sofia rather than Bucarest.

The great battle, of which the night attack was the opening incident, and which may be said to have continued uninterruptedly until 9th July, will live in history as the battle of Bregalnica, though of course it actually extended over a much wider front. The best proof of the scale upon which the attack was planned and of the fierceness with which it was conducted is supplied by the Serbian losses, which are officially admitted to have amounted to 3,500 within the first twenty-four hours.[1]

Parallel with their surprise attack, the Bulgarians took steps to convince Europe that it was their would-be victim who had commenced. " C'est le lapin qui a commencé." On 30th June it was officially announced from Sofia that the Serbian troops had opened sustained fire upon the Bulgarian lines between Zletovo and Štip, and early in the morning of that day the Bulgarian Minister in Belgrade actually went to the Serbian Foreign Office to lodge a protest against the Serbian attack ! At first sight it is difficult to understand how Mr. Tošev could have known in Belgrade at seven o'clock that fighting had begun on the Zletovska only two or three hours earlier. The explanation is that the attack had originally been planned for the night of 28th June, and that its postponement for twenty-four hours had been decided at the last moment and not intimated to Mr. Tošev, who thus through no fault of his own committed a fatal indiscretion.[2] Some days later the Serbs and Greeks captured the original orders for the attack issued by a divisional commander, and naturally hastened to supply facsimiles to the chancelleries and Press of Europe; yet the Bulgarian

[1] Barby, *Bregalnitza*, p. 38.
[2] *Revue Bleue*, first article.

Government had the effrontery to issue a formal statement, describing the captured document as a forgery.
It was not till after the war that the facts were finally
and irrefutably established by the rival Bulgarian fac-
tions washing their dirty linen in the face of the whole
world.

The utter failure of their original plan had filled the
conspirators of Sofia with dismay, and already on 3rd
July Savov was removed from his command and replaced
by General Radko Dimitriev, the hero of the Thracian
campaign.[1] Whether Savov's chief crime in the eyes of
King Ferdinand consisted in his issuing the order for
the attack or the order for the cessation of hostilities, is
still a matter of conjecture; but it is far more probable
that he was thrown to the wolves of public opinion the
moment that his failure became apparent. The mobilisation of the Roumanian army on 5th July came as a
further shock to the Bulgarian Government and
paralysed their whole plan of campaign. Instead of
rapidly strengthening Kovačev's hard-pressed army
by the transference of troops from the Pirot-Vidin
front, they denuded still further the army of Ivanov,
which was already threatened by the Greek advance
(see p. 276).

Mr. Danev, whose position was rapidly becoming
untenable, more than once placed his resignation in the
King's hands, but the continuance in office of a discredited Russophil was thought for the moment to be
convenient. A letter addressed to the King by Messrs.
Radoslavov, Genadiev, and Tončev, urging the need for
security against Turkey and Roumania and advocating
an intimate accord with Austria-Hungary as the sole
means of attaining this and of saving Bulgaria from

---

[1] There is said to have been a violent scene, almost degenerating
into a scuffle, between Savov and Todorov, the Minister of Finance.
See *Reichspost,* 30th July, 1913.

disaster,[1] throws light upon the real political background at Sofia and foreshadowed the return of long-
discredited statesmen to power. Not all the efforts of
the Bulgarian press bureau could avail to conceal the
gravity of the situation.[2] The first sign of impending
danger from the Turkish side was the Porte's invitation
to the Government of Sofia to withdraw its troops from
Rodosto to within the new frontier (8th July), and news
of the capture of Kočana by the Serbs and of Strumnica
by the Greeks coincided with Roumania's declaration
of war (10th). In breaking off relations the Roumanian
Government pointedly reminded Dr. Danev that he had
received fair warning from Bucarest, but had never even
condescended to reply. Bulgaria, on the contrary, had
attacked Serbia " without any observance of even the
elementary rules of preliminary notification which would
at least have testified to a respect for the conventions of
international usage." Next day Roumanian troops
began to cross the Danube, and Bulgaria announced that
they would not be opposed. Realising that the situation
was becoming desperate, Mr. Danev placed himself in
the hands of Russia, and appealed for mediation. But
naturally enough Mr. Sazonov no longer showed the
same eagerness to mediate, and declined to entertain the
idea, unless all the Balkan states were willing to submit
their claims. He made no concealment of his view that
Bulgaria's action had destroyed the original treaty of
1912, and that Serbia and Greece had a right to insist
upon a common frontier. Sofia was not yet prepared

[1] See full text in *Reichspost* of 12th October, 1913.

[2] According to the news supplied to Mr. Bourchier on 6th July,
the Serbs were "now completely repulsed." On 10th July the
Serbs were announced as retreating all along the line, pursued
by the Bulgars; while on 17th July he records a great victory
over the Greeks at Strumnica, hitherto "cancelled for political
reasons but now confirmed." See *Times* of 7th, 12th, and 19th
July, 1913.

for such humiliation, and events were allowed to take their course.[1]

With the capture of Egri Palanka on 14th July by the Serbs the struggle on their front reached its high-water mark. Next day the Bulgarian Fourth Army withdrew to strong positions round Pehčevo, thus reestablishing its connections with Ivanov's forces; and henceforth, though intermittent fighting, sometimes of a very fierce character, continued till the very eve of the armistice, something approaching a stalemate had been reached. It had become a war of frontal positions, and the Serbs could not hope to pierce the Bulgarian lines except at enormous cost. Their losses had already been extremely heavy, and as the result of difficulties in the supply of water to the troops, a serious epidemic of cholera had broken out in their ranks and was causing much alarm at headquarters. Above all, Serbia's aim had been attained. Her armies had defied all attempts to evict them from their much coveted Macedonian conquests; they were in occupation of all and more than they desired to keep. Any attempt to make fresh conquests would only have destroyed the reviving sympathies of Europe and increased still further the danger of an Austrian attack upon Serbia. As we shall see, the spectre of Austro-Hungarian intervention lurked

[1] The Russophobe tendencies which at this moment gained the upper hand in Sofia, are faithfully reflected in Mr. Bourchier's telegrams to the *Times*. On 16th July he writes that "the fatal mistake of believing that Russia would protect this country against the consequences of misadventure is now manifest. Russia has played a double *rôle*. She has witnessed complacently the denunciation of a treaty concluded under her auspices, she has allowed the Protocol of Petrograd, embodying the decision of Europe, to be set aside, and she has encouraged a neighbouring state to invade the territory of her defenceless *protégé*. Having sanctioned the unity of the Bulgarian race at San Stefano, she now proposes its dismemberment. She is even suspected of having instigated the advance of the Turkish Army." (See *Times* of 17th July, 1913.)

continually in the background and was probably only averted by the attitude of Roumania. In August Bucarest no longer availed to hold back Vienna, and the combined efforts of Berlin and Rome were needed to prevent the Ballplatz from taking action which would almost certainly have plunged Europe into war.

Almost simultaneously with the treacherous night attack upon the Serbs, and acting upon parallel orders, the Bulgarian Southern Army under General Ivanov assumed the offensive against the Greeks; and it was calculated that if the operations on the Bregalnica front followed the desired course, there would be no great difficulty in taking possession of Salonica. Savov, however, being obsessed with the idea of Greek inferiority, left Ivanov with quite inadequate forces, on a far broader and more open front than that between the Bulgar and Serbs. The number of men at Ivanov's disposal has been the subject of fierce controversy both in Sofia and Athens; and after the war the General himself, in the Bulgarian Press, accused Savov of deliberately leaving him to face an enemy which outnumbered him by three to one, out of revenge for their difference of opinion at the siege of Adrianople. A confidential Bulgarian report captured by the Greeks shows that on 4th June the strength of the Second Army was 83 infantry battalions and 216 cannon[1]; but this, of course, gives no clue as to its strength nearly four weeks later. It must also be remembered that the Bulgarian regiments were very often under strength. At the critical moment estimates vary between 30 and 66 battalions, and a French military expert accepts 57 as the true figure.[2] But it is certain that as soon as Kovačev's

---

[1] Crawfurd Price, *Balkan Cockpit*, p. 280.
[2] See *Revue Bleue*, *op. cit.* (first article). Captain Trapmann, who accompanied the Greek army, maintains that the Bulgarians

coup de main against the Serbs had failed, a considerable portion of Ivanov's forces were hurriedly diverted northwards, and consequently that the Greeks for the first three weeks of the campaign greatly outnumbered the Bulgars and were especially superior in artillery. The Greek plan consisted in holding the Bulgarian right wing by an attack upon Kukuš-Likovan, which if successfully maintained would have the effect of driving a wedge between the Bulgarian Fourth and Second Armies; meanwhile the Greek right was to cut the railway between Seres and Drama and thus restrict the arrival of Ivanov's supplies or reinforcements to a single road across the Rhodope Mountains. Ivanov gallantly tried to forestall this plan by prompt offensive operations; and on 30th June the Bulgarian left drove in the Greek advance guards between Lake Tachinos and the sea, while their right seized Gjevgjeli. But already lack of men fatally hampered his movements; and he found it necessary to transfer what troops he had at Seres with all possible speed in the direction of Kukuš. Meanwhile an abrupt end was put to the dream of a

---

numbered 80,000 on 2nd July, and 115,000 on 3rd July, as opposed to 60,000 and 80,000 respectively on the Greek side. This writer's statements, however, are to be accepted with great caution. What he says of the Bulgars is rant of the worst kind : "cold-blooded, cruel, ignorant, vicious, and lustful"—all this is thrown at their heads in a single sentence. "Tippoo Sahib, Nero, Robespierre, Catherine of Russia, and the Borgias were but mildly oppressive and unkind, as compared with the lustful brutes who wore the uniform of King Ferdinand of Bulgaria." After this the reader is apt to discount the absurd assertion that the Bulgars during the nine months preceding the Second War "have done to death between 450,000 and 500,000 peaceable inhabitants, men, women, and children, Turks and Greeks." On the other hand, we may accept his account, based upon his own investigations on the spot within a few days of the events, of the atrocities committed by the Bulgarians at Nigrita. (See his article in *Nineteenth Century* for October, 1913.)

Bulgarian seizure of Salonica. General Hasapčev's troops, abandoned by their officers with orders to resist to the death and the assurance that they would be relieved within twelve hours, offered a stout resistance, but eventually surrenderd when they realised they were caught like rats in a trap.

On 2nd July the Greek army, led by King Constantine in person, opened a vigorous offensive at Kukuš, with the object of capturing the Bulgarian base of supplies at Dojran and thus threatening Kovačev's rear during his struggle with the Serbs. The Greek superiority in mountain guns[1] and the King's able generalship were supplemented by the remarkable *élan* of the Greek infantry, who in spite of blazing heat forced the Bulgarians to yield ground and to evacuate Gjevgjeli (3rd July). Next day the Greek Third Division took positions of Lahana at the point of the bayonet, while the First Division forced the Bulgarians northwards towards Strumnica. That night General Ivanov, seeing his communications threatened, ordered a general retreat, and acting on instructions from Sofia, withdrew into the Struma valley, the one column direct from Seres and Demirhissar through the gorge of Rupel, the other across the Belašica Planina to Strumnica, a small town near the source of the river of the same name, itself a tributary of the Struma.

These operations involved very grave risks, owing to the wide front and very inferior numbers of the Bulgarians, but they were carried out with surprising precision and success, and though 21 cannon fell into Greek hands, the number of prisoners taken was insignificant. The fierceness with which the battle of Kukuš was contested may be judged from the Greek casualties, which amounted, according

---

[1] According to Colonel Immanuel, 60 to 12 (288 guns in all to 140 Bulgarian), *op. cit.*, p. 60.

to official admissions, to over 10,000 in three days, or fourteen per cent. of the forces engaged.[1]

On the evening of 6th July the town of Dojran, a valuable strategic point, filled with huge military stores, was occupied by the Greeks without a struggle; and their advance next day upon Strumnica at once began to affect the position of Kovačev's army, which was forced to evacuate Štip and Radovište to the Serbs. On 9th July the Greek advance, necessarily slow owing to the broken nature of the ground and the lack of good roads, placed Strumnica in their hands, but they had found it impossible to cut off the retreat of the Bulgars down the valley of the Strumnica. By 11th July Ivanov's army was safely ensconced in the Kresna Pass, and engaged in consolidating its position and linking up with the Fourth Army on the upper Bregalnica.

Meanwhile Seres, which had been evacuated by the Bulgars as early as 5th July, was not occupied by the Greeks till the eleventh; and in the interval large bands of Bulgarian komitadjis, armed with cannon and led by regular officers, sacked the town and committed hideous excesses against the Greek and Turkish population. The victors found more than half the town, including many of its rich tobacco depots, in ruins; and King Constantine himself lost no time in exploiting these and other "Bulgarian horrors" by sensational interviews in the European press.[2] By an irony of fate the memorable

---

[1] Price, op. cit., p. 299.

[2] The whole question of atrocities is exhaustively—and exhaustingly—dealt with by the *Report of the International Commission of the Carnegie Endowment for International Peace* (Washington, 1914), and it could serve no good purpose to deal with the question in detail in such a volume as the present. But it is essential that the reader should be informed of certain facts regarding the composition of the Carnegie Commission. If all its members had actually taken part in the investigations, as the reader is left to infer from an extraordinarily misleading preface by Baron D'Estournelles de Constant, its mission could hardly have been

phrase of Gladstone now became a reproach to the
nation in whose aid it had mobilised civilised opinion
a generation earlier.

opposed by the belligerent Governments, and its findings would
have commanded universal respect. In point of fact, Professor
Redlich (Vienna), Professor Paszkowski (Berlin), and Mr. F. W.
Hirst (London), were from the very first prevented, Baron
D'Estournelles remained at home, and Professor Schücking (Mar-
burg) got no farther than Vienna. Thus the Commission consisted only of four—two entirely non-committal, because un-
acquainted with Balkan problems, M. Godart (the French deputy)
and Professor Dutton (Columbia University), and two whose
knowledge and high reputation no one can fairly dispute, but
whose selection was bitterly and openly resented by the Serbian
and Greek Governments, and by public opinion in Belgrade and
Athens, owing to their pronouncedly Bulgarophil record—namely,
Professor Paul Miljukov and Mr. H. M. Brailsford. Personally
I have absolute confidence in their desire to be impartial, but none
whatever in a central committee which failed to realise the fatal
error of making such a selection, unless it were supplemented by
the appointment of other equally well-known friends of the Hellenic
or Serbian cause.

Those who desire to investigate the repulsive and thorny subject
of atrocities, may be referred to the following publications :—

(1) (Greek case) Professor Theodore Zaimis : *Atrocités bulgares
en Macédoine. Exposé soumis par le recteur de l'Université
d'Athênes aux recteurs des Universités d'Europe et d'Amérique.*

(2) (Bulgarian case) Professor L. Miletitch, *Atrocités Grecques
en Macédoine.* Sofia (Imprimerie de l'Etat), 1913, and *Réponse
à la Brochure des Professeurs d'Athênes,* by the University Professors of Sofia.

(3) (Serbian case.)

(4) (Turkish case) *The Balkan Massacres :* a Turkish appeal,
and, *Come Over to Macedonia and Help Us* (both published by
the " Balkan Allies Atrocities Publication Committee," of Constantinople), and Pierre Loti's *La Turquie Agonisante,* which
reveals its author's well-known qualities of imagination. For the
behaviour of the Turks on their return to Thrace, see statements
of an eye-witness, the Augustinian Father Superior Theophistus,
in *Reichspost* of 20th August, 1913.

There can be no question that the atrocities, bad as they were,
were magnified tenfold, and that this was due not merely to those
habits of mutual calumny and abuse and love of exaggeration
which Turkish rule has ingrained in the Macedonian population,

After the fall of Seres and Demirhissar there was an unaccountable delay of nearly a week in the Greek advance. King Constantine's aim was to isolate the Bulgarians at Nevrokop and Zernovo from the main forces further west, but above all to drive a wedge between the Second and Fourth Bulgarian Armies and link up with the Serbs on the Bregalnica. But the unquenchable Ivanov explained this unexpected respite from attack as a sign of slackening on the part of the Greeks, and was only prevented from resuming the offensive by the refusal of headquarters to supply him with the necessary reinforcements. Sofia was still completely paralysed by the rapid advance of the Roumanians, and while hesitating to involve itself in actual hostilities with the new invader, neglected to employ its surplus troops at the point where their appearance might possibly have turned the scale. On 15th July yet another stroke of misfortune befell Bulgaria. The Porte intimated to Sofia that it regarded the Treaty of London as no longer binding, in so far as Adrianople and the Marica were concerned, and that it intended to secure a real strategic frontier instead of the untenable Enos-Midia line. The same day a cavalry division under Enver Bey reoccupied Lüle Burgas and began to march upon Kirk Kilisse. The Bulgarian Government made a frantic appeal to Sir Edward Grey for action such as might enforce respect for the Treaty of London, " promoted and guaranteed by the Powers." But in London, as in Petrograd, these appeals met with scant sympathy; and whatever may be said of the wisdom

and to a lesser degree in some of its neighbours, but, above all, to the deliberate propaganda of occult influences which sought to discredit *all* the Balkan States with Western public opinion. The worst offenders were the Young Turks, with their invisible backers in the underworld of European finance, and many worthy people became their unconscious dupes.

of such an attitude, there can be little doubt that the *Times* was accurately interpreting the average public opinion, when, in a leading article of 17th July, it expressed doubt whether Bulgaria, having deliberately refused to listen to the counsels of Europe, had any right to expect Europe to save her from the consequences, or "any right, legal or moral, to regard the obligations of the Powers as intact, after she herself has rekindled the flames of war." Looking back upon these events in the light of what has happened since, it is easy to see that our complaisant attitude towards the Turks alienated the Bulgarians from the Entente and left them with a deep sense of grievance towards those who had imposed the Treaty of London upon them and then so soon consented to regard it as "a scrap of paper," and that while leaving Bulgaria to pay the penalty for her act of treachery towards Serbia and her neglect of Roumanian warnings, we should have been wiser to insist upon the Thracian arrangement remaining unaltered.

There can be no doubt that the indifference of the Entente Powers to Bulgaria's plight contributed very materially to the failure of Mr. Malinov to form a new Russophil Cabinet in succession to that of Dr. Danev. On 17th July his place was definitely taken by Mr. Radoslavov, who for a whole generation past has consistently represented Austrophilism in Bulgaria and whose attitude to Russia may be summed up in the famous phrase of Cankov:—"We want neither your honey nor your sting." The influence of Count Tarnowski, the Austro-Hungarian Minister in Sofia, thus became more powerful than ever, and to the very last it was hoped that a situation favourable to Austrian intervention might arise. The main factor in preventing this was undoubtedly Roumania, who, after being the faithful vassal of Vienna for a whole generation past,

seemed now on the point of self-assertion and who, therefore, had to be treated with special consideration and
tact. Much then as Austria-Hungary would have liked
to reinstate Bulgaria at the expense of the Serbs, she
still hesitated to take any action which might alienate
Roumania from the orbit of the Monarchy.

The Bulgars, realising the hopelessness of resistance,
did not oppose the Roumanian advance; and by 20th
July four army corps had been rapidly thrown across
the Danube and were holding a line within forty miles
of Sofia itself. This new threat forced the Bulgars to
withdraw their First and Third Armies, which in accordance with Savov's original plans, but at least a week too
late to be really effective, had invaded northern Serbia.
On 8th July Kutinčev had occupied Knjaževac in the
Timok valley and even threatened Zaječar, while General
Račo Petrov attacked Pirot, on the main line of the Orient
Express, and for a short time held the railway station
and seemed about to cut the connection between Belgrade
and Skoplje. On the 17th both armies withdrew once
more into Bulgarian territory, and some regiments, getting completely out of hand, sacked the town of Knjaževac, murdered and outraged many innocent civilians
and even killed the Serbian wounded in cold blood.
The Serbs followed them as far as the border fortresses
of Belogradčik and Vidin, but soon took up a waiting
attitude and contented themselves with occasionally
shelling the latter town.

By 23rd July Bulgaria's enemies were closing in upon
all sides. The Fifth Roumanian Army occupied the
Turtucaia-Balčik line, while the main forces arrived
within cannon shot of Sofia. On the same day the
Turks reoccupied Adrianople with very considerable
forces. They had employed the first half of 1913 in
making good their military deficiencies and were now
able to put into the field larger armies than those which

had been engaged in the First Balkan War.[1] Fortunately the Greeks had landed troops at Kavala and pushed them eastwards along the coast as far as Dedeagač; and the Turks hesitated to provoke the international complications which an attack upon them would have involved.

By 21st July the struggle on the Serbo-Bulgar front had passed its height and assumed the character of a war of positions in mountainous country, where enveloping movements were not easy and both armies held strongly fortified points of vantage. The Serbs had attained their object and were disinclined to increase their already heavy losses by operations on a large scale : while the Bulgars, after launching fierce assaults for five consecutive days (22nd-27th July) upon the Serbian positions near Egri Palanka and also to the east of Kočana, finally renounced the hope of breaking through towards Veles or Skoplje and devoted their whole efforts to crushing the Greeks.

On 21st July King Constantine opened an attack upon the Bulgarian defensive positions which lay across the mouth of the Kresna Pass, Pehčevo forming the link with the upper Bregalnica valley. The Greek aim was to outflank Kresna from the east, and thus force back the Bulgars within their old frontiers, while the latter hoped to draw on the Greeks towards Džumaja and then by an encircling movement to cut off their retreat down the Struma valley. With this end in view, a new army was formed under the command of General Savov, both Ivanov and Kutinčev being placed under

[1] The Eastern Army, under Ahmed Abuk Pasha, held Kirk Kilisse with 80,000 men, the Western, under Hurshid Pasha, held Adrianople and Dimotika with 90,000 men, while 60,000 more, under Djavid Pasha, were concentrated in Constantinople and Gallipoli (see Immanuel, *op cit.*, V. pp. 78–80).

him; and as the result of a steady flow of reinforcements from the north, the Bulgarians for the first time gained a numerical superiority over the Greeks. On 24th July the Fourth Greek Division stormed the lofty mountain position of Rujen, and the Second Division took possession of Susitsa. But after a couple of days of position warfare in the mountains, the Bulgars swiftly assumed the offensive, moving simultaneously south-eastwards up the Bregalnica and south-westwards from Belica. Their plan, which aimed at bottling six Greek divisions, was thwarted by the timely arrival of reinforcements, and after fierce fighting the Bulgars retired on the 27th to the outskirts of Džumaja. Next day the decisive battle began. At first the Greek right captured certain positions, but it was gradually forced back by the advancing Bulgars, who occupied Mehomija and Banjska, while the Greek left, consisting of the Third and Tenth Divisions, was seriously threatened by Bulgarian forces advancing up the Bregalnica, and found it necessary to withdraw to Pehčevo. On the 29th a counter-attack was ordered by King Constantine, and the Second and Fourth Divisions made a determined effort to ease the situation for their comrades of the Third by attacking their assailants in the rear. None the less the Bulgarian offensive continued, and on 30th July Colonel Gešev occupied Pehčevo and other points and seemed to be threatening the Greek main position on the Kadijica hill.[1] Moreover, the Serbs, who had renewed their activity in order to lighten the task of the Greeks, met with a decided check between Kočana and Carevoselo.

Desperate fighting still continued, when late in the evening of 30th July hostilities were suspended by the news that a five days' armistice had been concluded at Bucarest. Not unnaturally an acute controversy has

---

[1] Immanuel, p. 89.

raged over the respective positions and prospects of the
opposing armies, and the material for a definite judgment is not as yet at our disposal. The Bulgars claim
that their enveloping movement was on the very point
of succeeding, while the Greeks assert that the fall of
Hasan Pasha and Leska, two important strategic points,
was imminent, and that five Bulgarian brigades would
then have been caught between two fires by Greeks and
Serbs and forced to surrender.[1] While the orders issued
by King Constantine for a fresh offensive next day certainly prove that the Greeks were not yet exhausted, it
has been alleged by Sofia, and as vigorously denied by
Athens, that the Greek headquarters, alarmed at their
unfavourable situation, begged the Roumanians to insist
upon an immediate suspension of hostilities. What
truth there is in this allegation, and whether it was invented as a sop to Bulgaria's wounded pride or was
merely a perversion of the undoubted fact that the
Roumanians threatened to enter Sofia unless the
armistice were accepted by the night of 30th July, time
alone can show.

[1] Crawfurd Price, *op. cit.*, p. 340.

BIBLIOGRAPHY.

[Unfortunately Mr. Seton-Watson was unable to finish his bibliography, and he left it in my hands. I have made his scheme as complete as I could.—GEORGE GLASGOW.]

[*Books marked with a * are specially recommended.*]

1. GENERAL HISTORIES AND TEXTBOOKS.

*Bamberg, F., *Geschichte der orientalischen Angelegenheiten*, Leipzig, 1888.

Forbes, Nevill, and others, *The Balkans: a History*, Oxford, 1915.

*Iorga, Prof. N., *Histoire des Etats balcaniques*, Bucarest, 1914.

*Miller, W., *The Balkans*, London, 1896.

　　　　The Ottoman Empire, 1801–1913, Cambridge, 1913.

Roth, K., *Geschichte der christlichen Balkanstaaten*, 1907.

Sax, Carl Ritter von, *Die Wahrheit über die Serbische Frage und das Serbentum in Bosnien*, Leipzig, 1909.

Seignobos, Charles, *A Political History of Contemporary Europe since 1814* (translated from the French), London, 1901.

2. GEOGRAPHICAL, ETHNOGRAPHICAL, STATISTICAL.

Brancoff, D. M., *La Macédoine et sa Population Chrétienne*, Paris, 1905. Contains elaborate statistics; but no Macedonian statistics are of any real value, save as illustrating the psychology of the respective claimants.

Grothe, Hugo, *Zur Landeskunde von Rumänien*, Halle, 1907.

Jireček, K., *Die Heerstrasse von Belgrad nach Konstantinopel*, Prag, 1877.

Jireček, K., *Die Handelsstrassen und Bergwerke von Serbien und Bosnien während des Mittelalters,* Prag, 1879.

Lyde, L. W., and Mockler-Ferryman, A. F., *A Military Geography of the Balkan Peninsula,* London, 1905. A most admirable textbook.

Murgoci, G., and Popa-Burcă, I., *România şi Ţĕrile locuite de Români,* Bucarest, 1902.

*Newbigin, Marion I., *Geographical Aspects of Balkan Problems in their Relation to the Great European War,* London, 1915.

Robert, Cyprien, *Les Slaves de Turquie,* Paris, 1862.

3. TURKEY.

Bérard, Victor, *La Turquie et l'Hellénisme Contemporain,* Paris, 1897.

    Pro Macedonia: L'Action Austro-Russe, etc., Paris, 1904.

    Le Sultan, l'Islam et les Puissances, Paris, 1907.

    La Révolution Turque, Paris, 1909.

    La Mort de Stamboul, Paris, 1913.

*Brailsford, H. N., *Macedonia: Its Races and their Future,* London, 1906.

Creasy, Sir Edward, *History of the Ottoman Turks,* London, 1878.

Draganof, P., *La Macédoine et les Réformes,* Paris, 1906.

*Eliot, Sir Charles, *Turkey in Europe,* 2nd ed., London, 1908 (1st ed., 1900).

Gfrörer, A., *Byzantinische Geschichten,* 3 vols., Graz., 1872-7.

*Hammer-Purgstall, J. von., *Geschichte des Osmanischen Reiches,* 2nd ed., 4 vols., Pest, 1840. Will always remain a standard work.

Hertzberg, G., *Geschichte der Byzantiner und des Osmanischen Reiches,* Berlin, 1883.

*Iorga, Prof. N., *Geschichte des Osmanischen Reiches,* 5 vols., Gotha, 1908-14.

    The Byzantine Empire (Temple Primers), London, 1906.

*Jonquière, Vicomte de la, *Histoire de l'Empire Ottoman,* 2 vols., Paris, 1914.

Juchereau de St. Denys, *Histoire de l'Empire Ottoman depuis 1792 jusqu'en 1844,* 4 vols., Paris, 1844.

Lane-Poole, Stanley, *Turkey,* London, 1888.

Midhat, Ali Haidar, *Life of Midhat Pasha,* London, 1903.

Midhat Pasha, *La Turquie, son passé, son avenir,* Paris, 1878.

Pears, Sir Edwin, *Turkey and its People,* 1911.

Rosen, Georg, *Geschichte der Türkei,* 2 vols., Leipzig, 1866-7.

St. Priest, Comte de, *Mémoire sur l'Ambassade de France en Turquie,* Paris, 1878.

Sax, Carl Ritter von, *Geschichte des Machtverfalls der Türkei bis Ende des 19 Jahrhunderts und die Phasen der " orientalischen Frage " bis auf die Gegenwart,* Vienna, 1913.

Urquhart, David, *The Military Strength of Turkey*, London, 1869.
*Zinkeisen, J., *Geschichte des Osmanischen Reiches*, 7 vols. Gotha, 1840–63.

4. THE EASTERN QUESTION.

Abeken, *Das religiöse Leben im Islam*, Berlin, 1854.
　　Der Eintritt der Türkei in die europäische Politik des XVIII. Jahrhunderts, Berlin, 1858.
Bengescu, G., *Essai d'une Notice Bibliographique sur la Question d'Orient*, Brussels, 1897.
Cahuet, Albéric, *La Question d'Orient*, Paris, 1905.
Choublier, Max, *La Question d'Orient*, Paris, 1905.
Djuvara, T. G., *Cent Projets de partage de la Turquie*, Paris, 1914.
Driault, Edouard, *La Question d'Orient depuis ses origines*, 5th ed., Paris, 1912.
Eichmann, F., *Die Reformen des Osmanischen Reiches*, Berlin, 1858.
Engelhardt, A., *La Turquie et le Tanzimet, ou Histoire des réformes dans l'Empire Ottoman depuis 1826*, 2 vols., Paris, 1882–4.
*Goryainov, Serge, *Le Bosphore et les Dardanelles*, Paris, 1910.
Jovanović, V M., *English Bibliography on Eastern Question*, Belgrade, 1908.
　　The Emancipation and Unity of the Serbian Nation, 1871.
Juchereau de St. Denys, *Les Révolutions de Constantinople*, 2 vols.
Lecomte, F., *La Guerre d'Orient en 1876–7*, 2 vols., Paris, 1879.
MacColl, Canon M., *The Eastern Question, its Facts and Fallacies*, London, 1877.
Mischev, P. H., *La Mer Noire et les Détroits de Constantinople*, Paris, 1899.
*Pinon, René, *L'Europe et l'Empire Ottoman*, Paris, 1909.
　　L'Europe et la Jeune Turquie, Paris, 1911.
Roepell, Rich., *Die orientalische Frage in ihrer geschichtlichen Entwickelung*, Breslau, 1854.
Schopoff, A., *Les Réformes et la Protection des Chrétiens en Turquie (1673–1904)*, Paris, 1904.
*Sorel, Albert, *La Question d'Orient au XVIIIe siècle*, Paris, 1878.
Thouvenel, L., *Trois Années de la Question d'Orient (1856–9)*, Paris, 1897.
Ubicini, A., *La Question d'Orient devant l'Europe*, Paris, 1854.
　　Lettres sur la Turquie, Paris, 1854.
　　Les Serbes de Turquie, Paris, 1865.
*Villari, Luigi (ed.), *The Balkan Question*, London, 1905.
Zinkeisen, J. W., *Osmanisches Reich in Europa* (*Geschichte der europäischen Staaten*), Gotha, 1840–63.

5. Serbia, Montenegro, and the Southern Slavs.

Bérard, Victor, *Heroic Serbia*, London, 1916.

Civis Italicus, *Italy and the Jugoslav Peoples*, London, 1915.

Coquelle, F., *Histoire du Montenegro et de la Bosnie*, Paris, 1895.

Cuhibert, B. S., *Essai historique sur la Révolution et l'Indépendance de la Serbie*, 2 vols., Leipzig, 1855.

Cvijić, Prof. Jovan, *L'Annexion de la Bosnie et la Question Serbe*, Paris, 1909.

*Denis, E., *La Grande Serbie*, Paris, 1915.

Denton, Rev. W., *Montenegro: its People and their History*, London, 1877.

    Servia and the Servians, London, 1862.

Diplomatist, A, *Nationalism and War in the Near East*, Oxford, 1915.

Engel, J., *Geschichte von Serwien und Bosnien*, Halle, 1801.

Evans, Sir Arthur, *Illyrian Letters*, London, 1878.

Fournier, Prof. A., *Wie wir zu Bosnien kamen*, Vienna, 1909.

Gavrilović, M., *Miloš Obrenovic*, 2 vols., Belgrade, 1908–9.

Georgewitsch, Vladan, *Les Albanais et les grandes puissances*, Paris, 1913.

Gopčević, Spiridion, *Serbien und die Serben*, Leipzig, 1888.

Hilferding, A., *Geschichte der Serben und Bulgaren*, 2 vols., Bautzen, 1856.

*Jireček, C., *Die Romanen in d. Städten Dalmatiens*, Berlin, 1902–4.

    Serben (Geschichte der europäischen Staaten), Gotha, 1911.

Kállay, Benjamin von, *Geschichte der Serben*, Budapest, 1878.

Kanitz, F., *Das Königreich Serbien*, 2 Bde., Leipzig, 1904–9.

*Klaić, Prof. V., *Povjest Hrvata (History of the Croats)*, 5 vols., Zagreb, 1899–1913. The standard modern history.

    Geschichte Bosniens, Leipzig, 1885.

Lanux, Pierre de, *La Yougoslavie*, Paris, 1916.

Leger, L., *Le monde Slave*, Paris, 1873 and 1902.

Loiseau, Charles, *Le Balkan slave et la Crise autrichienne*, Paris, 1898.

Mallat, J., *La Serbie contemporaine*, 2 vols., Paris, 1902. Colourless.

Mijatović, Chedo, *Servia of the Servians*, London, 1908.

    A Royal Tragedy, London, 1906.

Mijatović, E. L., *History of Modern Servia*, London, 1872.

Novaković, Stojan, *Die Wiedergeburt des serbischen Staates (1804–1813)*, Sarajevo, 1912.

*Picot, Emile, *Les Serbes de la Hongrie*, Prague, 1873.

Piročanac, M., *Knez Mihajlo i zajednička Radnja balkanskih Naroda*, Belgrade, 1895.

Prezzolini, G., *La Dalmazia*, Rome, 1915.

Račic, F., *Le Royaume de Serbie,* Paris, 1901.

*Ranke, Leopold von, *History of Servia,* London, 1853 (2nd ed., German, 1879).

Ristić, Jovan, *Diplomatska Istorija Srbije,* 1875–8, 2 vols., Belgrade, 1896–8.

Spoljašnji Odnošaji Srbije novijega Vremena. 3 vols., Belgrade, 1887–1901.

Ružičić, N., *Das kirchlich-religiöse Leben bei den Serben* Göttingen, 1896.

St. René Taillandier : *Kara Georges et Milosch : La Serbie au XIXe Siècle,* Paris, 1873.

*Savić, V. R., *The Reconstruction of South-Eastern Europe,* London, 1917.

*Seton-Watson, R. W. *The Southern Slav Question and the Habsburg Monarchy,* London, 1911.

The Balkans, Italy, and the Adriatic, London, 1915.

German, Slav, and Magyar : a Study in the Origins of the Great War, London, 1916.

Sišić, Prof. F., *Hrvatska Povijest (Croatian History) (to 1847),* 3 vols., Zagreb, 1908–12.

Southern Slav Library, The, I., *The Southern Slav Programme,* II., *The Southern Slavs : Land and People,* III., *A Sketch of Southern Slav History,* IV., *Southern Slav Culture,* London, 1915, V., *Idea of Southern Slav Unity,* London, 1916.

Spalajković, M., *La Bosnie et l'Herzegovine,* Paris, 1899.

Stead, Alfred (Ed.), *Servia by the Servians,* London, 1909.

Stevenson, F. S., *A History of Montenegro,* London, 1912.

*Temperley, H. W. V., *History of Serbia,* London, 1917.

Thiers, H., *La Serbie, son Passé et son Avenir,* Paris, 1862.

Urquhart, David, *A Fragment of the History of Servia,* London, 1843.

Vivian, Herbert, *Servia, the Poor Man's Paradise,* London, 1897.

Wyon, R., *The Balkans from Within,* London, 1904.

Yakshitch (Jakšić), G., *L'Europe et la Résurrection de la Serbie,* Paris, 1907.

6. BULGARIA.

Avril, Baron d', *La Bulgarie chrétienne,* Paris, 1867.

Beekmann, Jos., *Die Wahrheit über Bulgarien,* Leipzig, 1898.

Crispi, Francesco, *Politica Estera,* Milan, 1913.

Dicey, Sir Edward, *The Peasant State : Bulgaria in 1894,* London, 1894.

Drandar, A., *Les Evénements Politiques en Bulgarie,* Brussels, 1896.

La Bulgarie sous le Prince Ferdinand, Brussels, 1904.

Gladstone, W. E., *Bulgarian Horrors and the Question of the East*, London, 1876.

Huhn, A. E. von, *Kampf d. Bulgaren um ihre Nationaleinheit: Gesch. d. bulgar.-rumel, Ereignisse*, 1885, Leipzig, 1886.

The Struggle of the Bulgarians for National Independence: History of the War between Bulgaria and Servia in 1885, London, 1886.

Hulme-Beaman, A. G., *Twenty Years in the Near East*, London, 1898.

*Jireček, K., *Geschichte der Bulgaren*, Prag, 1876.

Das Fürstentum Bulgarien, Leipzig, 1891.

Koch, A., *Prince Alexander of Battenberg*, London, 1887.

Lamouche, L., *La Bulgarie dans le passé et le présent*, Paris, 1892

Launay, Louis de, *La Bulgarie d'hier et de demain*, Paris, 1907.

Mach, Richard von, *The Bulgarian Exarchate*, London, 1907.

Minchin, J. G. C., *The Growth of Freedom in the Balkan Peninsula*, London, 1886.

Samuelson, James, *Bulgaria, Past and Present*, London, 1888.

Weiss-Bartenstein, W. R., *Bulgarien: Land, Leute und Wirtschaft zur Zeit des Balkankrieges*, Leipzig, 1913.

7. ROUMANIA.

Arion, V., Parvan, Papahagi, and others, *România şi Popoarele Balcanice*, Bucarest, 1913.

Barbulescu, Ilie, *Relations des Roumains avec les Serbes, les Bulgares, les Grecs et la Croatie*, Iaşi, 1912.

Bibesco, Prince Georges, *Le Règne de Bibesco*, 2 vols., Paris, 1893

Bratter, C. A., *Die Kutzowalachische Frage*, Hamburg, 1907.

*Charles I., King of Roumania, *Aus dem Leben König Karls von Romänien*, 4 vols., Stuttgart, 1894–1900. One of the most authoritative volumes of memoirs in modern times.

*Damé, F., *Histoire de la Roumanie Contemporaine*, Paris, 1900. Contentious, but highly instructive.

Dragu, T., *La Politique Roumaine après les troubles agraires de 1907*, Paris, 1908.

Fiedler, J., *Die Union der Walachen in Siebenbürgen*, Vienna, 1858 (*Akademie der Wiss.*, Bd. XXVII.).

Hauterive, Comte d', *Mémoire sur l'Etat ancien et actuel de la Moldavie*, Bucarest, 1902.

Hintz, J., *Geschichte des Bistums der griechisch-nichtunierten Glaubensgenossen in Siebenbürgen*, Hermannstadt, 1850.

*Honfalvy, Paul, *Die Rumänen und ihre Ansprüche*, Vienna, 1883. The best presentment of the Magyar case.

Hungaricus, *Das magyarische Ungarn und der Dreibund*, Munich, 1899. A very able Roumanian *plaidoyer*.

Hurmuzaki, Baron E., *Fragmente din istoria Românilor,* Bucarest, 1879–1900.

*Iorga, Prof. N., *Geschichte des rumänischen Volkes,* 2 vols., Gotha. 1905. The standard work.

Jonescu, Take, *La Politique Etrangère de la Roumanie,* Bucarest, 1891.

Mitrany, D., *Rumania, her History and Politics* [Oxford Pamphlet], 1915.

Murnu, G., *Vlahia Mare* (980–1259). *Istoria Românilor din Pind,* Bucarest, 1913.

Pič, J. L., *Ueber die Abstammung der Rumänen,* Leipzig, 1880.

Picot, Emile, *Les Roumains de la Macédoine,* Paris, 1875.

Rubin, A., *Les Roumains de Macédoine,* Bucarest, 1913.

Salaberry, Comte de, *Essai sur la Valachie et la Moldavie,* Paris, 1821.

Samuelson, James, *Roumania, Past and Present,* London, 1882.

Seton-Watson, R. W., *Roumania and the Great War,* London, 1915.
    Racial Problems in Hungary, London, 1908.

Slavici, Ioan., *Die Rumänen in Ungarn, Siebenbürgen und der Bukowina,* Vienna, 1887.

Sturdza, Demeter, *Le Roi Charles I. de Roumanie,* 2 vols., Bucarest, 1900–4. Documentary.

Ubicini, J. H. A., *La Question des Principautés devant l'Europe,* Paris, 1858.

Verax, *La Roumanie et les Juifs,* Bucarest, 1903.

Wace, A. J. B., and Thompson, M. S., *The Nomads of the Balkans,* London, 1914.

Witte, Baron Jean de, *Quinze Ans d'Histoire* (1866–1881) *d'après les Memoires du Roi de Roumanie,* Paris, 1905

*Xenopol, Prof. A. D., *Histoire des Roumains,* 2 vols., Paris, 1894. An admirable abridgement from the Roumanian original.
    Les Roumains, Paris, 1909. A brilliant course of lectures.

8. GREECE.

About, Edmond, *La Grèce Contemporaine,* 4e éd., Paris, 1860.

*Finlay, G., *History of Greece,* 2 vols., London, 1861.

Gordon, Thomas, *History of the Greek Revolution.* Edinburgh, 1832.

Grenier, A., *La Grèce en 1863,* Paris, 1863.

Jebb, Sir Richard, *Modern Greece,* London, 1880.

Martin, Percy F., *Greece of the Twentieth Century,* Pref. by A. Andréadès, London, 1913.

Nikolaides, Dr. K., *Griechenlands Anteil an den Balkankriegen,* Vienna, 1913.

Phillips, W. Alison, *The War of Greek Independence* (1821–33), London, 1897.

Pouqueville, F., *Régénération de la Grèce*, 4 vols., Paris, 1826.

Rodd, Sir Rennell, *Customs and Lore of Modern Greece*, London, 1892.

Sergeant, L., *Greece, 1821–97*, London, 1897.
     New Greece, London, 1878.

Toynbee, A. J., *Greek Policy since 1882* [Oxford Pamphlet], 1914.

9. ALBANIA.

Balkanicus, *Le Problème Albanais, la Serbie et l'Autriche-Hongrie*, Paris, 1913.

Boppe, C., *L'Albanie et Napoléon*, Paris, 1913.

Chlumecky, Baron Leopold, *Österreich-Ungarn und Italien. Das westbalkanische Problem*, 1907.

*Durham, M. Edith, *High Albania*, London, 1909.

Georgevitch, Vladan, *Die Albanesen und die Grossmächte*, Leipzig, 1913.

Grothe, Hugo, *Durch Albanien und Montenegro*, Munich, 1913.

*Hahn, J. G. von, *Albanesische Studien*, Vienna, 1854.
     Reise durch die Gebiete des Drin und Vardar, Vienna, 1867.
     Reise von Belgrad nach Salonichi, Vienna, 1868.

Ippen, Theodor, *Skutari und die nordalbanische Küstenebene*, Sarajevo, 1907.

*Juray, Gabriel Louis, *L'Albanie inconnue*, Paris, 1913.

Mantegazza, Vico, *L'Albania*, Rome, 1912.
     L'Altra Sponda, Milan, 1905.

Mihačevic, Fra Lovro, *Durch Albanien*, Prag, 1913.

Peacock, W., *Albania, the Foundling State of Europe*, London, 1914.

Question Albanaise, La, by Biancour, Chéradame, Wesselitsky, Yakshitch, etc., Paris, 1912.

Siebertz, Paul, *Albanien*, Vienna, 1910.

Woods, H. C., *The Danger Zone of Europe. Changes and Problems in the Near East*, London, 1911.

10. BOOKS OF TRAVEL.

Boué, Ami, *La Turquie d'Europe*, 2 vols., Paris, 1840.

Cambon, V., *Autour des Balkans*, Paris, 1890.

*Evans, Sir Arthur, *Through Bosnia on Foot*, 2nd Ed., London, 1877.

Fortis, Alberto, *Travels into Dalmatia*, London, 1778.

*Gelzer, H., *Geistliches und Weltliches aus dem türkisch-griechischen Orient*, Leipzig, 1900.

*Hahn, Johann Georg v., *Reise von Belgrad nach Salonik*, Vienna, 1861.

Hobhouse, J. C. [Baron Broughton], *Journey through Albania*, new ed., 2 vols., London, 1855.

*Irby, Miss A. P., and Muir-Mackenzie, Miss G., *Travels in the Slavonic Provinces of Turkey in Europe*, Preface by W. E. Gladstone, 2 vols., London, 1877.

Lamouche, L., *La Péninsule Balcanique*, Paris, 1899.

Laveleye, Emile de, *The Balkan Peninsula*, Preface by W. E. Gladstone, London, 1886.

Leake, W. M., *Travels in Northern Greece*, 4 vols., London, 1835.

Miller, William, *Travels and Politics in the Near East*, London, 1898.

Paton, A. A., *The Highlands and Islands of the Adriatic*, London, 1849.

*Pouqueville, F. C. H. L., *Voyage de la Grèce*, 6 vols., Paris, 1825.

*Robert, Cyprien, *Les Slaves de Turquie*, Paris, 1862.

St. Clair, S. G. B., and Brophy, C. A., *Twelve Years' Study of the Eastern Question in Bulgaria* (revised ed. of *Residence in Bulgaria*), London, 1877.

Tozer, H. F., *Lectures on the Geography of Greece*, London, 1873.

Urquhart, David, *The Spirit of the East, Illustrated in a Journal of Travels through Roumeli*, London, 1838.
    The Lebanon: A History and a Diary, London, 1860.

Wilkinson, W., *Wallachia and Moldavia*, London, 1820.

11. DIPLOMATIC AND BIOGRAPHICAL.

Albin, P., *Les grands traités polit*, Préf. de M. Herbette, Paris, 1911.

Avril, Baron d'A., *Négotiations relatives au Traité de Berlin*, Paris, 1886.

*Beer, Adolf, *Die orientalische Politik Oesterreichs seit 1774*, Prag and Leipzig, 1883.

Charmatz, R., *Adolf Fischhof: Das Lebensbilde österreich. Politikers*, St., 1910.

Crispi, F., *Memoirs*, London, 1912.

*Debidour, A., *Hist. diplomat. de l'Europe, 1814-78*, Paris, 1891.

Edwards, Henry Sutherland, *Sir William White: His Life and Corr.*, London, 1902.

Gauvain, A., *L'Europe avant la Guerre*, Paris, 1917.

Gourdon, *Histoire du Congrès de Paris*.

*Hertslet, Sir E., *The Map of Europe by Treaty*, 8 vols., London, 1875-91.

*Klaczko, Julien, *Deux Chanceliers: Gortchakof et Bismarck*, Paris, 1876.

Midhat, A. H., *Life of Midhat Pasha*, London, 1903.

*Morier, Sir Robert, *Memoirs, 1826-76*, London, 1911.
Noradunghian, G., *Recueil d'Actes internationaux de l'Empire Ottoman*, 4 vols., Paris, 1897-1903.
Sosnosky, Theodor von, *Die Balkanpolitik Oesterreich-Ungarns seit 1866*, 2 vols., Stuttgart, 1913-4.
*Stratford de Redcliffe, *The Eastern Question*, Pref. by A. P. Stanley, London, 1881.

Ubersberger, Hans, *Osterreich u. Russland seit d. Ende d. 15 Jhdts.*, Vienna, 1906.

12. THE BALKAN WARS.

Balkanicus [Stojan Protić], *The Aspirations of Bulgaria*, London, 1915. The chief Serbian source for the events of the Balkan Wars, by a former member of the Pašić Cabinet.
Balkankrieg, 1912-13, Der.
Barby, Henri, *Les Victoires Serbes*, Paris, 1913; *Bregalnitsa*, Paris, 1913; *L'Epopée Serbe*, Paris, 1916. Firsthand accounts by the correspondent of *Le Journal*.
Bartlett, E. Ashmead-, *With the Turks in Thrace*, London, 1913.
Breitner, B., *Kriegstagebuch: Balkankrieg 1913 (sic)*, Vienna, 1913.
Buxton, Noel, *With the Bulgarian Staff*, London, 1913.
Carnegie Endowment: *Report of the International Commission on the Causes and Conduct of the Balkan Wars*, Washington, 1914. To be used with the very greatest caution.
Cassavetti, D. J., *Hellas and the Balkan Wars*, London, 1914.
Fleck, Richard von, *Ueber den Balkankrieg*, Vienna, 1913. Slight, but able and suggestive.
*Goltz, Baron K. von der, *Der Türkei Niederlage*.
Gueshoff (Gešov) I. E., *The Balkan League*, London, 1915. The work of the Bulgarian Premier who concluded the League: moderate, though significant for its omissions. To be studied conjointly with the book of Balkanicus (see above).
*Hochwaechter, G. von., *Mit den Türken in der Front*, Berlin, 1913.
Howell, Major P., *The Campaign in Thrace*, London, 1913.
*Immanuel, Colonel Friedrich, *Der Balkankrieg*, 4 parts, Berlin, 1913.
James, Lionel, *With the Conquered Turk*, 1913.
Mahmud Mukhtar Pasha, *Mon Commandemant au cours de la Campagne des Balkans de 1912*, Paris, 1913.
Meyer, Major Alfred, *Der Balkankrieg*, 5 parts, Berlin, 1914.
Mondésir, Col. P. de, *Le Siège d'Adrianople*, Paris, 1914. The work of an able French officer, based on careful study of the ground.
Pelissier, Jean, *Dix Mois de Guerre dans les Balkans*, Paris, 1913.
Pennenrun, Alain de, *La Guerre des Balkans*, Paris, 1913.

Price, W. Crawfurd, *The Balkan Cockpit*, London, 1915. Contains firsthand information regarding Serbo-Greek relations.

    Light on the Balkan Darkness, London, 1915.

Puaux, René, *De Sofia à Tchataldja*, Paris, 1913.

*(Revue Bleue), Anonymous, *Questions Militaires: Bulgares contre Serbes*. 13th Dec., 1913, and 17th Jan., 28th Feb., 23rd May, and 20th June, 1914. Five articles of very high value by a French officer. Indispensable.

Ripert d'Alauzier, Capitaine de, *Sur les Pas des Alliés*, Paris, 1914.

Schurman, Jacob Gould, *The Balkan Wars*, 1912–13, Princeton (U.S.), 1914.

Taburno, J. de, *De Koumanovo à Monastir*, Paris, 1913.

Wagner, Hermenegild, *With the Victorious Bulgarians*, London, 1913. Entirely unreliable, based on faked news supplied by the Bulgarian Staff.

Zwenger, Major Eugen, *Meine Erlebnisse mit den Türken*, Berlin, 1913.

BIBLIOGRAPHY

INDEX

INDEX

A

Abdul Hamid, 105, 106, 125, 137, 146, 172
Abdulla Pasha, 170, 173, 180
Abdul Medjid, 100
Achmet Riza, 136
Acropolis, 52
Adrianople, 8, 33, 71, 74, 106, 159, 170, 174, 176, 186, 191, 207, 235, 273, 278, 280
Adriatic, 34, 76, 236
Ægean, 44
Aehrenthal, Count, 133, 149, 153
Albania, 23, 28, 48, 72, 88, 138, 139, 140, 151, 158, 172
Alessio, 175, 196
Alexander I. Tsar, 50, 89
  II., 103, 105, 115, 117
  III., 115, 118, 121
  of Battenberg, 116, 120, 147
  Prince Regent of Serbia, 173, 243, 250
  Karageorgevitch, 41
  the Good, 59.
Alföld, 34
Ali Pasha, 48, 51
Ali Riza Pasha, 189
Andrássy, Count, 103, 115, 119
Antivari, 110, 175
Apulum, 57
Arabs, 7
Arbanasi, 78
Armenians, 84, 127, 160
Arsenius, Patriarch, 13, 22, 35
Asenid Dynasty, 4

Athos, Mt., 45, 46, 219
Atrocities, 276
Aurelian, Emperor, 57
Austro-Russian Relations, 15, 85–93, 115

B

Bagdad Agreement, 127
Bakurna Gumna, 191
Balance of Power, 96
Baldwin, Emperor, 74
Balkan League, 141, 176, 206, 233, 240
Ballads, Serbian, 4
Banat, 16, 41
Bánffy, Baron, 137
Banica, 192, 200
Bardanjolt, 175
Baring, Mr. 84
Basil II, 2, 4, 73
Batak Massacre, 84
Bavaria, 18
Belašica, Battle of, 73
Belgium, 30
Belgrade, 13, 33, 36, 38, 40, 49, 61, 88
  Treaty of, 15
Belisarius, 3
Berana, 159
Berat, 195, 217
Berlin, Treaty of, 109–112, 141, 143, 163
Berlin-Bagdad, 2
Berchtold, Count, 141, 162, 240
Bersa, 139
Bessarabia, 60, 61, 62, 87, 99, 107, 111

DATE DUE

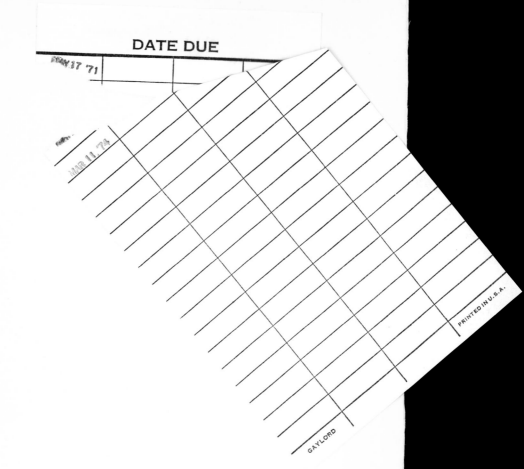

MAY 17 '71

MAR 11 '74

GAYLORD

PRINTED IN U.S.A.